Dedicated to the memory of Don C. Antley, 1942-2018
Point, Louisiana

American Patriot, stalwart Southerner,
and a life well lived in service to Jesus Christ.
Psalm 118:24

The Confederate Myth-Buster

Walter D. Kennedy

The Scuppernong Press

Wake Forest, NC
www.scuppernongpress.com

The Confederate Myth-Buster

By Walter D. Kennedy

©2019 The Scuppernong Press

First Printing

The Scuppernong Press
PO Box 1724
Wake Forest, NC 27588
www.scuppernongpress.com

Cover and book design by Frank B. Powell, III

All rights reserved

Printed in the United States of America

No part of this book may be reproduced or transmitted in any form or by any means, electronic or mechanical, including photocopying, recording, or by any information and storage and retrieval system, without written permission from the editor and/or publisher.

International Standard Book Number: ISBN 978-1-942806-22-6

Library of Congress Control Number: 2019908098

Contents

Part I

Preface 1

1. Secession 9
2. Constitution 27
3. Slavery 47
4. Racism 73
5. History 87
6. Lincoln vs. Davis 115
7. 100 Years of Failure 131
8. The Shield and Sword of Liberty 143
9. Consequences of Conquest 161

Part II

Pictures Worth a Thousand Words 183
Great Men of the US and CS 187
Northern Defenders of the Constitution 193
What Price Union 199

Part III

The Myth Lives On 203
Christians Marching with Marx 205
Paddling One's Own Canoe While Reflecting on Katrina 207
Ron Paul is Too Radical 213
Wall Street Journal's Confederate Animus 221

Conclusion 225

Bibliography 231

In a post-War speech at the dedication of a museum to the South, General Bradley T. Johnson made the following statement in part: "The time will come when all the world will realize that the failure of the Confederacy was a great misfortune to humanity, and will be the source of unnumbered woes to liberty."[1] The following pages will demonstrate the correctness of General Johnson's prediction.

---

1 General Bradley T. Johnson as cited in, John Levi Underwood, *The Women of the Confederacy* (The Neale Publishing Company, NY and Washington: 1906) 28. This speech was also published in *Southern Historical Papers*, Vol. 23, pp 368-70.

∾ Part I ∾

Preface

The *Confederate Myth-Buster* is the result of many interviews the Kennedy Twins have had with an antagonistic media dealing with the true history of the South. Many Americans believe the concept of "fake news" is something hit upon by Donald Trump to advance his 2016 Presidential campaign. Yet, the use of the news media to advance an agenda against one's opponent was introduced into American society in the early 1800s by radical abolitionists. These radical abolitionists desired to paint everyone down South with the tar-brush of being a vicious, inhumane slaveholder. This aggressive "fake news" narrative was so successful that by 1860 even Southerners who were non-slave holders were viewed as less than decent people. While going somewhat dormant post-Reconstruction, the promotion of an incorrect (fake news or false narrative) view of the South continues to this day. Today it is not unusual to hear news reporters, academicians, political figures, and ministers agree with the wildest charges of racism and intolerance against anyone who displays pride in their Southern and/or Confederate heritage.

The struggle to convey correct information about the War for Southern Independence to Americans in general and to Southerners in particular became the inspiration for this book. Here is a little background on how the Kennedy Twins of Louisiana began their defense of the rights and liberty of the people of Dixie.

In 1991 the Kennedy Twins (Ron and Donnie) of Louisiana published the first edition of *The South Was Right!* During the following three years the authors were both surprised and pleased with the reception of the little first edition of that book. Recognizing the limitations and foibles associated with their first effort at unequivocally defending the cause of the South during the War for Southern Independence, the authors began the process of improving their first book. That effort culminated with the publication of the Second edition of *The South Was Right!*, in 1994 by Pelican Publishing Company of Gretna, Louisiana. While revision of the first edition of *The South Was Right!* was underway, more than 5,000 copies of the first edition were sold. Since 1994 more than 135,000 copies of the second edition have been sold. The authors have been interviewed on numerous talk radio shows including the *Oliver North Show*, the *Ken Hamblin Show*, and *The Allen Colmes Show* as well as several hundred local talk radio shows; the authors and their book have been cited by many publications; they have made several trips to Hollywood to be interviewed on Bill Mahr's TV show, *Politically Incorrect*; and, they have been interviewed by the British Broadcasting Cooperation, French national television and Al Jazeera TV. Obviously, something about that book has caught the attention of quite a few people.

Having the opportunity to be interviewed by so many people, most of whom were antagonistic to the theme of Southern heritage and rights, the authors have had to answer some very interesting, difficult, intelligent, and, yes, some rather ignorant questions about Southern history and the War for Southern Independence. The very nature of an on-air interview does not lend itself to a well-thought-out and detailed answer to a question. Therefore, the authors have had to learn how to deal with these questions in a way which holds the attention and enlightens the minds of both the questioner and the audience. Adopting a system, we now refer to as Southern "shock and awe," the authors now feel quite secure when doing battle with politically correct anti-South bigots. The "shock and awe" system is a simple but very effective method of getting the Southern view across without losing the initiative in the process. The first part of an answer (the "shock") is designed to stop the questioner in his tracks and make him begin to question his viewpoint. It also makes the audience stop and listen to what is coming next (the "awe"). While answering the second phase of the question (i.e., the awe), one must succinctly offer a few proofs of why the questioner's belief structure is faulty. One important point any partisan supporter of a cause must remember about responding to an opponent is one does not have to convert every opponent at the first meeting. Partisans are usually so caught up in the advancement of their cause that they often overlook the steps taken by most people in changing a closely held viewpoint. The first step in changing a person's viewpoint usually begins by questioning that very same viewpoint. By giving a succinct and reasoned answer to an opponent, the process of "questioning" begins. Thus, it is not always necessary to win an argument, but it is essential to be correctly engaged in that argument. This "shock and awe" system is employed throughout this book in answering the type of questions put to the authors during our many interviews.

Late in 2004 a good friend of the authors called seeking advice about how to deal with a rather perplexing question on the issue of secession. Having just written a very politically incorrect book on American history, this author sought some advice from the Kennedy Twins on dealing with such perplexing questions. Thus, was conceived the idea of a book of questions and answers on the subject of Southern history and heritage. After reviewing tapes and transcripts of many interviews in which the authors have been engaged over the past ten years, the following questions and answers have been compiled. These questions deal with more than the so-called *Civil War* and its effect upon Southerners. It also demonstrates the deleterious results of the loss of real states' rights for all American, especially the malignant growth of big government.

In conjunction with the impetus to write a book of questions and answers about Southern issues, the publication and sale of more than 100,000 copies of the second edition of *The South Was Right!* was announced. With the total copies of *The South Was Right!*, both first and second editions, now amounting to more than 135,000 copies many people stated that it was time to publish a companion book to celebrate the success of *The South Was Right!* It is hoped *The Confederate Myth-Buster* will answer many questions which have surfaced since the original publication of our first book.

At the writing of this book America has just concluded celebrating the 150th (sesquicentennial) anniversary of the War Between the States. From Fort Sumter to Appomattox, America was embroiled in its most deadly war. Since the defeat of the South most Americans have been taught the Northern version of that conflict. Yet, there still remain staunch defenders of the South who refuse to kowtow to the victor's politically correct views of the War for Southern Independence and its consequences. Thus, it is hoped this book, among many other such books now in circulation, will give a voice to a defeated people and a conquered nation. The author trusts that this effort will serve as a creditable defense of the Cause of the South during this post-sesquicentennial era.

It is with great pleasure I now offer this book celebrating the success of this author and his twin brother has had defending the Cause of the South and American liberty. This book is divided into three parts. Part One contains nine chapters of questions and answers about why the Kennedy Twins hold the view that the South was right in 1861. Related questions have been grouped together to form each chapter. It should be noted that many questions could fit rather nicely into more than one chapter. Each question was placed in a chapter according to the nature of the discussion which was taking place at the time of its asking, as well as the direct intent of the question. Therefore, a question about secession that was asked during a discussion about slavery that also related to the issue of slavery was placed in the chapter on slavery. Part Two, is a collection of photographs and an explanation of the meaning of these photos to the South and to America. Part Three is a compilation of four articles written by the author defending life in Dixie and the Cause of the South.

One of the most common questions asked about *The South Was Right!* which is not included in this book is, "The South was right about what?" For those people raised on the common prejudices (false news) of modern America, the concept that the South could be right about anything sounds ridiculous. Upon a first viewing of the book, many people thought it was a defense of segregation or otherwise an anti-civil rights tome. Nothing could have been further from the truth but to the minds of those who only see racism and ignorance down South, this view was perfectly logical. With this thought in mind, it may be of some interest to the reader to learn just how the title of our first book was chosen.

For many years prior to the publication of the first edition, the authors had been doing research for a book in defense of the Southern cause during the War for Southern Independence. After several working titles were suggested, a tentative title, *To Live or Die for Dixie*, was chosen and used by the authors for several years while working on the manuscript. While on a business trip to Boston, Massachusetts, Ron was driven through a working-class Irish district of Boston. It was in this area during the infamous Boston busing crisis of the 1970s that so many demonstrations and outright acts of violence had taken place. While driving through this area, Ron noticed an old spray-painted graffiti sign that stated "The South WAS right!" It seems that at least some people in Boston had had enough of Federal interference in the lives of their children and remembered that the South had warned America of this danger. Returning home, Ron began lobbying for a name change of the book then in the process of completion. After due consideration it was agreed that the name of the forthcoming book would be *The South Was Right!*

How ironic, the name of a book about the correctness of the South's position during the War for Southern Independence was born during the civil rights struggle of forced school busing in Boston, Massachusetts! With three hundred state police patrolling every day just to keep the peace in the once sedate public schools of Boston, the schools began to look more like prisons or a war zone than schools. This of course led to the abandonment of those schools by many white parents. The end result after the expenditure of millions of dollars on busing, rather than on education, was a less sedate and less integrated student body. No wonder the people of that area of Boston, Massachusetts, expressed their feelings that "The South WAS right!" This example alone demonstrates the South was not the only section of this country struggling with the issues of civil rights during the sixties and seventies, yet it is the South which is routinely condemned and ostracized for the problems it had to face during those tumultuous years. This should not come as a surprise to Southerners. Since the end of the war, the North has routinely attempted to keep the South upon the "stools of everlasting repentance." With the least bit of falling Northern ego, one can expect to see the South paraded before the world so as to have all of its faults once again exposed, condemned, and corrected by morally superior Yankees. At that point in time, the self-same falling ego will have been sufficiently re-inflated so as to allow the South to once again go in peace — that is until it is once again needed to puff up the ego of its old self-righteous adversary.

Since the failure of the South to maintain its independence in 1865, the relationship between the North and the South has been at best one of overbearing paternal oversight or at worst one of a colonial people and an all-powerful imperial master. At best, the relationship is not the one envisioned by the founding fathers of these United States; at worst, it is a relationship backed by the moral suasion of bloody bayonets — it should be remembered that bloody bayonets are the instruments of tyrants.

Today, average Americans must work from January to mid-May just to pay their yearly tax burden. Every aspect of life from conception to burial is now under the regulation of an all-powerful Federal government. Even states north of the Mason-Dixon Line are beginning to complain about their rights being trampled upon by a Federal government that recognizes no limits on its perceived powers. It is hoped with the publication of *The Confederate Myth-Buster*, and the other Kennedy Twins' books, Americans, both from the North and from the South, will wake up to the dangers posed by an all-powerful and unlimited big government. After the defeat of the South, Vice President Alexander Stephens of the Confederate States of America noted, "The Cause of the South is the Cause of us all."[1] All people who love liberty more than government now have a stake in redressing the issues of 1861-65. Liberty, as established by our founding fathers both North and South, cannot survive in a post-Appomattox nation. Two themes run through *The South Was Right!* which are vociferously echoed in *The Confederate Myth-Buster:* (1) Southerners should be proud of their history and heritage, and (2) the defeat of the Confederate States of America at Appomattox destroyed true American liberty for all Americans, not just Southerners. Until Americans undo the ill effects of Appomattox, there is little hope of living as free as our founding fathers intended for us to live. As the Kennedy Twins often remind people, "The South was right in 1861 because America was right in 1776." Our hope is to see a day when our children's children enjoy the liberty that was established for Americans by our founding fathers in 1776. Liberty is what this book, as well as all the books written by the Kennedy Twins, is all about. Liberty — that happy condition of free people, that principle which Patrick Henry cherished above life itself, that stumbling block to tyranny — is most dear to all Americans who understand the cause of 1776. As Patrick Henry so ably put it, "The first thing I have at heart is American liberty; the second thing is American union."[2] The enjoyment of real American liberty in these United States would be the greatest blessing of all, but failing that, liberty will be enjoyed — even if it must be in a free and independent Southland. **Liberty, not geography, is what this struggle is all about!**

Deo Vindice

Walter D. Kennedy
www.kennedytwins.com
Point, Louisiana
March 13, 2019

---

[1] Alexander Stephens, *A Constitutional View of the Late War Between the States; Its Causes, Character, Conduct and Results* (1870, Harrisonburg, VA: Sprinkle Publications, 1995) II, 666.
[2] Patrick Henry, as cited in, William Wirt Henry, ed., *Patrick Henry: Life, Correspondence, and Speeches* (1891, Harrisonburg, VA: Sprinkle Publications, 1993) III, 449.

Patrick Henry

No other American Founding Father more correctly defined America's relationship with government than Patrick Henry when in 1775 he declared, "Give me liberty or give me death!" In 1788 Henry further defined the nature of government by announcing, "The first thing I have at heart is American liberty; the second thing is American union."³ According to Henry, liberty not union is the *sine qua non* (the essential element) of American government — Lincoln did not get that memo!

---

3 Ibid.

Chapter 1
Secession

The United States were formed into a federal body, with an express reservation to each state of its freedom, sovereignty and independence.[4]

For the Kennedy Twins, other than the issue of slavery, the issue of secession of a state from the Federal union has proven to be the most contentious subject to deal with on most talk radio shows. This is somewhat amazing when one realizes that in the early history of the republic, the right of secession was as American as apple pie. Yet, we must remember, it has been more than 150 years since the North won the war of 1861-65. For the most part in that time the South's view on the subject of the right of secession has gone under told or, worse yet, not given a hearing at all.[5] Therefore it should not come as a surprise most Americans, even Southerners, feel that to say that the South was right about the issue of secession sounds ludicrous. Yet, the principles for which the people of the South contended in 1861-65 had its antecedent in the American struggle of 1776. For this reason, the Kennedy Twins have often repeated the truism, **"The South was right in 1861 because America was right in 1776."** The "rightness" of the cause of the South, and therefore the right of secession, is based upon the presupposition of an unalienable right of free people to consent to the form of government under which they must live. After the establishment of this free government the right of secession then becomes the means by which a free people prevent the government that they have established from overstepping its authority and becoming a tyrannical government. Therefore, we maintain that the right of secession is both the author and preserver of free government. Without the right of secession, serfdom and eventual slavery will be the lot of a once free people.

---

4 William Rawle, *A View of the Constitution* (1825, Land and Land Press, Baton Rouge, LA: 1993) 37.
5 This should not be taken as just another gratuitous attack upon the liberal media and education systems in America. Even neo-conservative commentators such as Rush Limbaugh and Sean Hannity routinely dismiss as Neo-Confederate Nuts anyone who has a positive view of the right of secession. This author has on numerous occasions heard Rush Limbaugh dismiss out of hand Southerners who attempt to give the traditional Southern view of Southern rights and/or secession. The neo-conservatives of today are just as likely as any liberals to slander the good name of Southern leaders and the cause of the South.

1— Q. Where in the US Constitution is it written that a state has a right to secede?

A. Where in the US Constitution is it written that a person has a right to marry? You see, there is no guarantee in the Constitution for the vast majority of rights we enjoy as citizens. If the right of secession is denied because it is not written in the Constitution, then most of the rights we Americans hold dear are subject to abuse. The Constitution was never intended to be an itemized list of constitutionally protected rights. But this leads to an obvious question: What does the Constitution do if it does not grant us our rights or otherwise protect our rights? Many noted constitutional authorities tell us that the Constitution is mostly a grant of authority to the Federal government, a limitation of power of the Federal government, and a specific limitation on state powers.[6] In 1787 when our founding fathers gathered in Philadelphia to draw up a new constitution, they already enjoyed the rights and liberties of free men. They did not need a new constitution to grant these rights; they already had their rights. Each state had its own constitution that was drawn up by the people of that state. The various state constitutions spelled out what rights the citizens of that state were free to enjoy and the limits on the state government that they found necessary for guaranteeing their civil liberties. What was done in Philadelphia was to create a central government by granting to it certain powers that theretofore had belonged to the several states. The main desire of the vast majority of the delegates was to create a Federal government which was stronger than the government they then had, that is, the United States government under the Articles of Confederation. This desire to establish a stronger government was balanced by the fear of an overly powerful central government. The founding fathers had just successfully concluded their war of independence with Great Britain and had no desire to create another central government that would not respect their rights. Therefore, they established a limited central government that could exercise only those powers that had been specifically granted to it by the people of the states.

Now as to your question, we must insist that you ask a "constitutionally correct" question. Since the Constitution does not provide a list of "rights," your question cannot be answered. The correct ques-

---

6 Forrest McDonald, as cited in, M. E. Bradford, *Original Intentions on the Making and Ratification of the United States Constitution* (Athens, GA, and London: The University of Georgia Press, 1993) xi, xii.

tion to ask is, "Where in the US Constitution is the right of secession forbidden to the people of the states?" In Article I, Section 10, of the Constitution we find those things which the states mutually agreed they would not perform as members of the new Union. For example, the states cannot maintain a navy, coin money, wage war, or enter into treaties with foreign nations. But nowhere will you find the people of the states surrendering the right to judge for themselves how they should be governed. After all, the people of the individual states had already removed the British authorities from their state, entered a union with the other states under the Articles of Confederation, and at the time were looking at withdrawing from that government and establishing a new government for themselves. Such a people were loath to adopt a constitution that would limit their right to withdraw from a government that did not meet their needs. Americans at that time, both in the North and in the South, understood that free men in free states had the right to govern themselves.

2— Q. General Lee did not fight for the South, he fought for Virginia. How can you say he is a Southern hero?

A. You are right! As a Virginian, Robert E. Lee fought for Virginia, just as a Mississippian, Jefferson Davis, fought for Mississippi, and as a Louisianan, Pierre Gustave Toutant Beauregard, fought for Louisiana. As we have said, in 1861 Southerners believed in States' Rights. Lee became a "Southern" hero because he led Southerners from every Southern state as they defended their belief in States' Rights. Lee, not unlike Jefferson Davis, did not desire secession. After the war when testifying before Congress in Washington, Lee stated why he and his fellow Southerners seceded when he stated, "All the South ever desired was that the Constitution as given to us by our forefathers should be respected and honored."[7] Varina Davis, wife of Jefferson Davis, noted how Senator Davis struggled with the secession crisis. When word came to Washington from Mississippi that his home state had seceded from the Union, Davis at that time resigned from the United States Senate. In his farewell address Davis, the future president of the Confederacy, noted that Mississippi had seceded "…not even for our own pecuniary benefit; but from the high and solemn motive of defending and protecting the rights we inherited, and

---

7 Robert E. Lee, as cited in, Gamaliel Bradford, Jr., "A Hero's Conscience: A Study of Robert E. Lee," *The Atlantic Monthly* December 1910, 737.

which it is our duty to transmit unshorn to our children."[8] Lee was no different from most Southerners at the outbreak of the war. Few if any desired war. War was feared, but worse than the fear of war was the fear of the loss of liberty. As Patrick Henry noted in 1788, "The first thing I have at heart is American liberty; the second thing is American union."[9] Like Patrick Henry, no American should be ashamed of defending liberty first and foremost.

3— Q. According to your interpretation of the Declaration of Independence, a people have the right to secede from any government that does not meet their desires. Yet, when I read the Declaration of Independence what I see is a call for the people to have a voice, that is, a vote, in changing their government. Why do you insist the Declaration of Independence is about secession, that is, the destruction of a government, instead of voting, which is, changing what is wrong with a government?

A. The Declaration of Independence states free people have an unalienable right to "alter or abolish" the government under which they live. By voting we can alter the form of government under which we live. The right of secession is the means by which, when absolutely necessary, we abolish the form of our government. The founding fathers voted in their colonial elections. At no time did the founding fathers demand or request the right to vote in the British Parliament. Since each colony had its own legislative body which was freely elected by the citizens of that colony, there was no great demand to vote for a delegate in Parliament. Jefferson's words here "to alter or to abolish the government" should remind us of the words of John Locke: "Men can never be secure from Tyranny, if there be no means to escape it."[10] When tyranny threatens the liberty and rights of a people, secession becomes the final barricade behind which the defense of liberty is made.

---

8 Jefferson Davis, as cited in, James R. Kennedy and Walter D. Kennedy, *The South Was Right!* (Gretna. LA: Pelican Publishing Co., 1994) 319.
9 Patrick Henry, as cited in, William Wirt Henry, III, 449.
10 John Locke, *Two Treatises of Government* (1698, New York: *The Classics of Liberty Library*, 1992) 336. Thomas Jefferson, the author (actually he was more like the chief editor) of the Declaration of Independence, was greatly influenced by John Locke's *Treatises of Government*. In the preface of his book Locke warned about the evil that can befall a people who do not correctly understand the nature of legitimate government. Locke stated, That, there cannot be done a greater Mischief to Prince and People, than the Propagating wrong Notions concerning Government.

4— Q. Lincoln was justified in putting down the secession movement in 1861. If a state can secede from the Federal government, a county can secede from a state and a city can secede from a county. This would lead to complete anarchy. How can a nation survive such a situation?

A. The followers of King George, the Tories, made the same argument against the American Patriots in 1776. According to the followers of King George, if the colonies could break their union with the mother country, then counties and towns could do the same. Without King George and the union with the mother country, anarchy and chaos would destroy America. The Patriots of '76 replied that liberty and freedom is the greatest antidote for chaos. No one should ever fear freedom, whereas tyranny, no matter how paternalistic, produces chaos, fear, economic privation, and the loss of civil liberty. Tyranny is the ugly bride of big government. This is why our founding fathers feared big government. Now, as to your point about one secession leading to innumerable secession movements until America has been reduced to little tracts of land with no unity of purpose; let's take a close look at this assertion. Secession is the act of a sovereign community removing itself from one form of government and reasserting its rights of sovereignty. Historically, in these United States that action is performed by the people of a state (the first act was performed by the legislative body of each colony at which time it assumed the full rights of sovereignty). From removing the officials of King George, empowering delegates to go to Philadelphia to vote for independence, forming a Federal government under the Articles of Confederation, to withdrawing from that government and acceding to the new Federal government under the Constitution, all of this was done by the power of the people of each sovereign state. Note that in Article VII of the Constitution, it is the conventions of the people of the states who will bring the new Federal government into being. Also note that this article clearly states that this new Constitution will be established "between the states so ratifying the same." Those states who chose to remain outside of the new Union were treated as sovereign states, not as enemies that had to be invaded and conquered. Now, it should be plain who has a right to secede in America. The Federal government, and therefore the Union, is a product of the will of the people of the sovereign states. As Samuel Rutherford stated in *Lex Rex*, "Those who have the power to make have powers to unmake a king."[11] The people

---

11 Samuel Rutherford, *Lex Rex* (1644, Harrisonburg, VA: Sprinkle Publications,

of the states, who made the Union, and only the people of that particular state, could unmake the Union. Now, what about the secession of a city or of a county? The city, county, and other subdivisions of a state exist because they hold a charter from the state. A city or county did not create the state; therefore, a city or county cannot secede from a state. If one properly understands American history in regard to the right of secession, the fear of ultimate chaos due to unlimited secession movements is removed.

5— Q. You mentioned William Rawle, author of an 1825 textbook on the US Constitution. According to you, this textbook defends the right of secession. During the Whiskey Rebellion, the Federal government sent troops into Pennsylvania to put down this rebellion. Also, William Rawle was appointed by President Washington to try those men responsible for the Whiskey Rebellion. Obviously, George Washington and William Rawle believed rebels are traitors. Doesn't this prove that secession is illegal?

A. You are confusing secession with rebellion. William Rawle was an advocate of the right of secession of a state from the Union. Remember, this was the same Union the states had created. In these United States a state is sovereign, not a portion of a state. Therefore, the illegal act of a small portion of the population of a state in defiance of the lawful authority of a state is rebellion against the state, not secession from it. (See question and answer number 4 of this chapter.) Now, as for the Federal government sending troops into Pennsylvania to put down the rebellion, please note that the Constitution allows the Federal government to send troops into a state to uphold the law only upon the request of the legislature or governor of the state.[12] The governor of the state of Pennsylvania petitioned the Federal government for assistance in maintaining its lawful authority, whereupon President Washington requested the assistance of the militias of Virginia and Maryland to assist Pennsylvania in restoring order and its lawful authority. Once again, we see the Constitution working to maintain order and the lawful authority of the state. Rebellion is not

---

1982) 126.

12 Article IV, Section 4, of the United States Constitution states: The United States shall guarantee to every state in this union a republican form of government, and shall protect each of them against invasion; and **on application of the legislature, or of the executive, (when the legislature cannot be convened,) against domestic violence** (emphasis added).

the same action as secession. William Rawle understood this point, early Americans understood this point, and Confederate Americans understood this point. When will Americans of this age understand this point? (Did you know that early in the War for Southern Independence, Confederate soldiers detested having the term "rebel" attached to them? The reason was simple: they were not in rebellion against lawful authority, they were fighting to maintain their rights as Americans just as their grandfathers had done seventy-five years earlier. It was only after several years of being called "rebel" that they took the name to heart, much like early Christians had done with the slur "Christian" in the first century.)

6— Q. When Abraham Lincoln was elected, the South seceded from the Union. The South seceded because Lincoln and the Republican Party wanted to end slavery. Doesn't this prove that the South left the Union to protect slavery?

A. No major political party in 1860, including Lincoln's Republican Party, advocated the abolition of slavery in any Southern state. In his first inaugural address, Lincoln stated he had no desire or power to interfere with slavery anywhere that it existed. Lincoln stated quite clearly, "I have no intention, directly or indirectly, to interfere with slavery in those states where it exists. I believe I have no lawful right to do so. Those who nominated and elected me did so with full knowledge that I had made this and many similar declarations and had never recanted them."[13] Prior to this statement in February of 1860 in New York, Lincoln declared, "We can yet afford to let it [slavery] alone where it is." Just after the election of Lincoln, the future vice president of the Confederate States of America noted that the institution of slavery would be safer if the South remained in the Union.[14] While pledged to limiting the geographical growth of slavery, Lincoln and the Republican Party were equally pledged to protecting slavery "where it is." Lincoln and the Republican Party did pose a threat to the South, but it was not the supposed threat to slavery that drove the South to the expediency of secession. The straw the broke the proverbial camel's back was the election to the presiden-

---

13 Abraham Lincoln, First Inaugural Address, March 4, 1861, Washington, DC.
14 Alexander Stephens, *The Correspondence of Robert Tooms, Alexander H. Stephens, and Howell Cobb* U. B. Phillips, ed. (Washington, DC: American Historical Association, 1913) 487.

cy of the leader of an unbalanced party ticket. Up until the election of Lincoln, every major national political party nominated a presidential candidate from one section of the nation and balanced it with a vice presidential nomination from the other section. For example, in 1860 the Northern Democrats nominated Stephen Douglas from Illinois for president and Benjamin Fritzpatrick of Alabama for vice president; the Southern Democrats nominated John Breckinridge of Kentucky for president and Joseph Lane of Oregon for vice president; the Whig Party nominated John Bell of Tennessee for president and Edward Everett of Massachusetts for vice president; the Republicans nominated Abraham Lincoln of Illinois for president and Hannibal Hamlin of Maine for vice president. For the first time in American history a party had captured the chief executive office of the nation without having a balanced ticket. The South believed that its interests, not just its slave property but all its property and constitutional rights, would no longer be protected by a political party that had no standing in the South and had won only 39 percent of the national vote. Even after defeat, the South tried to maintain its attachment to the original Constitution. When in 1865 the Thirteenth Amendment (the abolition of slavery amendment) was sent to the states for ratification, every Southern state ratified the amendment. Yet, when the Fourteenth Amendment was sent to the states, every Southern state with only one exception refused to ratify it. Even when threatened with military occupation, the South still refused to ratify the Fourteenth Amendment. Why were Southern states willing to ratify the Thirteenth Amendment (ending forever any hope of regaining their slaves), but yet not be willing to ratify the Fourteenth Amendment? The Thirteenth Amendment ended slavery, something that was important only to a few Southerners, whereas, the Fourteenth Amendment struck a blow at the heart of States' Rights, and the American Republic as originally founded, which was very important to most Southerners. Unlike slavery, this issue was something that was near and dear to a large portion of Southerners. In essence the Fourteenth Amendment changed the nature of American government from a republic of republics into a unitary state otherwise known as an all-powerful central government, like unto an empire. This was the end of real States' Rights; therefore, the South refused to go along with such a draconian measure. The fear of 1861 was the same fear of 1866 — the fear of a Federal government so powerful no one could check its action. Ultimately, the fear of creating an all-powerful Federal government was the cause of secession and the reason the South refused to ratify the Fourteenth Amendment.

7— **Q.** You cite a lot of Southerners in defense of the right of secession. Where are the Northern voices favoring the right of secession?

A. One of the first Northern voices for secession was that of Representative Josiah Quincy from Massachusetts. On the floor of the United States House of Representatives in January 1813, Quincy stated that the fair state of Massachusetts would secede from the Union if the "mixed breed Creoles of Louisiana were allowed into the Union."[15] William Rawle of Pennsylvania, the author of the textbook on the United States Constitution that was used at the United States Military Academy at West Point, is another Northerner who believed in the right of secession. But you miss the point about the right of secession. The right of secession does not exist in a political vacuum. Secession is a right that exists only for a sovereign state. This is the meaning of the term of "States' Rights." Because a state is sovereign it has all the rights and privileges of any other sovereign state. By its own action, a state can limit certain portions of its rightful power, authority, or privileges. Thus, when the thirteen sovereign states of America acceded to the new Union under the Constitution, they mutually agreed to a self-imposed limit on certain actions that sovereign states have the power to perform. This limitation is clearly seen in Article I, Section 10, of the Constitution. In Article I, Section 10, you will note the words, "No state shall…." The Federal government did not force this concession upon the states; after all, the Federal government did not even exist at that time. Also, by granting to the central government certain rights, the states were empowering the Federal government to act as their mutual agent in those areas. Therefore, we see in Article VI that the "Constitution, and the laws of the United States, which shall be made in *pursuance thereof*…shall be the supreme law of the land" (emphasis added). The states are sovereign, and every right that they exercised before entering the Union are retained, unless such rights have been attenuated by their own action. The fact of state sovereignty, which is apparent in the acts of all the states as well as specially being announced in their various state constitutions, makes secession a right of the people, Northern as well as Southern. For

---

15 Josiah Quincy, as cited in, Kennedy and Kennedy, *The South Was Right!* 299.

example, the constitution of the state of Massachusetts proclaims: "The people of this commonwealth have the sole and exclusive right of governing themselves, as a free, sovereign and independent State."[16] The state constitution of Massachusetts was written before the adoption of the Federal Constitution. But even after the adoption of the Federal Constitution, the constitution of the state of New Hampshire also made an announcement of its belief in state sovereignty. New Hampshire's constitution states: "The people of this state have the sole and exclusive right to govern themselves as a free, sovereign and independent state."[17] A list of those Northerners who believed in state sovereignty and/or the right of secession would include the names of the most prominent men in early American history.

8— Q. Secession seems to be a favorite subject of yours. How could having this great nation broken into many little warring factions be a good idea?

A. As for your fear of America becoming a society of "little warring factions," let us remind you there are a dozen nations in South America. There has been less bloodshed, less loss of life, and less loss of private property in the past 150 years of South American history than in one year of the Federal government's War of Northern Aggression against the Confederacy. It seems that the nations of South America could teach the United States a lesson or two on how to mind our own business and be a good neighbor. Also, you seem to place a lot of stock in the landmass of America as if this is the source of its greatness. We believe that our country's greatness resides in the principles of free government as announced to the world in 1776 with the adoption of the Declaration of Independence. Principles of free government, not landmass, is what made America great. These principles and that greatness were surrendered at Appomattox.

9— Q. When the states ratified the Constitution, they became part of a great Union. They went into the Union for their own benefit, knowing that it was a "marriage for life" commitment. Why do you think states could take advantage of the Union and then just leave it at will?

A. Nowhere in the Constitution is there an announcement of the forming of a "perpetual" government. The only place one can find

---

16 Walter D. Kennedy, "SECESSION: The American Way," *Southern Mercury*, Vol. 1, No. 3, 18.
17 Ibid.

such a proclamation of the formation of a perpetual government is in the Articles of Confederation. This was the government the states had to withdraw from in order to form a new government under the Constitution. So much for "perpetual" government! If the states had the right to withdraw from the government under the Articles of Confederation that proclaimed its government to be perpetual, how can you maintain that the states did not have the right to withdraw from the new government when its constitution never proclaimed that it was forming a perpetual government? Logic is not on your side. But even more evidence can be found that points to the right of a state to withdraw from the new government. Let's look at what two states proclaimed in their official ratification of the new Constitution. One state, Virginia, made this bold statement: "We the delegates of the people of Virginia, etc., do, in the name and in behalf of the people of Virginia, declare and make known that the powers granted under the constitution, being derived from the people of the United States, may be resumed by them, whensoever the same shall be perverted to their injury or oppression, and that every power not granted thereby remains with them, and at their will; that therefore, no right, of any denomination, can be canceled, abridged, restrained, or modified, by the Congress, by the Senate, by the House of Representatives, acting in any capacity, by the President, or any department or officer of the United States, except in those instances in which power is given by the constitution for those purposes."[18] At this point you are probably thinking, "Oh yes, that is what Southerners thought." Well, let's look at what New York had to say about the nature of the new government it was forming in 1787: "That the powers of government may be resumed by the people whensoever it shall become necessary to their happiness; that every power, jurisdiction, and right, which is not by the said constitution clearly delegated to the Congress of the United States, or the department thereof, remains to the people of the several States, or to their respective State governments, to whom they may have granted the same."[19] You see, when these states acceded to the new form of government, they clearly stipulated that they reserved the right to withdraw whenever they determined. In the early history of these United States this was how free men in a free society viewed

---

18 Virginia's ratification of the United States Constitution, as cited in, E. A. Pollard, *Southern History of the War* (1866, New York: The Fairfax Press, 1978) II, 538.
19 New York s ratification of the Constitution, ibid., 539.

their right to "consent" to the government under which they lived: Free men in free society — what's wrong with that?

10— Q. Southern secession would have destroyed the United States. What kind of country would we have if the South had been allowed to go free?

A. What kind of country would we have if the South had been allowed to "go free"? We would have a free country! What's wrong with freedom? How would the secession of thirteen Southern states have destroyed the United States? After all, the United States managed to fight one of the bloodiest wars in Western history up until that time, and yet it was not destroyed. Now think about it; the Southern states never desired to invade or conquer the United States. If the Federal government had chosen peace rather than war, US trade and commerce would have commenced and gone on with the South just as it had commenced and gone on with the nation to the north of the United States, Canada. Does the existence of Canada to the north of the United States pose a threat to the existence of the United States? Has the economy of the United States suffered irreparable damage because a sovereign nation sits to its north? Such rhetorical questions don't even need an answer. By merely stating the question, we know the answer. A free Canada to the north of the United States or a free Confederate States of America to the south of the United States would not have caused the destruction of America. The invasion, conquest, and continual occupation of the Confederate States of America by the United States did indeed destroy America — the real America of 1776. A nation founded upon the right of free men living in a government of their own free choice, that is, a government by the consent of the governed, is a noble American principle and not a threat to America. This loss is a loss that is suffered not just by Southerners but by all Americans.

11— Q. Whether defending slavery or racial segregation, States' Rights seems to have always been a Southern doctrine used to defend the indefensible. Why should the rest of America embrace this Southern doctrine?

A. The South uniquely defended States' Rights (with the blood and the treasure of its people), but States' Rights is not a uniquely Southern doctrine. No doubt the strongest argument for the existence of States' Rights is the Tenth Amendment to the Constitution. Every state who ratified the Constitution in 1787-88 did so with the stipulation that an amendment be added to the Constitution that expressed the principle that states retained all rights that were not delegated to the new government. Here is how one such state expressed itself: "That it be explicitly declared that all Powers not expressly delegated by the aforesaid Constitution are reserved to the several States to be by them exercised."[20] The state who demanded the addition of this amendment to the Constitution was not South Carolina, Virginia, or any other Southern state; it was the great Northern state of Massachusetts. So impressed were the folks of Massachusetts of the need to protect the rights of the states that this was the very first amendment that Massachusetts recommended to be adopted. As has already been pointed out, every state demanded this protection for States' Rights. How many times must it be pointed out, States' Rights is an American principle of government, not a Southern principle. Yes, a good principle can be misused. The misuse of a good principle should be condemned, not the good principle. States' Rights is an American "good principle" of government.

12— Q. I am a veteran of the United States Army. Like my father before me, I risked my life for this country. You sound more like what I was fighting against; people who wanted to destroy America. Why shouldn't I call people like you traitors?

A. No section of the United States has responded with more enthusiasm to the call of this nation in time of war than the Southland. This is not just a twenty-first-century phenomenon but has been going on ever since the founding of this nation. In 1812 when the United States declared war on Great Britain, the people of the territory of Mississippi were so caught up in the spirit of patriotism that the territorial legislature had to "draft" men to stay at home rather than leave for the war. In every war this nation has fought, the people of the South have been in the forefront of the defense of American liberty. In the War of 1812 and in the Mexican War it was Southerners who comprised the majority of troops in defending this nation.[21] During both World War I and World War II it was Southerners, Alvin

---

20 Arthur T. Prescott, *Drafting the Federal Constitution* (Baton Rouge: Louisiana State University Press, 1941) 171.
21 Edward A. Pollard, *Southern History of the War* (1866, New York: The Fairfax Press, 1978), 64..

York of Tennessee and Audie Murphy of Texas, who were the most decorated soldiers of those wars. Your question is about "patriotism," but we must ask the question, "What is the emphasis of your patriotism?" Remember what Patrick Henry said, "The first thing I have at heart is American liberty; the second thing is American union."[22] How would you describe Patrick Henry, as a traitor or as a patriot? The view the Kennedy Twins espouse parallels the view Patrick Henry announced when he stated that he believed in liberty over union. American soldiers did not face death and the terror of battle to maintain a government, but rather to maintain liberty. Government is worthy of the sacrifices of these noble men only in and as much as it defends liberty first. Patrick Henry got it right; that is why we say, "The South Was Right!"

13— Q. Other than a few radical Southerners, who in the world cared if the rebellious effort of a few secessionists was a failure?

A. For various reasons many people outside of the United States or the Confederate States did bemoan the South's loss of the War for Southern Independence. France's last hope of an American empire or an influential ally in the Western Hemisphere was lost with a large and aggressive United States just north of its Mexican ally. Great Britain faced the same problem with its Canadian possessions. Remember, just after the North had conquered the South many Americans were pushing the idea of sending the giant army into Canada to remove any chance of Great Britain using Canada as a base for action against the United States.[23] Within thirty years of Appomattox, the Kingdom of Hawaii was overthrown by Yankees; Spain was stripped of its colonial empire both in the Western Hemisphere and Eastern Hemisphere; Panama was taken from Columbia by America and a big ditch was dug across it for the benefit of Yankee commerce; Latin America became an "American" protectorate with the United States exercising the right to send troops into any Latin American country at will; and China was invaded by American troops by the new and "improved" (i.e., improved as to its ability to create and maintain an empire) United States of America. In 1866, a well-known British libertarian and historian, Lord Acton, wrote General Lee and expressed his remorse for the South's loss of its war for independence. Lord

---

22 Patrick Henry, as cited in, William Wirt Henry, III, 449.
23 James R. Kennedy and Walter D. Kennedy, *Was Jefferson Davis Right?* (Gretna, LA: Pelican Publishing Co., 1998) 114.

Action stated, "I saw in States' Rights the only availing check upon the absolutism of the sovereign will, and secession filled me with hope, not as the destruction but as the redemption of Democracy.... I deemed that you were fighting the battles of our liberty, our progress, and our civilization, and I mourn for the stake which was lost at Richmond more deeply than I rejoice over that which was saved at Waterloo."[24] What did Lord Acton see as the great features of true States' Rights and the right of secession? As he noted, States' Rights and secession put a check on the "absolutism of the sovereign will." In other words, any government that could exercise its will unchecked was a government of tyrannical powers. The right of secession would be a people's avenue of escape from tyranny. But with the loss of the War for Southern Independence, as Lord Acton correctly noted, tyranny became more likely and liberty less safe. Southerners were not the last people in America who felt the weight of the tyrant's heel upon their neck. During the war the United States had already begun its campaign against the Native American population in the American West.[25] Once again, we must point out that secession is not rebellion; therefore, your remark about "rebellious secessionists" is way off mark. (See questions 4 and 5 of this chapter for a contrast between rebellion and secession.)

Summary

In launching their new Union in 1789, the founding fathers of the United States renewed and strengthened their confederacy of free, sovereign, and independent States.[26]

— John Remington Graham

The right and act of secession in this post-Appomattox age is little understood and surely very little appreciated by the average American. As Graham points out in the above-mentioned citation the founding fathers understood that they lived in "free, sovereign, and independent States." Graham also points out that, "this primordial and universal right did not suddenly appear...."[27] The act of secession

---

24 Lord Acton, as cited in, Thomas E. Woods, Jr. *The Politically Incorrect Guide to American History* (Washington, DC: Regnery Publishing, Inc., 2004) 74.
25 Kennedy and Kennedy, *The South Was Right!* 292.
26 John Remington Graham, *A Constitutional History of Secession*, (Pelican Publishing Co., Gretna, LA: 2002), 18.
27 Ibid.

has a long and remarkable history in these United States and in fact the very existence of this nation is predicated upon an act of secession, which was announced in the Declaration of Independence. One of the most often cited authorities our founding fathers quoted in defense of their right to withdraw from the union with Great Britain was John Locke. In Locke's *Two Treaties of Government*, he clearly points out that "Men can never be secure from Tyranny, if there be no means to escape it."[28] Secession was the "means" by which our founding fathers secured their liberty from an abusive central government in London. The right of secession acts as a warning to the powers that be within the central government of a federation that it is the people at the local level who hold ultimate power over how they shall be governed. Acknowledging the very existence of the right of secession puts the supreme power of government in the hands of the people at the local level and not in the hands of politicians, bureaucrats, and judges of the central government be that government in London or in Washington. Men who desire a big, strong, indivisible and therefore supreme Federal government detest the notion of secession. Hitler, Stalin, or any other tyrant, abhors a government that recognizes the right of secession. A federal republic that embraces the idea of secession will always die when tyrants become the leader of that federal republic — one more reason to embrace the right of secession.

---

28 Locke, 336.

William Rawle

A friend of George Washington and Benjamin Franklin, Rawle, a Northerner, was an abolitionist who worked closely with Southerners to end slavery in the United States. He also was the author of one of the first textbooks (1825) on the United States Constitution. Rawle was a strong advocate of States' Rights. In his textbook he stated, "The secession of a state from the Union depends on the will of the people of such state."[29]

---

29 William Rawle, *A View of the Constitution of the United States of America* (1825, Land and Land Publishing Co., Baton Rouge, LA: 1993) 238.

Chapter II
The Constitution

The history of man does not present a more illustrious monument of human invention, sound political principles, and judicious combinations, than the constitution of the United States.[30]

— William Rawle

The Constitution of the United States is so highly praised yet so little understood. The following questions need to be answered before any correct in-depth study of the Constitution can be made. First, why was the Constitution written; second, who authorized the writing of the Constitution; and third, who endowed the Constitution with the power it possesses?

Why was the Constitution written? The Constitution was written in the year 1787, eleven years after the states had declared their independence from Great Britain. At the time of the writing of the Constitution each of the thirteen states had its own state constitution that delineated the liberty to be exercised by its citizens and the scope of the power to be exercised by the state government. These constitutions were written and enforced by the people of each individual state. The drawing up of these state constitutions was performed by the people, a sovereign community, thus forming their own state government. In other words, it was the act of a people exercising original sovereignty. Unlike the English Constitution that was unwritten, these constitutions were written. There was a well-founded purpose in having a written constitution rather than an unwritten constitution. It was written so the people could easily understand what powers they had granted their state government and what rights they had retained for themselves. An unwritten constitution was the source of one of the problems the colonists had faced with the mother country. The colonists would demand their rights as protected under the English Constitution, and the mother country would change the law and declare that no such rights existed in the English Constitution. Therefore, the colonists demanded that their state constitutions be written. When they determined that a stronger central government was needed, it was natural the new constitution would also be a writ-

---

30 Rawle, 31.

ten constitution; thus, insuring this protection against abuse of their liberty by the central government.

Who authorized the writing of the Constitution? Unfortunately, most Americans seem to think the people of America in some form of a democratic mass got together and wrote and adopted the Constitution. Nothing could be further from the truth. In 1787 a convention of delegates, appointed by the legislature of each state, met in Philadelphia to consider reforming the government under the Articles of Confederation. Rather than reform the existing government under the Articles of Confederation, the delegates began deliberations that led to a new government under the Constitution. This document was then submitted to the states. The various state legislatures then appointed delegates to the State Constitutional Convention. Notice that all the action, which led to the adoption of the Constitution, was centered upon the free action of the people of each state. Notice also that the action of one state did not bind another state to any new government. Here we see the action of a sovereign community granting to an agent of its own creation portions of its sovereign power. This grant of power to the central government was done by the free and unfettered will of free men in sovereign states.

Who endowed the Constitution with its power? As William Rawle noted in his textbook on the United States Constitution, Article I, Section 1, which clearly states that "all legislative powers herein granted," gives evidence of the formation of a limited, not general government. Also, it reminds us that the power of the Federal government does not originate with the Federal government but is a "grant" from some other power.[31] The creation of the Federal government by the actions of sovereign states is an example of a government based upon secondary sovereignty. The central government of a federal republic cannot be sovereign because its existence is dependent upon the powers granted to it by the republics, i.e., states, which created the federal republic. The federal republic is "sovereign" only in those areas that the states have granted authority to the federal government. As we are instructed in the Ninth and Tenth Amendments, all power that is not granted to the Federal government by the Constitution is reserved to the people and the several states.

---

31 Ibid., 44.

1— Q. The Constitution states that "we the people" created the Union. Why should states be allowed to destroy that which "we the people" established?

A. Your question makes the false assumption that "we the people" mean "we the people in one common mass." Nowhere in the Constitution or the deliberations on the adoption of the Constitution is that notion even remotely indicated. Actually, the phrase "we the people" means "we the people of the sovereign states." Our founding fathers made it clear in the Declaration of Independence that a people have the right to "alter or abolish" any government they have established at their will. Now, if we follow the logic of the founders of this nation, all we must do is determine who established this nation. At that point we can "constitutionally" answer the question: "Do the people of the states have the right to alter or abolish their government?" After all, as we have seen, those who establish a government are the ones who have the power and the right to "abolish" that government.[32] Let me ask you, how many Americans voted for ratification of the Constitution? Answer: Not many! Only those Americans chosen by the people of sovereign states as their delegates voted yea or nay to ratify the Constitution. You see, the Constitution was ratified by a convention of the people of the individual sovereign states. This convention was called into being by the legislative will of each of the sovereign states. Can't you see a pattern here? Here we see the action of the state government calling the convention, and the people of that sovereign state choosing the delegates to determine whether their state would or would not join this new government. The action of all the other state conventions is not binding upon any other state or the people thereof. The history of the ratification of the Constitution clearly demonstrates that the Constitution was ratified by the independent actions of the people of sovereign states. Unfortunately, most Americans today seem to think that some form of general plebiscite of the American people ratified the Constitution. If the Constitution had been ratified by a national plebiscite, your assertion that a state does not have the right to secede (or as you incorrectly stated the issue "destroy the American government") would be valid. But as we see, we the people of the sovereign states and not we the people of America in a common mass ratified the Constitution. One final point must be made on this argument about "we the people" forming the Consti-

---

32 Rutherford, 126.

tution. You will note that this phrase "we the people" is found in the preamble of the Constitution and not in any article or section of the Constitution. As the United States Supreme Court correctly noted in Jacobson v. Massachusetts,[33] the preamble of a document cannot be used to change the meaning or intent of an article or section of the document. In other words, even if the phrase "we the people" meant the American people in a common mass, that phrase could not change the meaning of the words of any article of the Constitution. Note that in Article VII, the Constitution tells us who the agent is that will ratify the Constitution — the states.[34] Article VII makes it clear that it is the positive action of the states, more correctly nine of the thirteen states, which would give life to the new Constitution. Also of note, only nine of the thirteen states were needed to ratify the Constitution; but of equal note, the nine ratifying states could not mandate ratification by the remaining four states. The choice to join the new union and therefore withdraw from the former union under the Articles of Confederation was left completely in the hands of the people of the sovereign states. Even the notable American George Washington spoke of anticipating the accession of the remaining states to the new union.[35] Accession is the political antonym of secession. The same states that seceded from the union with Great Britain were the states that acceded to the union under the Articles of Confederation, and these same states seceded from the union under the Articles of Confederation when they acceded to the new union under the Constitution. With such a history of secession and accession by the people of sovereign American states, how could one ever think that the people of these very same American states do not have the right to "alter or abolish" the government they established themselves?

2— **Q.** The supremacy clause of the Constitution states that the laws of the Federal government are supreme to that of the states. How can a state law to secede be supreme to the Federal law?

A. Every good States' Rights advocate from Thomas Jefferson to John C. Calhoun believed in the supremacy clause of the Constitu-

---

[33] Jacobson v. Massachusetts, 197 US 11 (1905), pts. 23 & 39.
[34] Article VII of the Constitution states, The ratification of the conventions of nine states, shall be sufficient for the establishment of this Constitution between the states so ratifying the same (emphasis added).
[35] George Washington, as cited in Albert Taylor Bledsoe, *Is Davis A Traitor?* (1866, St. Louis: The Advocate Publishing House, 1887) 14. Also see, Kennedy and Kennedy, *Was Jefferson Davis Right?* 292.

tion. The so-called supremacy clause of the Constitution is found in the second paragraph of Article VI: "This Constitution, and the laws of the United States which shall be made in pursuance thereof; and all treaties made, or which shall be made, under the authority of the United States, shall be the supreme law of the land; and the judges in every State shall be bound thereby, anything in the constitution or laws of any State to the contrary notwithstanding." As Article I, Section 1, states, all the powers exercised by the Constitution are "granted" by some other source. This grant of power is clearly spelled out and delineated. Note also that in the Ninth and Tenth Amendments it is affirmed that all power that is not granted to the Federal government by the Constitution is reserved to the people of the several states. Yes indeed, in all areas where the states agreed to grant certain powers to the Federal government, the Federal government is supreme. Yet, this does not by any stretch of the imagination mean that in all areas of government the Federal government is supreme. If this is the case, what is the purpose of the Ninth and Tenth Amendments? Within the Constitution there are two areas in which the Federal government is rightfully denoted as supreme. The first area of Federal supremacy is derived from a specific grant given to the Federal government by the states — for example, the power to make treaties or build post roads. The second area of Federal supremacy is derived from an expressed negative to state action — for example, as seen in Article I, Section 10, in which the right to maintain a navy is denied to the states. Article I, Section 10, begins with the words, "No state shall...." Here the states mutually agreed that their Federal agent would be given an exclusive in particular areas. Therefore, in these areas the Federal government is supreme. Nevertheless, there are many more rights and privileges that are not granted to the Federal government or denied to the states. In all these "ungranted" areas the will of the people of the states is supreme. The supremacy clause states that the Constitution and the "laws made in pursuance" of the Constitution will be the law of the land. This word "pursuance" has great meaning in this discussion. Both Alexander Hamilton and James Madison in the Federalist Papers stated that in those actions in which the Federal government acted beyond (not in pursuance of) its constitutionally mandated powers, the Federal government's acts were void.[36] These

---

36 Alexander Hamilton, James Madison, *The Federalist Papers* No. 33 and 45, as cited in George W. Carey and James McCellan, eds., *The Federalist, Student Edition* (Dubuque, IA: Kendall-Hunt Publishing Company, 1990) 161, 237.

founding fathers understood that not all actions of the Federal government would be lawful; only those acts that were pursuant to or "in line with" the Constitution would be binding upon the people of the states. Thus, is demonstrated the proper understanding of the so-called supremacy clause of the Constitution.

3— Q. In Texas v. White the Supreme Court proved that secession was unconstitutional; therefore, how can it be legal?

A. Oh yes, the Federal Supreme Court has determined that the Federal government acted appropriately in its invasion and conquest of the Southern states. Not exactly an impartial umpire you have here, is it! If your child was an all-star athlete and was trying out to be on an exclusive all-star team, how would you feel if the judge charged with selection of athletes had children competing with your child? Would you feel secure that your child's talents would be judged fairly? Surely you would not feel secure about the impartiality of the judge, and with good cause. If this scenario is true in athletics how much more would it be true in the guardianship of our dearest interest — our liberty? For this very reason Thomas Jefferson and James Madison wrote, and the legislatures of Kentucky and Virginia passed, the Kentucky and Virginia Resolves of 1798. Here is what Thomas Jefferson had to say about who was empowered to be the judge of the use of Federal power when that power came into conflict with the rights of the people of the sovereign states: "Resolved, That the several states composing the United States of America, are not united on the principle of unlimited submission to their general government.... That the government created by this compact was not made the exclusive or final judge of the extent of the powers delegated to itself; since that would have made its discretion, and not the Constitution, the measure of its powers; but that, as in all other cases of compact among parties having no common judge, each party has an equal right to judge for itself, as well of infractions, as of the mode and measure of redress."[37] Two points thrust themselves to the forefront when reading Jefferson's "Kentucky Resolution:" one, Jefferson did not believe that the Federal government was created as a lord and master of the states, and two, that the Federal government was not granted an exclusive on the right to judge whether its acts were within the Constitution. As Jefferson pointed out, to do so would mean an end to the limitations

---

37 Kentucky Resolution of 1798, as cited in, Kennedy and Kennedy, *Was Jefferson Davis Right?* 282.

placed upon the Federal government by the Constitution — which is one reason that modern liberals and neo-conservatives insist that the Federal government is the only judge of its actions. By making the Federal government the sole judge of its actions, the government can be empowered to engage in any number of things from innumerable social welfare schemes to unlimited foreign military adventurism. Jefferson, the author of the Declaration of Independence, and Madison, the Father of the Constitution, agreed on the issue that the Federal government could not be empowered with the right to judge for itself whether its actions were within the limits of the Constitution. Therefore, your suggestion that the Federal Supreme Court "proved" that secession was not valid is untenable, that is, if you have faith in the founding fathers, the men who drafted, ratified, and enforced the Constitution. My faith is placed in the Original Constitution, the original republic of republics, and our founding fathers — not in Abraham Lincoln's court appointees.

4— Q. You keep talking about the "Original Constitutional Republic" as if we don't live under the same Constitution today. Other than a few amendments, the Original Constitution is the same Constitution we have today. How can you maintain that the Federal government today is not the same as the one given us by our forefathers?

A. During the time of the "Original Constitutional Republic," the average American citizen was taxed less than one percent of his income by the Federal government, and the only time he came into contact with the Federal government was during a visit to the post office. Today the average American's Federal tax burden will amount to somewhere between 20 and 40 percent of his income, and anything from buying gasoline to visiting the physician falls under the prying eye of the Federal government. Yes, I do believe we live in a different republic from the one established by our forefathers. Few historians will maintain the Constitution as originally written endowed the Federal government with the multiplicity of powers that it now exercises. If these new powers that have been added were in response to a constitutional change in that document, we would have little to complain about. Therefore, we must ask, what is the constitutional mode for granting additional powers to the Federal government? The constitutional mode for granting more power to the Federal government is by amending the Constitution. The only thing close to amending the Constitution in order to grant more power to the Federal government was the enforced adoption of the Fourteenth Amendment. After Appomattox, Republicans in Congress refused to allow Southern states representation in Congress. To be in the Union one must be represented in Congress and to hold membership in Congress is evidence of membership in the Union. The only way Southern states would be allowed full citizenship (to be allowed back into the Union) was if they would ratify the Fourteenth Amendment to the Constitution — in legal jargon this act is called "duress" or simply put, coercion. Now remember, these were the same Southern states that Lincoln and the Northern war party said were never out of the Union. Nevertheless, while maintaining that these Southern states were outside of the Union, the Federal government ordered them to perform an act that can only be performed by states within the Union in order to get back into a Union that the North said the South was never out of, and one in which the South did not wish to be part of any longer! Under these circumstances, the Southern states refused to ratify the Fourteenth Amendment. Remember, these were the same Southern states that had just ratified the Thirteenth Amendment, which abolished slavery in the United States. Why were these same Southern states that were willing to ratify the Thirteenth Amendment not willing to ratify the Fourteenth Amendment? The South has always maintained that the war was fought over States' Rights and not slavery. After being defeated by the Federal government, the South had no problem ending slavery in the United States, but when it came to giving up the principle of States' Rights they would not budge. You see, the Fourteenth Amendment placed every reserved right, that is, States' Rights, under Federal supervision; therefore, the South refused to ratify the Fourteenth Amendment. The South understood that with the passage of the Fourteenth Amendment, States' Rights would be dead. Even in defeat, the South refused to go along with this abominable and nefarious amendment. The nation was at a logjam. The radicals in Congress desired a strong Federal government, one that they could control and use for the benefit of their clientele. The South and many Northern Democrats feared the radical change in the form of government that the radicals were pursuing. In order to achieve victory for the radical scheme, the radical-controlled Congress overthrew all elections in the Southern states, disenfranchised large numbers of white voters, and made voters of former slaves, the majority of whom could not even read. Remember, this was done while most Northern states did not allow black people to vote, sit on juries, or even move into their states.

Backed by an occupation army, the Federal government held new elections in the Southern states, and guess what? Congressmen and senators loyal to the Radical Republican cause were elected all across the South. With Radical Republican control of the South, and with gross illegal action in several Northern states (New Jersey and Oregon being just two), the Fourteenth Amendment was, at the point of a bloody bayonet, forced into the Constitution. Does any of this sound like the grand and noble exercise of freedom that was displayed in the adoption of the Original Constitution? No, it does not. It was not legal, and still is not legal, but it did change the nature of our once free republic of republics into a Federal empire or more appropriately, a Yankee Empire! The great fear of the South and Northern Democrats was realized. This is a mere summation of this and other unconstitutional acts by the Federal empire that has changed our once free republic of republics. Don't even think about telling us that we have the same government as the one established by our founding fathers.

5— Q. Abraham Lincoln, Daniel Webster, and Joseph Story all stated that the Federal Union existed before the states. How can you maintain that a state can secede from the Union when it was the Union that created the states?

A. It would be easier to prove that a child could beget his parents than to prove that the Federal Union created the states. Think about it, the legislature or a general assembly of the freemen of a colony led the movement to eliminate Royal authority in each colony. After Royal authority was removed, the legislative body of each separate colony sent delegates to Philadelphia and empowered those delegates to vote for independence. After the war for independence began, the states acceded to a government under the Articles of Confederation in which each state was declared to be a "free, sovereign, and independent state."[38] After Great Britain recognized the independence of each state,[39] not one nation, the individual states sent delegates to Philadelphia and empowered those delegates to draw up a new constitution; thereupon, each state, acting for its own benefit and not compelled by any outside force, ratified the new constitution. It was at this point in time that the present Federal government or Union was brought into existence. This record clearly demonstrates that it was the action of individual, sovereign states that created the Federal the

---

38 Article II, Articles of Confederation.
39 Treaty of Paris, September 3, 1783.

Union. The Federal government or Union is a creature of the will of so many sovereign states, acting for their mutual benefit. The Union and its government was intended to be an agent of the states, not their parent, master, or lord.

6— Q. Daniel Webster was a great American defender of freedom and the Constitution. How can you say he supported the Southern view of the fugitive slave law?

A. Daniel Webster stated, "A bargain can not be broken on one side, and still bind the other side."[40] Webster appreciated the constitutional mandate to return fugitive slaves. The fugitive slave section was part of the Constitution,[41] and as long as it remained in the Constitution everyone was under a constitutional mandate to uphold the law. When Northerners, incited by radical abolitionists, refused to return runaway slaves as the Constitution mandated, Webster correctly noted that by willingly and continuously breaking this constitutional mandate, Northerners were destroying the Union. To prevent the destruction of the Union, Webster urged Northerners to uphold the Constitution while working to change those areas of the Constitution that had fallen into disfavor. Because of his unwillingness to trample upon the Constitution in the pursuit of a worthy goal, Webster lived out the final days of his life as an enemy of the radical abolitionists. Nevertheless, it should never be inferred that Webster was attempting to defend slavery; he was only attempting to defend the Constitution, and therefore the Union.

7— Q. Your faith in States' Rights is misplaced; after all, don't most states trample upon civil liberties as much as the Federal government?

A. Would you rather be stepped on by a midget or a giant? A fundamental concept among States' Rights advocates is that all government tends toward tyranny. Simply put, the larger the government the greater the tyranny. Thus, States' Rights advocates see small government not as a panacea for the evils of government (we are not foolish

---

40 Daniel Webster, as cited in George T. Curtis, *Life of Webster* (New York: D. Appleton and Company, 1870) II, 519.
41 Article IV, Section 2, paragraph 2 of the Constitution: No person held to service or labor in one state, under the laws thereof, escaping into another, shall, in consequence of any law or regulation therein, be discharged from such service or labor, but shall be delivered up on claim of the party to whom such service or labor may be due.

socialist utopians) but as a bulwark to slow the advance of tyrannical government. The further government is removed from the eyes of the people, the more likely that government will insidiously encroach upon the liberty of the people. This does not mean that we of the States' Rights camp believe that government can be made perfect by placing it close to the people. Yes, it is easier for citizens to observe and control government at the local level, but even there the people must be vigilant in the defense of their liberty. Governmental perfection is not a reasonable goal; therefore, eternal vigilance is necessary if liberty is to be protected. As many have stated, "Eternal vigilance is the price of liberty."

8— Q. Even if the South had a right to secede in 1861, didn't that end with the passage of the Fourteenth Amendment?

A. (For a more complete discussion of the Fourteenth Amendment, see question 4 in this chapter.) In 1776 our founding fathers declared certain principles to be unalienable — which is to say, these principles cannot be destroyed. Why would you want to argue with the authors of the Declaration of Independence? Jefferson, speaking for the Patriots of '76, clearly noted that man is endowed by his creator with certain unalienable rights such as life, liberty, and the pursuit of happiness. As Jefferson noted, one aspect of life and liberty that man has been endowed with is the right to "alter or abolish" his government. These principles, as Jefferson noted in the Declaration of Independence, are beyond the scope of man to negate. Yes, tyrants can and often do trample upon man's unalienable rights, but tyrants cannot destroy those rights. An Adolph Hitler may destroy the lives of millions of people, but the right to life lives on after the holocaust. Marxist tyrants may fill their gulags to the brim with political prisoners, but the right of liberty lives on, even in the midst of tyranny. Abraham Lincoln may have been able to suppress the free exercise of the right of secession, but that right lives on today. Tyrants cannot negate the God-ordained and unalienable rights of free people.

9— Q. The Constitution is a document by Americans for Americans. Where do you get the idea that the power it grants to the Federal government comes from the states?

A. (For a more complete answer to the question of who established the Constitution, see question 1 in this chapter.) Where do we get the idea that the Federal government derives its power from the states? Very simply, we get it from the Constitution. Or to be more specific, we get it from Article VII, the "ratification" article of the Constitution. Other than in the preamble, which has no binding legal force,[42] the people of "America" are only recognized in the Constitution in relation to their respective states. Electors from each state elect the president; each state elects its own two senators (prior to the adoption of the Sixteenth Amendment senators were elected by the legislature of each state); people within political subdivisions of a state elect representatives to Congress. Nowhere is there a general mass of "Americans" steering the ship of state in these United States. After completing their work of drafting the Constitution and before sending that document to the conventions of the states, the founding fathers added these words to the document: "Done in convention by the unanimous consent of the **states**...." (Emphasis added). You see, in 1787 the delegates who drafted the Constitution understood the states were creating the new government. The very first amendment added after the adoption of the Bill of Rights demonstrates this point. Notice that in the Eleventh Amendment the term "citizen" is coupled with the word "state."[43] Once again this points out American citizens did not exist in some sort of political vacuum but existed as citizens of their respective states. A year before the War for Southern Independence broke out, Jefferson Davis spoke to a cheering crowd in Portland, Maine.[44] At that time Jefferson noted when united against a common foe, the citizens of the United States stood as brave Americans. Jefferson Davis understood, as did most Americans at that time, that when dealing with those things purely local, a citizen was a loyal member of his state; but when faced by a common foe, citizens of all the states would unite as Americans for their mutual protection. At the formation of these United States, it was understood that the citizens of every state would be Americans, but that not all Americans would be citizens of every state.

---

42 Jacobson v. Massachusetts, 197 US 11 (1905) pts. 23 & 39.
43 The Eleventh Amendment of the Constitution states: The judicial power of the United States shall not be construed to extend to any suit in law or equity, commenced or prosecuted against one of the United States by citizens of another state, or by citizens or subjects of any foreign state.
44 J. Williams Jones, *A Memorial Volume of Jefferson Davis* (1889, Harrisonburg, VA: Sprinkle Publications, 1993) 154.

10— Q. The Confederate Constitution protected slavery in each of the Southern states. How can you say the Confederate Constitution went further in ending slavery than the United States Constitution?

A. The Confederate Constitution unequivocally outlawed the African slave trade, whereas, the United States Constitution protected the African slave trade for twenty years after its adoption. The only additional slaves that were allowed into the Confederacy were slaves from the slaveholding states of the United States, and the Congress of the Confederacy could stop that additional flow as it saw fit. As for the African slave trade, the Confederate Constitution was far superior in fighting that nefarious trade. Your suggestion the Confederate Constitution "protected" slavery is unfounded. Nowhere in the Confederate Constitution was there a mandate to maintain slavery. What the Confederate Constitution did state is the "Confederate" government would not interfere with the institution of slavery. This is absolutely the same stance that was taken by the founding fathers of the United States in regard to slavery in the United States in 1788 at the adoption of the United States Constitution. The abolition of domestic slavery was deemed to be a purely local matter. It was thought wiser to leave that issue in the hands of the people at the local level to deal with, as the exigencies of the local situation proved necessary. The situation varied from state to state as it related to the elimination of slavery. For example, Massachusetts with less than three percent of its population of African descent found it easier to end slavery and make adjustments in its society for the newly freed slaves than Virginia with 50 percent of its population of African descent. Nevertheless, by the outbreak of the war, Virginia had freed more slaves than all of New England combined! The idea the elimination of slavery should be a task for the states and not the Federal government was not a Southern idea. At the time of the drafting of the Constitution, Oliver Ellsworth of Connecticut stated, "The morality or wisdom of slavery are considerations belonging to the States themselves…the States are the best judges of their particular interest."[45] The Confederate States Constitution treated the institution of slavery just as the United States Constitution treated it, as an issue to be adjudicated by the people of each sovereign state.

---

45 Oliver Ellsworth, as cited in, M. E. Bradford, *Founding Fathers*, Second Edition (Lawrence: University of Kansas Press, 1982) 33.

11— Q. You claim that you love liberty. Yet, the Confederate Constitution does not even have a Bill of Rights. How could your rights be protected by such a constitution?

A. The Confederate "Bill of Rights" is an integral part of the entire Confederate Constitution, not an afterthought as it is in the United States Constitution. The reason the Bill of Rights is located at the end of the United States Constitution is because when it was drafted there was no guarantee of civil liberties within the Constitution. Due to the efforts of the anti-federalists, the precursors of the advocates of States' Rights, the states ratified a Bill of Rights. It was the descendants of these anti-federalists who drafted the Confederate Constitution. For them it was only reasonable that all the rights that had been protected as an afterthought in the United States Constitution should be protected in the actual body of the Confederate Constitution. Most of the United States Bill of Rights can be found in Article I, Section 9, of the Confederate Constitution. The first paragraph of Article I, Section 9, declares an unequivocal end to the African slave trade and requires the Confederate Congress to "pass such laws as shall effectually prevent the same." Not only does the Confederate Constitution protect civil liberties just as the United States Constitution does, it also goes much further in ending the African slave trade than did the United States Constitution.

12— Q. Didn't the United States Constitution state it was creating a perpetual union? How can a state secede from a perpetual union?

A. Nowhere in the United States Constitution can one find a statement, demand, or claim of a perpetual union. You must understand that the current Constitution is not the first "constitution" for the United States. The first American government was under the Articles of Confederation. This "constitution" did indeed assert the government under that "constitution" would be perpetual.[46] What became of that perpetual union? The states of that federation seceded from it in order to form a new government under the Constitution of the United States. Conspicuous by its absence in the new Constitution is the call for a perpetual union.

---

[46] The first paragraph of the Articles of Confederation states, Whereas the Delegates of the United States of America in Congress assembled did on the fifteenth day of November in the year of our Lord One Thousand Seven Hundred and Seventy seven, and in the Second Year of the Independence of America agree to certain articles of Confederation and perpetual Union. …

13— Q. The Declaration of Independence speaks of human rights that are unalienable and ordained by God. This is nothing less than natural law, the law upon which America was founded. Slavery runs counter to America's concept of natural law. Why defend a system of government, that is, States' Rights, that runs counter to natural law?

A. Indeed, slavery runs counter to any theory of natural law, but Americans are bound by a written constitution and not by a metaphysical concept. The Constitution and the founding fathers left the subject of ending slavery in the hands of the people of the states (see question 10 of this chapter). There was a constitutional method for ending slavery at the Federal level, the constitutional amendment process. If the North had approached ending slavery just as the British had done in its slaveholding areas, slavery may very well have ended in the United States just as it ended in the colonies of Great Britain. States' Rights did not stand in the way of the elimination of slavery; therefore, your statement that the principle of States' Rights "runs counter to natural law" is unfounded. By overruling the Constitution and by force of arms or strong-arm politics we may achieve a worthy objective, but in the process cause immense and lasting damage to the very document we depend upon to protect our liberty. Only by usurpation of the written law, i.e., the Constitution, could one use metaphysical law, i.e., natural law, to run counter to the Constitution. President George Washington warned Americans about this dangerous process of changing the Constitution in his farewell address when he stated, "If in the opinion of the people the distribution or modification of the constitutional powers be in any particular wrong, let it be corrected by an amendment in the way which the Constitution designates. But let there be no change by usurpation; for though this in one instance may be the instrument of good, it is the customary weapon by which free governments are destroyed."[47] Simply put, Washington stated that the end does not justify the means. The worthy goal of ending slavery does not justify any method of fulfilling this goal. This is something that President Washington understood, but the radical abolitionists and modern politically correct liberals still don't understand.

---

47 George Washington, as cited in, Clarence B. Carson, *Basic American Government* (Wadley, AL: American Textbook Committee, 1993) 561.

14— Q. The Constitution was written more than two hundred years ago by rich white men. Women, blacks, and Native Americans were excluded. Why act like this document is holy writ? Times change, we have to change with it or die. You wouldn't want to go to a doctor who used eighteenth-century medicine, would you? Then why try to take modern America back to the days before the Civil War?

A. The Constitution and the Declaration of Independence were both written more than two hundred years ago, but does that mean the principles enshrined in these documents are no longer valid? Let's hope not; after all, the right to life, liberty, and the pursuit of happiness is something we hold dear even more than two hundred years after the writing of these documents. The Constitution is not written in such a manner as to make it impossible to be changed as time and circumstances require. As President George Washington pointed out in his farewell address (see question number 13 in this chapter), when a needed change in the Constitution is demonstrated, there is a constitutional means for changing it. Now, as for your assertion the Constitution is not "holy writ," we could not agree with you more. The Constitution is not holy writ, or even close to it, but as originally written and enforced, outside of the Holy Bible it is as close to holy writ as we will ever get in this world.

15— Q. You said that in ratifying the Constitution, Virginia reserved unto itself the right of secession. Isn't Virginia a Southern state? I do believe that the whole war was fought because the South said it had a right to secede and the North said the South did not have a right to secede. How can you justify secession of the South by citing what a Southern state said it was justified in doing?

A. Virginia was not the only state to reserve the right of secession when it ratified the Constitution; New York and Rhode Island did the same. According to Article VII of the Constitution, each state, acting for itself only and not being forced by any other state, ratified the Constitution. Some states such as Rhode Island and North Carolina did not join the new Union until more than a year after the new government had been established. During this time no one suggested the Federal government should invade those states who were reluctant to join the new government and force them into the Union — why? The answer is simple; everyone understood at that time that each state was a sovereign state and could not justly be forced to do anything against its will. In other words, the people of each state were free men with the right to consent to the form of government under which they would live. Now, that is real freedom; those men did indeed live in the "land of the free." When these two states (New York and Rhode Island) later acceded into the new Union, they were accepted with the said provision to withdraw from the Union if at some future time the people of either state desired to do so. Because each state within the Union is considered equal, no one state can have a right that another state does not possess; they are co-equal members in the Union. As co-equal members of the Union, the right reserved by Virginia, New York, and Rhode Island now equally belongs to all states. For this reason alone, secession must be viewed as constitutional. It should be noted that although you are critical of Virginia, a Southern state, claiming the reserved right of secession, we see that at least two Northern states were just as anxious to reserve the right of secession as a Southern state. At that point in time very few people in these United States doubted the right of a state, composed of free men, to withdraw from any compact, alliance, or federation that it had freely entered. The American states were so jealous of their individual independence that in the government under the Articles of Confederation they proclaimed to the world, "each state retains its sovereignty, freedom, and independence, and every power, jurisdiction, and right, which is not by this Confederation expressly delegated to the United States, in Congress assembled."[48] As they entered the new government under the Constitution, the states carried into the new Union every right and power that was not granted to the Federal government or denied to the states. To make sure everyone understood this point, the anti-federalists, led by Patrick Henry, demanded and received an amendment to the Constitution stating that every right that was not granted to the Federal government was retained by the people and the states; we call this statement the Tenth Amendment to the Constitution. The right to judge for themselves how they would be governed and what type of government they would live under was never surrendered by the states nor denied to the states. If the right of secession is not denied or surrendered, where does it reside? It resides with the people of the states. Secession is constitutional, and it is inherently American.

---

48 Article II of the Articles of Confederation.

Summary

A fig for the Constitution! When the scorpion's sting is probing us to the quick, shall we pause to chop logic? Shall we get some learned and cunning clerk to say whether the power to do this is to be found in the constitution, and then, if he, from whatever motive, shall maintain the affirmative, like the animal whose fleece forms so material a part of this bill, quietly lie down and be sheared?[49]

— John Randolph of Roanoke, 1824

Randolph, an "Old Republican" of the Anti-Federalists school was very leery of the protection a parchment or paper document could offer the liberty of citizens of a republic. Randolph did not despise the Constitution; rather he understood that more than a paper barricade needed to stand between a powerful government and individual liberty. "When the scorpion's sting is probing us to the quick, shall we pause to chop logic?" In this statement Randolph is pointing out how foolish it would be, while enduring an odious Constitutional wrong, to stand and debate Constitutional principles. While proving said Constitutional wrong is unjust, the wrong will not be removed until a power sufficient enough to compel the government to remedy the wrong is vigorously applied. This principle has application for twenty-first century Americans. It must be pointed out that although Louisiana had every right to protect its wetlands from the Deepwater Horizon Gulf oil spill of 2010, the Federal government refused to allow state action; Arizona had every right to protect its borders (2010) but the Federal government nullified Arizona's right; Obama's Health Care law is blatantly un-Constitutional, yet the Federal Supreme Court has told every American (2012) to obey a blatantly un-Constitutional action. What good is it to stand and debate these issues when we know that the Federal government has all the power to enforce its will upon American citizens? What is needed are tools in the hands of "we the people" of each sovereign state that would force the Federal government to abide by the Constitution. If the Federal government still persists in its odious act then "we the people" would be left with no other option than firing our agent (the Federal government) and establishing a government that will abide by our wishes. In a free society liberty should always trump government.

---

49 John Randolph, as cited in, Russell Kirk, *John Randolph of Roanoke: A Study in American Politics* (Liberty Press, Indianapolis, Indiana: 1978) 61.

"'You may entrench yourself in parchment to the teeth,' says Lord Chatham, 'the sword will find its way to the vitals of the constitutional.'"[50] Randolph here is pointing out that even with the best-written constitution, if there be no means of opposing the power of the government, the constitution is a dead letter. This is why REAL States' Rights was such an essential part of the formation of these United States. These United States as given to us by our founding fathers were a republic of republics, that is, a federal republic. A federal republic is one composed of sovereign states (republics) that are federated together for their mutual benefit and well-being. The right to judge whether this arrangement is indeed mutually beneficial does not belong to the federal government but to the local republic, i.e., each sovereign state. As Randolph points out, the Constitution is an instrument for the protection of our liberty but it is not the final judge of whether "we the people" are being governed well. Whether "we the people" are being govern well is the job of the people of each state acting for their own benefit and wellbeing.

---

50 Ibid.

Levy Carnine, Confederate Veteran

The complexities of the relationship within the system of African slavery in the South and race relations itself is demonstrated in the life of Levy Carnine. Born a slave in Northwest Louisiana, Carnine entered the War with his master in the 2nd Louisiana Volunteer Infantry serving in Virginia. After his master was killed in action, Carnine remained with the 2nd Louisiana Infantry until he volunteered for a dangerous cross-country mission to get letters back home to his friends' family. Successfully completing his perilous mission, he became a local hero. After the War, Carnine became a faithful member of the United Confederate Veterans. At his death his fellow white Confederate Veterans insisted that Carnine be buried in the same cemetery alongside his white friends and fellow veterans. His grave and the graves of these Confederate Veterans are maintained today by the members of the Sons of Confederate Veterans.

Chapter 3
Slavery

No subject [slavery] has been more generally misunderstood or more persistently misrepresented.[51]

— Jefferson Davis

It would be difficult to find any subject in American history that has been the source of more debate, argument, or outright anger than the issue of American slavery. In the simplistic minds of the modern politically correct liberals and neo-conservatives, the issue of slavery is reduced to the following formula: The North hated slavery and loved freedom, whereas the South loved slavery and fought to keep America as a slave nation. The role of the North in promoting and in benefiting from slavery is either not mentioned or is downplayed to the point of insignificance in the discussion of slavery. At the same time, the North's role in promoting and profiting from slavery is downplayed; the South's role in promoting the end of the African slave trade, establishing some of the first abolition organizations and at its own expense manumitting (freeing) large numbers of slaves is either not mentioned or is downplayed to the point of insignificance in the discussion of slavery. Unfortunately for the truth, this overly simplified and false concept of slavery in America has become the centerpiece of liberal and neo-conservative ideology as it relates to both slavery and modern race issues. Anyone who dares to stand in opposition to the "standard" philosophy of "the North is good, the South is bad" ideological cult is sure to bring down upon himself the wrath of both the liberal and neo-conservative establishments. When President Ronald Reagan nominated an unapologetic Southerner, Professor M. E. Bradford, as chairman for the National Endowment for the Humanities, it was neo-conservatives who demanded that Reagan not allow anyone who did not believe in the Lincoln myth to head this Federal agency. Part of the Lincoln myth Dr. Bradford did not embrace was the myth of Lincoln as the Great Emancipator. When white students in a Georgia high school planned a party outside of and not supported by the school system, i.e., a private party, it was neo-conservative Bill O'Reilly who

---

51 Jefferson Davis, *The Rise and Fall of the Confederate Government* (1881, Nashville, TN: William M. Coats,) I, 3.

night after night castigated his perception of racism down South. The truth is there are more segregated schools in New York City than in the South! Is there no racism in New York? If we remember correctly it was in New York that a quasi-ethnic war existed between orthodox Jews and African-Americans. It was in New York that the local police shot an unarmed black man from Haiti more than fifty times while he stood in his doorway. Yet Mr. Neo-conservative, Bill O'Reilly, spent hours castigating Southern young people for having a private party. Does no one in New York City have private parties? Both liberals and neo-conservatives embrace the "North equals good — South equals bad" mentality as it relates to Southern issues on race. Embracing the false notion of Northern moral superiority is bad enough, but liberals and neo-conservatives compound the evil by doing all in their power to suppress a fair discussion of the issue of race and/or slavery. A free people should never be cowered into silence when discussing issues that are vital to the well-being of their republic. As William Rawle stated in 1825, "The foundation of a free government begins to be undermined when freedom of speech on political subjects is restrained; it is destroyed when freedom of speech is wholly denied."[52] No subject has been more politicized in America than the subject of race and/or slavery. Nevertheless, fair minded people must insist that telling the whole truth about the issue of slavery is not tantamount to defending slavery. There is a pervasive notion within modern American society that anyone who says anything out of line with the officially accepted norm about slavery is trying to defend the institution of slavery. Nothing could be further from the truth. Many opponents of the institution of slavery were slaveholders. Although sounding like a philosophical oxymoron, i.e., slaveholders who opposed slavery, the previous statement is historically correct. Men such as George Washington, Thomas Jefferson, John Randolph, and numerous other slaveholders were some of America's first and strongest advocates for (1) the elimination of the African slave trade, (2) the manumission of slaves, and (3) the adoption of a system of gradual emancipation. With America's strong attachment to liberty and freedom, few people in the South or the North believed that slavery was a noble institution, but neither did they believe in the confiscation of millions of dollars of property by instantaneously abolishing slavery. Up until the American "Civil War," no European power had abolished slavery by confiscating the legal property of its citizens. That form of tyr-

---

52 Rawle, 108.

anny would be demonstrated in Europe by the Fascist and Marxist tyrants of the twentieth century who believed that all property of a nation belonged to the government and not the individual. Even men such as the president of the Confederate States of America, Jefferson Davis, condemned the institution of slavery. Most Americans of the mid-nineteenth century had little love for the institution of slavery. Even the most ardent Southerners understood that something had to be done about the institution of slavery. Here are President Davis's thoughts on slavery: "The idea of freedom is captivating, that of slavery repellent to the moral sense of mankind in general."[53] General Robert E. Lee went even further in his denunciation of the institution of slavery when he said, "In this enlightened age, there are few I believe, but what would acknowledge, that slavery as an institution, is a moral and political evil in any country."[54] As President Jefferson Davis noted, the institution of slavery, especially Southern slavery, has been misrepresented.

1— Q. How can you say the South was fighting for freedom and independence when all eleven Southern states had laws protecting slavery?

A. How can you say that America was fighting for freedom and independence in 1776 when all thirteen states had laws that protected slavery and the slave trade? Only a hypocrite would condemn the South for slavery while praising the United States for doing the very same thing. Yes, the first president of the Confederacy, Jefferson Davis, was a slaveholder; therefore, should he and the nation he led be condemned? If so, what shall we do with President George Washington and the nation he led? After all, President Washington, the first president of the United States, was a slaveholder. The institution of slavery that includes the trans-Atlantic commerce in slaves, i.e., Yankee slave traders, has deep roots in American history, not just Southern history. It was a well-established fact in early American history that the abolition of slavery was a matter that was best left to the states (see question 10, chapter 2). The Confederate States Constitution demanded an unequivocal end to the African slave trade, which itself proves that nation was not promoting slavery. The very first veto that President Jefferson Davis of the Confederacy issued was in

---

53 Jefferson Davis, 6.
54 Robert E. Lee, as cited in, Douglas Southall Freeman, *R. E. Lee* (New York: Charles Scribner's Sons, 1934) I, 372.

response to a bill from the Confederate Congress that Davis said impinged upon the spirit of the Confederate Constitution's prohibition on the African slave trade. Davis' veto was upheld by the Confederate Congress, making the point that the Confederate government was opposed to the African slave trade. As for the national government of the Confederate States, the issue of abolishing slavery was denied to the central government and left where it had been under the United States Constitution — with the states. Slavery in the South would have ended peacefully, just as it had done in every other Western Hemisphere nation (with the exception of Haiti), if radicals in the North had not seized upon the issue of slavery as a weapon to use against the South, thereby promoting their special interests. With the advent of modern technology and the mechanical advantage of machines and the internal combustion engine, the market system alone would have made slavery a costly relic. The anachronistic nature of slavery in a modern age, along with the tendency of society to embrace a more enlightened and liberal view of slavery when it becomes less costly to do so, would have spelled sure death to the institution of slavery. This was the feeling of the founding fathers in 1776 and in 1861; therefore, we can say that both the United States and the Confederate States were fighting for freedom and independence.

2— Q. The Confederate flag is the flag of slavery. As a symbol of slavery shouldn't it be banned?

A. The only flag of slavery that we know of is the flag of the United States of America. Are you suggesting that we ban the United States flag? When the US flag was first raised in this nation, all thirteen American states had laws protecting the institution of slavery. When African slave traders needed a flag to protect their slave cargo from being liberated by English or French naval vessels, an American flag and an American citizen were kept handy for this purpose. At the approach of a naval vessel, the foreign slave vessel would sell the ship and its cargo to the American citizen, raise the United States flag, and go unmolested with its slave cargo. Please note this was being done long before there was a Confederate nation or flag. We are sure there are some people who associate the Confederate flag with slavery and would like to see it banned. Likewise, we are sure there are some people who view the United States flag in the same light, for example the Native Americans or Hispanics of the Southwest. How long after banning the Confederate flag do you think it would be before an equally strident call for banning the United States flag would be heard? During the War for Southern Independence it was not uncommon to see mottoes written on the Confederate battle flags given to troops by the ladies of the area from which the troops were raised. We have viewed hundreds of these flags and have never seen one Confederate battle flag with a motto that demanded the protection of slavery. Most of these flags bore mottoes demanding faithful service in the defense of the Southern homeland and freedoms. One of the most poignant mottoes we ever read on a Confederate battle flag was on the flag of the troops raised from King's Mountain, South Carolina. These men were the descendants of the patriots who defeated the British at the pivotal Battle of King's Mountain in 1780. Their flag's motto simply stated, "Like our ancestors, we will be free." So you see, the flag of the Confederate States of America was and still is the flag of freedom and independence — not the flag of slavery.

3— Q. The South attempted to extend slavery into the territories of the United States. Didn't the North have a right to keep slavery out of the rest of America?

A. The North had no more constitutional right to keep slavery out of the commonly held territories of the United States than the South had a constitutional right to force slavery upon those same territories. The question to be answered is how was the issue of slavery to be determined in those territories? The South always maintained that only the people of a sovereign state could determine whether slavery was to be allowed within that state. This is after all the method the founding fathers had chosen as the proper means of eliminating slavery. Neither the Congress of the United States nor the people of a territory could determine the status of slavery within the commonly held territory of the United States (the only exception would be the Northwest Territory as will be explained). Only when the people of a territory had met the requirements of statehood could they then determine for themselves whether slavery was to be allowed or restricted within their state. Now as to your assertion that the South tried to "extend slavery into the territories," the facts just don't support your theory. Early in the history of these United States, Virginia granted to the United States all of the Northwest Territory that it had conquered during the War for American Independence. No "Federal" troops or monies were used in this endeavor, i.e., the capturing of the Northwest Territory. Virginia and Kentucky militia units, under orders of Governor Patrick Henry of Virginia, defeated the British and their Indian allies and laid claim on the vast territory. When Virginia ceded this huge landmass from which no less than five Northern states were created, Virginia requested slavery not be allowed in this new territory. When this measure was brought before Congress, every delegate both from the North and from the South voted to disallow slavery in the Northwest Territory. Now if, as you contend, the South sought to extend slavery into all the territories of the United States, why did the South unanimously vote to restrict slavery in the Northwest Territory? The only issue about slaves in the territory either purchased from France, the Louisiana Purchase, or acquired after the defeat of Mexico at the end of the Mexican War was the right of Southerners to carry their property into the newly purchased or captured territory. Unlike the North, the South never insisted that all or any states carved from the new territories be "slave" states. The North did demand that Southerners not be allowed to take into the new territories any property that was recognized by the Constitution as legal property. Most Southerners never believed slavery in the new territories would be economical; therefore, few if any new "slave" states would have been admitted to the Union from those territories even if no opposition to slavery were made. What the South demanded was fair treatment as an equal partner within the Union. If Northerners were allowed to carry their property into the new territories, then Southerners insisted they should be allowed to do the same. If at the time a territory had enough population to become a state, then and only then could the people of that territory determine the status of slavery in their new state. One point that really upset many Southerners in the debate over slaves in the new territories was the fact that more Southerners fought, bled, and died in the Mexican War than did Northerners; yet, it was the North that was trying to set rules that would discourage Southerners from moving into the territories purchased by their own blood. This was by no means an effort by the South to make any territory of the United States a "slave" territory. As good States' Rights advocates, Southerners believed, and rightfully so, that these matters were to be determined by the people of the state involved, and that state only.

4— Q. Representative David Wilmot of Pennsylvania was a defender of freedom and equality. The purpose of his Wilmot Proviso was to keep America free of slavery. Notwithstanding this fact, the South fought against the Wilmot Proviso. Doesn't this prove that the South wanted America to be a slave nation?

A. Representative David Wilmot of Pennsylvania was a typical nineteenth-century racist, not a defender of the downtrodden, friend of the African American, or liberator of the slave. His Wilmot Proviso was written with two objectives: (1) to keep the South from gaining more states from the newly acquired territories, and therefore more power in Congress, and (2) to keep the states to be formed from the new territories free of black people. As for the welfare of African Americans, Wilmot stated that he had "no squeamish sensitiveness upon the subject of slavery, no morbid sympathy for the slave... I plead the cause and the rights of white freemen... I would preserve to the free white labor a fair country, a rich inheritance, where the sons of toil, of my own race and own color, can live without disgrace which association with Negro slavery brings upon free labor."[55] Nothing in the Wilmot Proviso can be said to advance the cause of equality in America. As we see from Wilmot's statement, he was anything but an advocate of equality for African Americans. Yes, he did desire to keep the territories free of slaves, but this desire was in response to his racist attitude toward blacks and his desire to increase the power of his own section of the nation at the expense of the South. We find nothing noble or uplifting about David Wilmot's attitude or proviso. Only if one totally embraces the Northern myth of "North good — South bad" could one find David Wilmot a man to be emulated and to be held up as a patriotic American.

5— Q. The greatest spokesman for the South before the Civil War was John C. Calhoun. This man was a defender of slavery! How could any American respect the man or follow his teaching?

A. John C. Calhoun defended slavery no more than another great Southerner, Thomas Jefferson, defended slavery. Both Calhoun and Jefferson were strong advocates of strict construction interpretation of the Constitution and States' Rights. If you condemn Calhoun, who was the student and follower of Jefferson, then what are you going to do with President Thomas Jefferson, author of the Declaration of Independence and the Kentucky Resolve of 1798? Some people have

---

[55] David Wilmot, as cited in, Leon P. Litwack, *North of Slavery: The Negro in the Free States, 1790-1860* (Chicago: The University of Chicago Press, 1961) 47.

incorrectly asserted that since Calhoun defended the right of the people of each sovereign state to determine how or if they would end slavery, he was defending slavery. As we have demonstrated elsewhere (see question 10, chapter 2), this right was not a Southern right but a right accepted by the founding fathers both Northern and Southern. Like many Southerners, when the radical abolitionists issued scurrilous statements about the institution of Southern slavery, Calhoun responded with the truth. Senator Calhoun was no different from the vast majority of Americans or of Europeans in his day; he believed that the black man was inferior to the white man. But on that issue, he merely stood where even Abraham Lincoln stood some fifteen years later.[56] Calhoun believed that the Constitution did not grant to the Federal government the right to interfere with the domestic institutions of the sovereign states; nor did he believe that the South should be made the scapegoat for American slavery. What Calhoun did was fight to keep the Federal government within the limitations of the Constitution. Northerners did not appreciate Calhoun's strict construction view of the Constitution because it stood in their way of using the power of the Federal government to enrich themselves at the expense of the South. Remember, the greatest conflict between the Federal government and a Southern state during Calhoun's reign of power was over tariffs, and not slavery. Tariffs are an economic issue not directly related to the issue of slavery. Nevertheless, the issue of tariffs almost led to a violent conflict between the state of South Carolina and the Federal government. The issue of slavery is a moot question in today's political environment, but the issue of an all-powerful Federal government is all-pervasive in the lives of modern Americans. There are very few activities that do not fall under the scrutiny and regulation of the Federal government today. From gasoline to health care; education to unemployment; public worship to retirement plans, an all-powerful Federal government is our constant companion and supervisor. The growth of the Federal government from a small, frugal, and respectful entity to one that knows no limit to its power, nor any end to its demand for more contributions (taxes) from its tax serfs, was made possible by the rejection of the principles of John C. Calhoun. Americans are paying a high price in lost property that is being taken from them by the IRS and in liberty that is being trampled upon by an all-powerful government as a result of the defeat

---

56 For more information on Lincoln's racist opinions see Walter D. Kennedy, *Myths of American Slavery* (Gretna, LA: Pelican Publishing Co., 2003) 163-82.

of Calhoun and his principles. His States' Rights philosophy of limited government and a Federal government that is forced to respect the will of "we the people" of the sovereign states is the death knell to Federal tyranny. Unfortunately for all Americans, Appomattox was the death knell of limited government and States' Rights.

6— Q. Since African Americans have been forever harmed by the institution of Southern slavery, why shouldn't your people pay them reparations?

A. The descendants of slaves living in Mississippi today have a higher life expectancy, a higher per capita income, a higher level of literacy and education, and a lower infant mortality rate than any Africans outside of the United States.[57] Now, please tell me, where is the harm to these descendants of slaves? There is no doubt that African Americans have faced discrimination from the very first time they set foot upon these shores. The fact is that all new groups have faced discrimination to some degree since the time they first entered this country. The greater the differences — social, religious, cultural, and yes, racial — the more discrimination a group has had to overcome. That being the case, it must be noted that even during the heyday of Jim Crowism, i.e., racial segregation, the African American was still far ahead of his counterpart in the rest of the world. For example, an African American living in Mississippi in 1940 had a longer life expectancy than a modern Sub-Saharan African.[58] Even though the average African-American of the South did not vote after Reconstruction, white voters of the South taxed themselves in order to provide an education system that was second to no African nation or major African country in the world. Better housing, education, life expectancy, and income, and a more stable civic, social, and spiritual life, all these things were the common experience of African Americans in the South or in the United States during and after the age of segregation. These United States, both North and South, did practice slavery and discrimination against African Americans; nevertheless, it was these United States, both North and South, where the sons and daughters of Africa have made the greatest economic and social gains. Also, remember that it was here in these United States where white citizens, both from the North and from the South, fought to end the African slave trade, abolish slavery, and end discrimination against

---

57 Ibid., 214-17.
58 Ibid.

The Confederate Myth-Buster

people of color. Your demand for reparations is akin to the demands of those who would kill the goose just to get the golden egg.

7— Q. The fugitive slave portion of the Constitution was added to the Constitution by Southern slaveholders. Why should the rest of America honor a hideous Southern section of the Constitution?

A. You honor the Constitution by following it and constitutionally changing those parts that you find disagreeable. If a man steals from you, you don't have the right to kill him. You do have a right to have him arrested, tried, and once convicted, imprisoned. The Constitution is a document written for all citizens of each state to follow. When your state either ratified the Constitution or was admitted into the Union, the Constitution plainly stated what was required of your state. Why expect the South to follow the Constitution in every point but allow Northern states to abridge the Constitution at will? Now, as for your statement that the fugitive slave section of the Constitution is a "hideous Southern element," you could not be further from the truth. The origin of the fugitive slave section of the United States Constitution extends back to an agreement between the people of New England and the Dutch colony of New Netherlands in 1646.[59] As long as New England needed a fugitive slave law, that law was retained and enforced. Only after slavery had been eliminated in New England did the good people of New England and the rest of the North discover scruples that forced them to condemn the fugitive slave law. Remember, this section of the United States Constitution had its origin in New England; it was approved by the conventions of all the states when they acceded to the new government under the Constitution. Just because the South was the only part of the nation in the mid-1800s that required the enforcement of this section of the Constitution that does not make this section a "Southern" section. In the early 1800s, virtually all states of this nation had, at one time or another, utilized this portion of the Constitution and all states in the nation at that time had approved the Constitution knowing full well that the fugitive slave section was part of the Constitution. As Daniel Webster noted, "A bargain broken on one side is broken on all sides." If the North did not keep its side of the bargain that created the Union, then why do you think the South should be held to a higher

---

59 George H. Moore, *Notes on the History of Slavery in Massachusetts* (New York: D. Appleton and Company, 1866) 27-28.

standard? Webster was right on this point! The Union was broken long before South Carolina seceded from the Union. Once again, we must point out that "The South Was Right!"

8— Q. You condemn Northerners for being "slave traders." If you Southerners were not buying those slaves, how could Northerners have been slave traders? Can't you see that the problem was caused by Southerner plantation owners seeking more slaves, and not Northern merchants selling those slaves?

A. Ninety-four percent of all slaves brought to the Western Hemisphere were sold in non-Southern markets. The slave markets of the South amounted to around four to six percent of slaves sold in the New World. We don't see how that small number could be the culprit in the Yankee slave trade. The very nature of the so-called three-corner or triangular slave trade demonstrates that most slaves were not brought into the United States but rather were sold in the Caribbean. For example, Yankee merchants would outfit slave ships with local products such as cloth, rum, and dried fish, and sail to the coast of Africa. At the coast of Africa, they would trade such articles for slaves; loaded with slaves, the vessel would sail to the Caribbean where it would exchange its human cargo for sugar. Once a load of sugar and other articles was obtained, the vessel would sail for homeport, usually somewhere in New England. Back home the ship's owner would trade sugar and other articles for more rum, cloth, fish, etc. With each "trade" along the three corners of the voyage, a small profit was made until the ship was back in homeport. As you can see, the South did not play a large role in the Yankee commerce in human flesh. In the 1700s, long before American independence, various Southern colonies had already attempted to end the African slave trade. After the adoption of the Constitution, the African slave trade was outlawed in 1808. Even before that time, every Southern state had already passed laws to limit or prohibit the importation of more African slaves into their state. No, the South was never a big player in the African slave trade; whereas, Cuba, Brazil, and the islands of the Caribbean did indeed play a large role in keeping the Yankee commerce in slaves booming. This commerce was so intense that five years after the defeat of the Confederate States of America, the United States Congress was still appropriating monies for the policing of this nefarious trade.

9— Q. Do you really think anyone is going to believe that slaves freely fought for the South during the Civil War?

A. Slaves fighting alongside their masters against the central government that had promised the slaves freedom does sound improbable. Yet that is what happened — but not only did it happen during the War for Southern Independence but also during the War for American Independence. One example of this fact occurred during the Battle of Cowpens, South Carolina, in 1781. Toward the end of the battle, the life of Colonel William Washington, a commander of continental cavalry, was saved when his servant shot a British officer before the officer could deliver a deadly blow to Colonel Washington.[60] Foreign, Federal, and Southern accounts of slaves going to war with their masters and faithfully discharging their duty abound in the written record. Yes, not only in the War for Southern Independence but also in every war, including several Indian War campaigns, slaves went to war with their masters and served not only their masters but also their nation on the field of battle. One must remember that in 1861 few people in America viewed the War for Southern Independence as a war of liberation of the slaves. Even when it became obvious that the South would lose the war, and therefore slavery would soon end, the vast majority of slaves remained loyal to the only family and home they had ever known. For many slaves, staying with a sure thing, a master they knew, was preferable to surrendering to a master they did not know. In either condition the slaves understood that they would have many obstacles to overcome. The slaves who chose to go to war with their masters did so for many different reasons. Some slaves wanted the adventure that going into the army offered — in that respect, they were no different from many white soldiers. Other slaves desired to prove their loyalty to their masters with the hope of future reward. Regardless of the reason, many African-Americans served with the Confederate Army. Most slaves served as body servants, nursing the sick and wounded, as messengers, and sometimes as soldiers fighting alongside their master and his friends. In Louisiana no less than two companies of free men of color remained in Confederate service until after the surrender of General Robert E. Lee's Army.[61] What was true during the War for American Indepen-

---

60 R. L. Barbour, *South Carolina's Revolutionary War Battlefields* (Gretna, LA: Pelican Publishing Co., 2002) 78.
61 Gary Mills, *The Forgotten People: Cane River's Creoles of Color* (Baton Rouge: Louisiana State University Press, 1977) 230-46.

dence was equally true during the War for Southern Independence—African Americans both slave and free fought in the military forces of the South.

10— Q. You put a lot of faith in the writings of Thomas Jefferson. Jefferson said, "All men are created equal." If men are equal, how can you or the South defend the institution of slavery?

A. Of all men, Jefferson never defended slavery, and neither do we defend the indefensible. Remember, the same Thomas Jefferson who penned the famous phrase "all men are created equal" is the same Thomas Jefferson who owned slaves and never freed them. The correct question to ask here is not, "How could Jefferson believe in human equality and own slaves," but, "What did Jefferson and the founding fathers mean by the phrase 'all men are created equal'?" You appear to take the equality phrase in the Declaration of Independence as meaning absolute human equality, which is a Marxist concept. Jefferson and the founding fathers were republicans, not Marxists. For Jefferson and the founding fathers, the equality phrase in the Declaration of Independence was an attack against a society based on a hereditary aristocratic social concept. Also, they did not believe in the concept of a king having the "divine" right to rule a nation. As republicans, the founding fathers adhered to the concept of the people's right to "alter or abolish" their government at their volition. Among the founding fathers there were men who owned slaves, participated in the African slave trade, and believed in a social organization in which people of different and varied talents would move up or down the social ladder within society. As republicans, they did not believe that anyone was born, as Thomas Jefferson stated, "booted and spurred to ride them."[62] This is the same Jefferson who was a life-long slaveholder. The emphasis on freedom and liberty in the Declaration of Independence and the establishment of a republican government in the United States did have the effect of promoting the ending of both the African slave trade and slavery itself. Slaveholders such as Thomas Jefferson spoke out against the African slave trade and encouraged those working to abolish slavery. Other slaveholders such as John Randolph and George Washington, at their own personal expense, manumitted (i.e., freed) their slaves. Your attempt to slander

---

62 Thomas Jefferson, as cited in Adrienne Koch and William Peden, *The Selected Writings of Thomas Jefferson* (New York: The Modern Library, 1944) 729-30.

The Confederate Myth-Buster

Southerners as "defenders of slavery" just does not hold water.

11— Q. You say slavery could have been abolished by a system of gradual emancipation. How fair would it have been to ask slaves to remain in slavery while rich plantation owners worked these slaves to death? Your system of gradual emancipation sounds more like a gradual death sentence, doesn't it?

A. How fair would it have been to steal someone's legally obtained property? Dealing with the abolition of slavery and respecting the property rights of slave owners has always been a difficult task. One of America's earliest critics of slavery and discrimination against people of color, St. George Tucker, noted, "There are other considerations not to be disregarded. A great part of the property of individuals consists in slaves. The laws have sanctioned this species of property. Can the laws take away the property of an individual without his own consent, or without just compensation?"[63] Great Britain solved this problem by instituting a system of gradual emancipation with compensation for slave owners. Granted, the system of gradual emancipation was not perfect, but a system of immediate emancipation had its own problems as well. Not only would immediate emancipation rob people of their legal property, but also the slaves would not be served by this system either. Where would the newly freed slaves live? How would they make a living for their families? Who would take care of the old "retired" slaves if they were just set free? Even if the aforementioned problems were addressed, what would be the status of the newly freed slaves within "white" America? Remember it was common practice among Northerners to pass laws that would exclude free people of color from moving into their states. Color and race issues had to be addressed by Americans both in the North and in the South even if the slavery issue disappeared. Most Northerners who had a strong desire for the elimination of slavery had a parallel desire for the elimination of the Negro as well.[64] Early in the history of America, the lot of free people of color in New England was that of second-class citizens. For example, most New England states barred free people of color from sitting on juries, bearing arms, and by social pressure or by law, from voting. In Massachusetts, black and white people were

---

63 St. George Tucker, as cited in, Clyde N. Wilson, ed., *A View of the Constitution of the United States: With Selected Writings* (Indianapolis, IN: Liberty Fund, 1999) 214.
64 Joanne P. Melish, *Disowning Slavery: Gradual Emancipation and Race in New England 1780-1860* (Ithaca, NY: Cornell University Press, 1998) 53.

barred from marrying outside of their race.[65] So, as you can see, there were no "simple" solutions for the problem of slavery in America. As for your assertion that "rich" slaveholders would "work their slaves to death," you don't understand plain economics if that is your concept of slave ownership. A slave was a large capital investment — why on earth would anyone deliberately damage his own valuable property? Slaves were owned for one major purpose, the economic betterment of the slave owner. Most slaveholders understood that good treatment of their slaves meant more profits for themselves. This fact plus the social pressure of their fellow citizens was more than enough reason for the bulk of slaveholders to treat their slaves quite well.

12— Q. Other than the slaveholding South, Americans have always recognized the radical abolitionists as American heroes. Why don't you Southerners just recognize the greatness of the radical abolitionists?

A. The antics of the radical abolitionists were so offensive to Americans that President Andrew Jackson referred to their activity as a "wicked plan."[66] In 1835, William Lloyd Garrison, a leading radical abolitionist, was beaten and dragged through the streets of Boston, Massachusetts, and his press was destroyed by an angry mob of Northerners.[67] At the same time a mob of Northerners broke up an antislavery convention in Utica, New York.[68] These are only a few anti-radical abolitionist acts that took place in the North early in American history. It was not just Southerners who viewed the radical abolitionists as enemies of the Union (remember, it was a radical abolitionist, William Lloyd Garrison, who demanded "no union with slaveholders" and referred to the United States Constitution as "an agreement with hell"). Even a slave in Georgia, Harrison Berry, wrote an article in which he condemned the actions of the radical abolitionists as causing more trouble for slaves and making it more difficult to end slavery.[69] In 1845, a debate on the issue of slavery was held in

---

65 Lorenzo J. Greene, *The Negro in Colonial New England*, 1620-1776 (Port Washington, NY: Kennikat Press, Inc., 1966) 208, 300-302, 303.
66 Andrew Jackson, as cited in, Francis B. Simkins, *A History of the South* (New York: Alfred A. Knopf, 1959) 106.
67 Melish, 200-201.
68 Ibid.
69 Harrison Berry, *Slavery and Abolitionism, as Viewed by a Georgia Slave*, as cited in Afro-American History Series (Wilmington, DE: Scholarly Resources, Inc., 1970) VII, Preface.

Cincinnati, Ohio, between a radical abolitionist and a moderate abolitionist. Dr. N. L. Rice, speaking for the moderate view, noted that the problem with radical abolitionism was not that it "tends to abolish slavery, and improve the condition of the slave, but because, as I firmly believe, it [radical abolitionism] tends to perpetuate slavery, and to aggravate all its evils. That such is its tendency, that such have been its effects, I think I can prove to every unprejudiced mind."[70] The words of a respected president of the United States, elected by the people of all the states of the Union; the actions of the citizens of New England and the North against the radical abolitionists; the words of a Georgia slave; and the words of a Northern moderate abolitionist minister all dispute your concept of the radical abolitionists as "great Americans." Until the arrival of the radical abolitionists, both the African slave trade and slavery itself were considered a common problem to be dealt with by all Americans. The North was not stigmatized for the African slave trade, and the South was not stigmatized for its slave holdings. Northerners and Southerners worked together for the common good of the elimination of these evil systems. But with the advent of the radical abolitionist movement, rational thought and action were slowly subverted, and the South, not just slavery, became the focus of vitriolic hate speech. Slavery was then redefined from being a common American problem to being a uniquely Southern problem. According to the radical abolitionists, the new solution for ending slavery in America was to purge the nation of Southern political power, and if necessary, to purge the nation of Southerners. Summing up the radical abolitionists' view about the South, Ralph Waldo Emerson said, "If it takes ten years, and ten to restore the general prosperity, the destruction of the South would be worth so much."[71] According to Emerson, it was the South that was the cause of the blemish of slavery in America. Ralph Waldo Emerson must have forgotten about his great-grandfather Cornelius Waldo who was a slave trader.[72] This

---

70 N. L. Rice, as cited in, Walter D. Kennedy, *Myths of American Slavery*, 77.
71 Ralph Waldo Emerson, as cited in, Otto Scott, *The Secret Six* (New York: Times Books, 1979) 319-20.
72 Greene, 28. Cornelius Waldo was the maternal great-grandfather of Ralph Waldo Emerson. Cornelius Waldo was a merchant who sold items as diverse as Irish Duck to Negro slaves. Waldo was not alone in this venture, as many leading men in New England were involved in this nefarious trade. A very abbreviated list of famous New England slave traders would include such names as: Andrew and Peter Fanueil of Boston; Jonathan Belcher, governor of Massachusetts (1730); James Brown and family, one of the largest slave traders in New England and benefactors of Rhode Island College before its name change to Brown (as in the slave trading

selective memory is a common characteristic of Northerners when they are discussing the institution of slavery in America.

13— Q. Everyone knows New England and the North led the way in the elimination of slavery. Even still, you keep saying that the slaveholding South was a leader in the abolition of slavery. How can this be true?

A. Virginia was the first colony in America to protest against the importation of African slaves into the colonies, not Massachusetts or any other Northern colony. When you speak of slavery and do not include the African slave trade, which New England and the North were very much beholding to for their economic well-being, you are giving New England a "pass" on the issue of slavery. Nevertheless, we insist that trading in slaves was just as much a part of the system of slavery in America as owning slaves. It was in the case of ending the African slave trade that the South took the lead. For example, while Virginia was still a British colony, Virginia's House of Burgesses petitioned London to end the importation of African slaves into the colony. Virginia's petition to London stated in part, "The importation of slaves into the colonies from the coast of Africa hath long been considered as a trade of great inhumanity, and under its present encouragement, we have too much reason to fear will endanger the very existence of your majesty's American dominions."[73] At or about this same time, other Southern colonies also were attempting to convince the government in London to end the further importation of African slaves into their colonies.[74] After the adoption of the Constitution and before Congress had legislated against the African slave trade in 1808, most Southern states had already passed laws to eliminate the further importation of African slaves. As for freeing slaves, the South was light-years ahead of the North in breaking the shackles of slavery. Also remember it was a Southerner, St. George Tucker, who first encouraged not only the ending of slavery but also the ending of laws that discriminated against free people of color. Many early New Englanders understood the connection of their society with the infamous institution of slavery. At a meeting of abolitionists in

---

family) University; and Mark Anthony DeWolf. The DeWolf family continued their slave trading ventures even after the United States Constitution outlawed the slave trade: So many slaves, so much money, and so little recrimination; ah, the joy of living north of the Mason-Dixon Line.
[73] *Journal of the House of Burgesses*, as cited in, Clyde N. Wilson, 417.
[74] Walter D. Kennedy, *Myths of American Slavery*, 30.

Concord, New Hampshire, in 1823, Daniel Dana made note of New England's support of slavery: "In New England are the forges which have framed fetters and manacles for the limbs of unoffending Africans. In New England are found the overgrown fortunes and proud palaces, which have been reared up from the blood and sufferings of these unhappy men."[75] In 1828, Jonathan M. Wainwright delivered an address to an African missionary society in which he pointed out not only was New England the homeland of slavery itself and the African slave trade, but also New England was enriching itself on the same slave-grown cotton, rice, sugar, and other commercial ventures just as much as Southern slaveholders.[76] Good men in the North and South at one time worked together to promote the elimination of slavery in America. With the advent of radical abolitionism and a parallel Yankee sense of moral superiority of the North over the South, it was easy for Northerners to rationalize away their connection with the institution of slavery as they pursued their goal of cultural, economic, and ultimately political domination of the South.[77] Even into the twentieth century, Southerners were aware of the North's sense of moral superiority and domination. In 1930, a noted Southern historian, Frank L. Owsley, pointed out that the North had defeated the South, impoverished the South, and was attempting to "write error across the pages of Southern history which were out of keeping with the Northern legend, and set the rising and unborn generations upon stools of everlasting repentance."[78] The inference in your question is just another example of self-righteous Yankees attempting to keep Southerners upon the "stools of everlasting repentance."

14— Q. It is obvious you have a high regard for John Randolph of Virginia. He was after all a leading figure in early Virginia, but he was a lifelong slaveholder and defender of slavery. Is this what makes a Southerner a great man?

A. This Southerner did what few Northerners were ever willing to

---

[75] Daniel Dana, *A Discourse Addressed to the New Hampshire Auxiliary Colonization Society at the First Annual Meeting, Concord, New Hampshire*, June 2, 1825 (Concord, NH: Shepard & Bannister, 1825) 8.
[76] Jonathan M. Wainwright, *A Discourse on the Occasion of Forming the African Mission School, Christ Church, Hartford Connecticut* (Hartford, CT: H & F. J. Huntington, 1828) 18.
[77] Melish, 220-23.
[78] Frank L. Owsley, *The Irrepressible Conflict, I'll Take My Stand* (Baton Rouge: Louisiana State University Press, 1983) 66-67.

do, free slaves at his own personal expense. The radical abolitionists were ever willing to see slaves freed, provided that the cost of that liberation was borne by Southerners. Men such as John Randolph, who was a leading figure in the defense of States' Rights and republican values, were very serious about seeing to the well-being of their slave property. During his life Randolph often spoke of how easy it would be to rid himself of his slaves, but feeling a strong sense of respect for his friends he would rather suffer with them than enrich himself by selling them. In 1814 his estate was hard pressed by natural and financial woes. He could have sold his property and lived a secure and pleasant life; nevertheless, he would not do so. Writing to a friend about his troubles Randolph noted, "It is easy to rid myself of the burden if I could shut my heart to the cry of humanity and the voice of duty. But in these poor slaves I have found my best and most faithful friends; and I feel that it would be more difficult to abandon them to the cruel fate to which our laws would consign them, than to suffer with them."[79] Discharging his responsibility to his slaves, Randolph made provision for land and training so that when freed, his slaves would be fully capable of functioning without his care. At his death Randolph's slaves were freed and provided with land in Southern Ohio, all at his expense. It should be noted the good folks of Ohio would not allow Randolph's freed slaves to move into their fair state. It took ten years after Randolph's death for suitable lands in Western Virginia to be found where homes for his freed slaves were established, no thanks to the "freedom-loving" folks north of the Ohio River. Yes, John Randolph of Roanoke is the type of man who should be considered an American hero. John Randolph defended the Constitution against those who would make of it a *tabula rasa*, a blank sheet of paper upon which one could write at will from time to time anything that the majority wished, and he treated his slaves with respect and saw to it that they were freed. Many Southern slaveholders were men of heroic proportions who diligently worked to end slavery; John Randolph and George Washington being only two of many.

15— Q. The Second Amendment seems to be rather special to you. Yet, before the war, free men of color and especially slaves could not own guns. If you are a true believer in the Second Amendment, how can you defend such a record?

---

[79] John Randolph, as cited in, Russell Kirk, *John Randolph of Roanoke: A Study in American Politics* (Indianapolis, IN: Liberty Press, 1978) 159.

A. The Second Amendment does not protect a child's right to own a gun, nor does it protect a criminal's right to own a gun. The Second Amendment protects the free citizens of each state from having their weapons confiscated by the Federal government. When this amendment was adopted, slavery existed by law or tradition in every state in the new union. Now that you understand what the Second Amendment is all about, let's look at your suggestion that free men of color and slaves could not own guns in America. In his journal of life in Natchez, Mississippi, William Johnson, a free man of color, gave several accounts of his prowess as a hunter.[80] Johnson was a well-known and respected citizen of the city who rode to and from his hunts on horseback through the streets of Natchez, yet he never recorded one time in which anyone objected to his owning or using a gun. The use of guns by slaves is also recorded in the antebellum South. It was not uncommon for masters to keep hunting weapons on their plantations for the use of the male slaves. None other than Jefferson Davis described an occasion when he armed his slaves in order to expel a rather large group of white trespassers from his property.[81] In Northwest Louisiana at a place called Germantown, merchants of that place often sold slaves knives and accoutrements for firearms. Why would slaves be buying such items if they were not using them?[82] Laws, customs, and traditions of gun ownership by free people of color varied from place to place within the South; nevertheless, the use of guns and ownership of guns by free people of color was not uncommon. Although the ownership of guns by slaves was not accepted, it is obvious from the local historical record that many slaves were rather accustomed to the use of firearms. After the war and Reconstruction, Holt Collier, a former slave and Confederate soldier, became one of the South's most famous hunting guides. Collier is the man who was the hunting guide for Theodore Roosevelt on Roosevelt's famous "Teddy Bear" hunt.[83] Collier was well known for his ability to use a gun before, during, and after the war. During Reconstruction Collier even killed a Yankee carpetbagger.

---

80 Hogan, William R. and Edwin A. Davis, eds. *William Johnson's Natchez: The Ante-Bellum Diary of a Free Negro* (Baton Rouge: Louisiana State University Press, 1993) 214.
81 Kennedy and Kennedy, *Was Jefferson Davis Right?* 40.
82 For more on the subject of slaves in Northwest Louisiana buying products with their own money, see Walter D. Kennedy, *Myths of American Slavery*, 122-23.
83 Minor Ferris Buchanan, *Holt Collier: His Life, His Roosevelt Hunts, and the Origin of the Teddy Bear* (Jackson, MS: Centennial Press, 2002) vi, vii.

16— Q. The Federal government had to act to end slavery. If left up to the states, slavery would still be alive and well today. Isn't it true the South's claim that the right to end slavery belonged to the states was just a ploy to defend slavery?

A. The Federal government waited twenty years after the ratification of the Constitution before it ended the African slave trade. This was almost one hundred years after many Southern states had already petitioned the government in London to end this nefarious trade. During the drafting of the Constitution it was determined that the issue of domestic or local matters would remain in the hands of the people of the local area. Therefore, the Federal government was not granted authority to legislate on the matter of domestic slavery. Each state had to determine for itself how it would deal with the issue of slavery. Allowing the people at the local level to determine how they would organize their society was and is a very American method of government, not a Southern idea. By the early part of the nineteenth century, slavery was a dying institution. All European powers with the exception of Spain had begun a system of gradual emancipation of slaves. Well after the War for Southern Independence, Cuba in 1875 and Brazil in 1888 abolished slavery. Slavery ended twenty-three years after Appomattox in the Western Hemisphere and still exists today in Africa. Economic necessity and technical advances in farming would have doomed slavery in America at or about the same time it ended in Cuba or Brazil; without the loss of one-half million lives in bloody warfare.[84]

17— Q. As a libertarian I find it regrettable that conservative Southern Christians stood in the way of the liberation of the slaves. How can you say these people were lovers of liberty?

A. Step number one in ending slavery in America was putting an end to the African slave trade. It was here the South led the way (nothing to regret so far). By including the slaves in the religion of their masters, Christians were recognizing slaves were human and not animals. By including slaves in the religion of their masters and in making slaves more than just property, the second step in the elimination of slavery was taken. This advance led to a relationship be-

---

[84] The figure of one-half million is the cost of human life of the military personnel of the United States and the Confederate States; it does not take into consideration the almost equal loss of civilian life, both black and white in the South.

tween slaves and masters that were more paternalistic and less harsh. It was the feelings of paternalism that prompted men such as George Washington and John Randolph, among many others, to provide for their slaves and ultimately free them. This same sense of paternalism led other Southerners like Jefferson Davis to begin a system of training slaves for future freedom. Ultimately, this sense of paternalism led Southerners like Robert E. Lee to openly speak out against the institution of slavery itself. Rather than standing in the way of the liberation of the slaves, Southern Christianity was the driving force in a system of abolition that was mutually agreeable to both slaves and masters. With the advent of the radical abolitionists, the moderate voices for the elimination of slavery were drowned out by the harsh rhetoric of death and war (see question 12 in this chapter).

18— Q. As a Christian, Southerners using the Bible to defend slavery offends me. How can you be a Christian and not condemn slavery?

A. The first American Christians who used the Bible to defend the ownership of slaves were the Puritans of Massachusetts, and not Southerners. A Boston judge, John Saffin, wrote one of the most interesting tracts published in New England in 1700 on the subject of the biblical authority of slavery. This tract was in response to a tract published by another judge who did not approve of slavery. It should be noted the majority of the people in New England held Judge Saffin's pro-slavery views at that time.[85] Not only did New Englanders approve of slavery, but even Quakers in the colony of Pennsylvania got into the business of slave ownership. Just three years after the establishment of the colony of Pennsylvania, a shipload of 150 African slaves arrived in port. How do you think the Quaker colonists reacted? Did they rush to the dock and liberate their enslaved brothers? The Quakers did indeed rush to the port, but not to liberate slaves; rather they came, money in hand, to buy slaves.[86] It was almost seventy-five years from the time that these Quakers bought their first slaves until the Religious Society of Friends, i.e., the Quakers, abolished slavery within their fellowship. It was no easy task for the Quakers to end slavery, and it took much effort by many Quakers before slavery was abolished within their society. It should be noted that slavery within the Quaker community was not eliminated until after suffi-

---

85 Judge John Saffin, *A Brief and Candid Answer to a Late Printed Sheet, Entitled, The Selling of Joseph*, as cited in, George H. Moore, 55-60.
86 Water D. Kennedy, *Myths of American Slavery*, 51.

cient free white labor was available to meet the needs of the Quaker community.[87] This is just one more bit of evidence that slavery existed for one basic reason, to meet the demands for labor to maintain a community. Once the labor problem was solved, usually by the influx of free white laborers, then and only then did moral scruples sway the general public to end slavery. This included the reinterpretation of the Bible to promote the abolition of slavery. As for the defense of slavery, most theologians who were accused of being "defenders of slavery" were not defending slavery itself. Just because a theologian disagreed with the radical abolitionists' view of slavery as a sin in and of itself, does not mean that he was a "defender of slavery." It must be understood those who said slavery was not a sin in itself were not promoting slavery but rather promoting a "strict construction" view of the Bible. Most reasonable people understood that much sin could and did take place in the institution of slavery, which was a very good reason for Christians to work to bring about the end of slavery, but that did not mean that slavery was a sin. For example, sin can take place within marriage, but marriage is not sinful. Just because a person does not believe slavery to be a sin in and of itself does not make him a defender of the institution of slavery. Many theologians both from the North and the South disapproved of slavery and sought an introduction of a system of gradual emancipation all the while holding to the view that slavery was not a sin in itself. (For a more complete look at this vexing question, see chapter 3, "Abolitionism Versus Christianity" in *Myths of American Slavery* by Walter D. Kennedy.)

Summary

Among the blessings which the Almighty hath showered down on these states, there is a large portion of the bitterest draught that ever flowed from the cup of affliction. Whilst America hath been the land of promise to Europeans, and their descendants, it hath been the vale of death to millions of the wretched sons of Africa. The genial light of liberty, which hath here shone with unrivalled luster on the former, hath yielded no comfort to the latter, but to them hath proved a pillar of darkness, whilst it hath conducted the former to the most enviable state of human existence. Whilst we were offering up vows at the shrine of Liberty, and sacrificing hecatombs upon her alters; whilst we swore irreconcilable hostility to her enemies, and hurled defiance in their faces;

---

87 Ibid., 52.

whilst we adjured the God of Hosts to witness our resolution to live free, or die, and imprecated curses on their heads who refused to unite with us in establishing the empire of freedom; we were imposing upon our fellow men, who differed in complexion from us, a slavery, ten thousand times more cruel than the utmost extremity of those grievances and oppressions, of which we complained.[88]

— St. George Tucker, 1796

For those unacquainted with the writing and life of St. George Tucker, the preceding quote surely sounded like the furious ranting of a Radical Abolitionist or perhaps the mournful groaning of Abraham Lincoln. Yet, these are the words on one of the South's earliest advocates of REAL States' Rights — including of course the right of secession. Not only did St. George Tucker speak out against slavery but 133 years before the birth of Martin Luther King, this Southerner and defender of REAL States' Rights was speaking out against law that discriminated against free people of color. Tucker's views were on the cutting edge of the American liberty movement but as stated he was a strong supporter of the rights of "we the people" of sovereign states and opposed a strong, all-powerful, indivisible, Federal government. For those who would insist that Southerners who favor limited government, that is, REAL States' Rights are just using those principles as cover for racism, St. George Tucker surely will burst that liberal notion.

St. George Tucker is just one of many Southerners who worked to end the African slave trade, promoted the formation of abolition societies, and otherwise worked for a freer society.

---

[88] St. George Tucker as cited in, Clyde Wilson, editor, *View of the Constitution With Selected Writings* (Liberty Fund, Inc., Indianapolis, IN: 1999) 403

Saint George Tucker

Tucker, a veteran of the War for American Independence and noted legal scholar from Virginia, was a strong advocate of the independence, freedom, and sovereignty of the states. His essays on the Constitution of Virginia and the Federal Constitution were some of the earliest definitive work on those documents. Although a firm advocate of States' Rights including the right of secession, Tucker was an early abolitionist and critic of laws that discriminate against people of color. Tucker describes slavery as existing in three forms: (1) domestic slavery, where one person owns the labor of another person; (2) civil slavery, where the government implements laws that impacts one class of people to the advantage of another class of people; and, (3) political slavery, where a government does not recognize the right of a people to consent to the government they are forced to live under. Tucker equally condemns all three forms of slavery. According to Tucker's definition of slavery and with the post-Appomattox death of the right of secession, all Americans live under a system of political slavery — if you can't leave, you are not free!

Chapter 4
Racism

[I] profess to ... fight for but one single purpose, viz, to sustain a government capable of vindicating its just and rightful authority, independent of niggers, cotton, money, or any earthly interest.[89]
— General William T. Sherman

It is my purpose to utterly exterminate the Sioux.[90]
— General John Pope

In the minds of modern Americans racism, like slavery, is usually associated with the South. Many times, when specific acts of violence against people of color happen somewhere outside of the South, a tearful moan is uttered, "This is not Mississippi, why is this happening up here?"[91] The tender sensibilities of a morally superior people or at least a people raised on the myth of their innate moral superior nature, cannot fathom the idea they may be as evil as their arch villain. Unfortunately, facts have a way of shocking people into some semblance of reality. In November of 1988, an Ethiopian (black) man was bludgeon to death by a group of neo-Nazis in Portland, Oregon. The Portland community had to come to grips with the fact evil does indeed exist even in a liberal paradise.[92] To make matters worse for the liberals of Portland, the young men who committed this heinous act were not from the South. The myth of racism as a Southern phenomenon has spread from the South and infected the rest of morally superior America is a near constant theme of the victor of the so-called Civil War.[93] The myth of the South as the source of the evil of racism in America parallels the myth of the South as the source of the evil of slavery in America. By making the South the object of

---

89 William T. Sherman, as cited in, *Official Records War of the Rebellion*, XXX, pt. IV, 235.
90 John Pope, as cited in, David A. Nichols, *Lincoln and the Indians* (Columbia: University of Missouri Press, 1978) 87.
91 Joe Uris, A racist legacy taints this state, *Portland Tribune*, October 17, 2003 @ www.portalndtribune.com/archview
92 Ibid.
93 Melish, XI-XIII, 2.

scorn for the dual evils of slavery and racism, the North is left with its sense of moral superiority untouched and intact. Nevertheless, we must insist that evil, or if you prefer, sin, is not something unique to the southern region of these United States. Yes, there was and is much evil in the South, but as the "Good Book" tells us, "all have sinned" (Romans 3:23), and "let those without sin cast the first stone" (John 8:7, paraphrased). As we have shown in chapter 3, slavery is a global not just an American problem. Furthermore, in the United States of America, slavery is not simply or solely a Southern problem. Likewise, discrimination against people of color and various acts of racism were and are still common throughout these United States, not just something that happens down South. Even in places as far removed from Dixie as the state of Oregon, one can find abundant proof of anti-black acts and actions by some Northern people. For example, when Oregon was admitted to the Union as a "free" state in 1858, its state constitution not only denied slavery a home in Oregon, it also denied free people of color a home in the "free" state of Oregon. Even after the so-called Civil War was over and slavery had been outlawed, Oregon refused to allow interracial marriages, the Ku Klux Klan was a dominate force in state politics, and lynching and mock lynching were part of vigilante justice in the state.[94] Oregon was no different from any other state in the Union, North, South, East, or West of the Mason-Dixon Line. Yes, there have been injustices done in America, but it is in America that these same injustices have been corrected.

1— Q. General Nathan Bedford Forrest massacred African American soldiers at Fort Pillow. Why should Americans respect such a man or the cause of Southern independence for which he was fighting?

A. Listening to the report of the Battle of Little Big Horn from a Native American is very different from the "official" report one gets from the Federal government. Why is this true? Is it because Native Americans are uncivilized and therefore cannot be trusted with the truth? No, the truth of the matter is often discovered when both sides of an issue are given the opportunity to be heard. That which is true when discussing the Indian Wars is also true when discussing the War for Southern Independence. After all, one must remember, the victor writes the official view of any conflict. Yes, the Battle of Fort

---

[94] Uris, A racist legacy taints this state.

Pillow was a bloody affair, but it was General Forrest who at the close of the battle and at great danger to himself rode into the middle of the carnage to order an end to the shooting. General Forrest did not order a massacre of prisoners nor did he stand by or encourage the firing into surrendering soldiers. Much of the carnage can and should be laid at the feet of incompetent Federal officers who allowed their soldiers to obtain alcohol and to continue firing when surrender was offered. By looking at both the Federal and Confederate records of this battle, one will come away with a better understanding of what really happened. There was no massacre of Federal soldiers by Confederate General Forrest or his men at the Battle of Fort Pillow; rather, it was just one more hard-fought and bloody fight. This type of incident was not uncommon during the war.

2— Q. General Forrest started the Ku Klux Klan, an anti-black organization. Is this the type of man you would have Southerners idolize as an American hero?

A. General Forrest was neither the man, nor one of the men who founded the Ku Klux Klan. He did however in an effort to rid the South of carpetbagger rule, play a large part in the original Klan movement. As progress was made in removing foreign control of the Southern states, General Forrest ordered the Klan disbanded. He even rode with the local sheriff as he put an end to Klan activity. One fact must be pointed out when we are discussing the Klan: there have been several, no less than three, different organizations known as the Ku Klux Klan, the KKK, or simply the Klan. The first Klan was organized by Southerners in an effort to rid the Southern states of Yankee carpetbagger rule. This Klan was not organized as an anti-black, anti-Jew, or anti-Catholic group as was common in the twentieth-century Klan. During this fight against Yankee carpetbaggers, it was not unusual for former black Confederate soldiers to give assistance to those who were fighting their former enemies. When a Yankee carpetbagger was found dead, Holt Collier, a former slave and Confederate veteran, was charged with the Yankee's death. The Yankee carpetbagger had a history of insulting Holt's former master, and Holt was known as a man of action. When the Yankees put Holt on trial, the white citizens of the community came to his defense, and Holt was found innocent.[95] Here we see a black Confederate veteran who was known as a man of action, defending his former mas-

---

95 Buchanan, 110-17.

ter against the actions of a carpetbagger, and the white community coming to his aid. This is just one example of the fact that the original Ku Klux Klan was not anti-black, it was anti-carpetbagger. Yes, since the freed blacks had been enlisted by the Yankees to be used as a weapon against the white community, many blacks were the object of the Klan, but only because they were allies of the conquering Yankees, not because they were black. Like Holt Collier, some blacks assisted in the fight against the carpetbaggers. Likewise, Jews and Catholics were also part of the original Klan movement. It was not until the advent of the twentieth-century Klan that racism, anti-Semitism, and anti-Catholicism became issues promoted by the new Klan. It must be pointed out that the twentieth- and twenty-first-century Klan has no connection with the original Klan. As a matter of fact, most of the members of the twentieth- and twenty-first-century Klan live outside of the South. Don't confuse the nineteenth-century group with the twentieth- and twenty-first-century groups. General Forrest had great respect for his black soldiers and often spoke highly of them. On July 4, 1875, in Memphis, Tennessee, General Forrest had the honor to speak to a group of black citizens. After receiving a gift of flowers from ladies representing the black citizens, the general said in part, "I accept these flowers as a token of reconciliation between the white and colored races of the South.... I take this occasion to say that I am your friend.... I assure you that every man that was in the Confederate army is your friend. We were born on the same soil, breathe the same air, live in the same land, and why should we not be brothers and sisters.... I think it is right, and will do all I can to bring about harmony, peace and unity.... Do your duty as citizens, and if any [of you] are oppressed, I will be your friend."[96] This is the kind of man most Southerners would consider a hero.

3— Q. The Confederate flag is offensive to many people, especially African-Americans; therefore, why shouldn't it be banned?

A. The United States flag is offensive to many Native Americans and Hispanic Americans who see it as a symbol of Yankee imperialism and genocide. Should we ban the United States flag? Every reliable poll that has been conducted about the use of the Confederate flag has shown the vast majority of Americans and especially Southerners view the Confederate flag in a positive rather than a negative light. Even among African Americans these polls show a strong belief

---

[96] General Nathan B. Forrest, *Memphis Daily Avalanche*, July 6, 1876, I.

that the Confederate flag is a symbol of heritage or history and not a symbol of hate. The voters of Mississippi, both black and white, spoke with a loud voice when given a chance to vote to keep the Confederate emblem on their state flag. More than 75 percent of the voters were in favor of the Confederate emblem. Even many predominately black districts voted in favor of the Confederate emblem! Some people will be offended by anything. If we start banning everything that offends someone, soon nothing will be left. It's okay to be offended. The offended person has the right to voice his opinion and try to get something done about the source of his displeasure. But once the people have spoken, it's time to get over it! (See question 2, chapter 3, for more information about the Confederate flag and slavery.)

4— **Q.** The Confederate flag is the flag of the Ku Klux Klan. Why should an emblem of a hate group be allowed public display?

A. In the mid-1920s several very large Klan marches were held in Washington, DC. At that time thousands of Klansmen carrying hundreds of flags were seen marching down Pennsylvania Avenue in Washington. How many Confederate flags were displayed in these parades? There were no Confederate flags in the Klan parades, but there were hundreds of United States flags.[97] The Klan has used many symbols during its history. The cross, the Bible, and the United States flag are just a few items used by the Klan. Shall we ban these items that are routinely used by the Klan? Where do we stop once we start banning items that have been misappropriated by hate groups? Neither the Confederate flag, nor the United States flag, nor the Bible should be banned because the Ku Klux Klan has used it. The Klan and not items it has misused should be the object of your rage.

5— **Q.** After the South was forced to free its slaves it passed the infamous Black Code laws that discriminated against the newly freed slaves. Don't these Black Code laws of the South prove that the South was and is a racist place?

A. As long as slavery existed, the South did not need any Black Code laws like the ones that were in place in the North before the war. You see, Black Code laws were born in the North. It was in New England where schoolchildren were segregated by race before the

---

[97] Walter D. Kennedy, *Myths of American Slavery*, photo section 6-7.

war.[98] One of the first acts against the freed slaves by Northern states was to pass laws to eliminate free black citizens from voting. New Jersey was one of the first Northern states to do so in 1807, Connecticut followed in 1814, and Pennsylvania's free people of color lost the right to vote by a state court decision in 1837.[99] Other Northern states followed suit not only by eliminating the ability of black citizens to vote, but also by excluding them from moving into their states. The same radical-controlled Congress that demanded integrated schools in the South during Reconstruction was the same radical-controlled Congress that established segregated public schools in Washington, DC.[100] Under the system of gradual emancipation in which slaves were taught how to provide for themselves, and where newly freed slaves were provided a place to live and work, Black Code laws were never needed. But with the advent of radical emancipation a very new and different set of problems faced the states of the South, one that had never been faced by any other American state — a very large, uneducated, and unprepared group of free Africans living within the borders of a state. When faced with a very small portion of its population being African before the war, Northern states quickly passed and enforced their very own Black Codes. The Northern states passed Black Code laws long before any Southern state passed such laws. Why do you insist on attacking the South for doing what the North had already done? Why are you so prejudiced — prejudiced against the South?

6— Q. Why shouldn't the South be set upon "stools of everlasting repentance"— not only because of its practice of slavery but also because of its legacy of segregation, an outgrowth of Southern slavery?

A. No Americans should be made to sit upon "stools of everlasting repentance." Surely, when we discover an injustice, that injustice should be challenged and corrected. But to have the Northern section of the United States telling the Southern section of the United States that it must forever play the role of the villain in America is hypocritical and unjust. (See the previous question and answer for related answers to this question.)

---

98 George H. Moore, 54-55.
99 Edgar J. McManus, *Black Bondage in the North* (Syracuse, NY: Syracuse University Press, 1977) 183-84.
100 Kennedy and Kennedy, *The South Was Right!* 53-58.

7— Q. With such a history of slavery and racism in the South, how can you defend Southern heritage?

A. It must be nice to live in Utopia, as you do, but the rest of us don't live there. As for your place of residence, Utopia is an air castle that does not exist. The North has its record of slavery, slave trading, and of course discrimination against people of color, yet no one is demanding that Northern heritage and/or history be eliminated. Southern heritage is more than just reliving the days of slavery. Although slavery is part of Southern history as well as American history, it is not the central theme for those who love the South. Those of us who see the South as a wonderful place to live and raise a family see the South as the land of George Washington, Patrick Henry, Thomas Jefferson, Robert E. Lee, Stonewall Jackson, and Jefferson Davis among many other great Americans of the South. We see a South that has led the way in promoting limited government, establishing republican institutions, ending the African slave trade, and manumitting slaves. These are just a few reasons we see the South as a great place, whose heritage and history should be preserved and promoted.

8— Q. Even the vice president of the Confederacy, Alexander Stephens, stated that the Confederacy was based upon slavery and white supremacy. What more proof do you need to establish the fact that the Confederacy was a racist nation?

A. Even President Abraham Lincoln believed in white supremacy and had often spoken in favor of keeping the white race the superior race in America. To be more specific, in the famous Lincoln-Douglas Debate of 1858 Lincoln stated, "I, as much as any other man, am in favor of having the superior position assigned to the white race."[101] Both Abraham Lincoln and Alexander Stephens were strong advocates of the nineteenth-century philosophy of white supremacy. Accordingly, Vice President Stephens noted slavery was also based upon that theory, and the Confederate government recognized this fact. Commenting on the theory of absolute human equality, i.e., as in Marxist ideology, which a small element in Lincoln's party had already embraced, Stephens made the comment that the Confederate government was established on the opposite idea. The idea of human inequality was the prevalent view held by people in both the North

---

101 Abraham Lincoln, as cited in, R. W. Johannsen, *The Lincoln Douglas Debates of 1858* (New York: Oxford University Press, 1965) 162-63.

and the South during the nineteenth century. In his speech Stephens was pointing out that the Confederacy was organized in a manner that was in keeping with the normal philosophy of the time. On this point, Lincoln and Stephens were in agreement.

9— Q. Where was it that an African American man was dragged behind a truck until dead? Wasn't it in Texas? Texas is part of the South. Lynching and other types of murder of African Americans in the South have become a common legacy of the South. Doesn't this fact just prove to the rest of America that the South is a racist place? Why shouldn't you Southerners be treated differently from other Americans?

A. The beating of Rodney King to the point of bloody unconsciousness was an act of the Los Angeles police, not the Birmingham police. Mulugeta Seraw, an Ethiopian, was bludgeoned to death by a mob of neo-Nazis in Portland, Oregon, not in Laurel, Mississippi. A black man was severely beaten by a white mob in Yonkers, New York, not in Rome, Georgia. Do you get the message? Evil exists everywhere, and bad things happen in the North and the South. Why is it some people cannot see the evil within their society but never fail to point it out in someone else's society? Don't we have a name for people who can find fault with others and never themselves? I think we call those people "hypocrites." Let's take the Texas "dragging" incident as an example. In Texas, two convicted white criminals murdered by dragging to death a black criminal (whom they had met in jail — how appropriate). When this event became known, every liberal and neo-conservative news outlet talking-head, professional "insult warrior" from Al Sharpton to Jesse Jackson, and every liberal minister and evangelical "I want to be as famous as Al and Jesse" minister began crying and pounding their chest about the horror of this incident. Yes, it was horrible, but not uniquely horrible. At or about the same time the murder of this black man took place in Texas, in Kansas two African American brothers raped two white girls, murdered one of them and attempted to murder the other, and murdered the two girls' white boyfriends.[102] This case is as equally horrible as the Texas incident. Yet few if anyone in the media or ministry found the time to decry the loss of these young white people in Kansas. Why is the murder of a black criminal in Texas by two white criminals

---

102 Walter D. Kennedy, *Myths of American Slavery*, 224.

considered more newsworthy than the rape of two white girls and the murder of three young white people in Kansas by blacks? It all goes back to the problem of the North's sense of moral superiority over the South. Anything in the news that will stroke and massage this sense of moral superiority of the North is given front-page billing by all media outlets. The South is once again reminded why it exists in this nation — to sit upon the stool of eternal repentance to make Yankees feel and look good!

10— Q. Racism is epidemic in the South. African Americans earn less money than Southern whites, and they own less real property than Southern whites. Most schools and colleges for African Americans in the South are under-funded when compared to white educational institutions. Doesn't this disparity prove that the South is a racist section of America?

A. Yes, evil is epidemic in the South, but that does not make the South unusual in that respect. Evil is epidemic in all of America. What makes the South unusual is that Southerners have the ability to recognize the evil in them and among them. You condemn Southerners for "under-funding" black schools and colleges in the South. Your condemnation is also a revelation in itself. Nowhere in the world have more Africans been given more education or have attained a higher literacy rate than in the South. Even after Reconstruction white-dominated Southern legislatures passed taxes to fund black schools and colleges. Nowhere outside of the United States do people of African descent own more property, have a higher per capita income, or enjoy a longer life span than in the South. Yes, more can be done, but that is no reason to discount what has already been done. As to your point about "under-funding" of black schools and colleges in the South, when Southern white schools and colleges are compared to Northern schools and colleges, it is revealed that an equal amount of under-funding of Southern schools and colleges exists. Can we surmise from this comparison that Northerners mistreat Southerners of all races?

11— Q. Everyone knows not all people down South are evil racists. Yet, it was in the South were most of the killings went on during the civil rights movement, and it was in the South where most of the evils of slavery took place. Aren't you just trying to cover up this sorry history of the South by saying that the North was also full of people with racist attitudes?

A. Malcolm X was killed in New York, not New Orleans, and the Los Angeles police, not the Birmingham, Alabama, police, beat Rodney King nearly to death. Due to the innate sinful nature of all humanity (this statement reflects orthodox Christian theology as accepted by most Southerners), evil resides in the heart of human beings regardless of where they reside. The problem, which your question points out so well, is that for far too long the North, assuming the position of moral superiority, has attempted to paint the South with the tar brush of racism while claiming moral purity for itself. Appreciating this truth makes it easier to understand your characterization of Southern history as "this sorry history of the South." Racism existed in the North before the time of the War for Southern Independence and continues to this day. The North is not now, nor has it ever been, the land of human brotherhood and equality. Ralph Waldo Emerson, a very prominent Northerner, had this to say about the reason many abolitionists desired to abolish slavery: "The abolitionist wishes to abolish slavery, but because he wishes to abolish the black man."[103] Emerson was merely giving voice to the majority of Americans of the nineteenth century who held to the opinion that white people and black people could not live together in a free society. The idea that blacks and whites could not live in the same country was so strong that Thomas Jefferson in his famous "these people will be free" statement went on to say that "once free we cannot live in the same country."[104] Abraham Lincoln voiced the same opinion in his famous Lincoln-Douglas debates.[105] So strong was this fear of living in a society of free black people and white people, the state of Illinois passed the following resolution in January of 1863 in response to Lincoln's Emancipation Proclamation: "Resolved: That the emancipation proclamation of the President of the United States is as unwarranted in military as in civil law; a gigantic usurpation, at once converting the war, professedly commenced by the administration for the vindication of the authority of the constitution, into a crusade for the sudden, unconditional, and violent

---

103 Ralph Waldo Emerson, as cited in, William H. Gillamn, ed., *The Journals and Miscellaneous Notebooks of Ralph Waldo Emerson* (Cambridge, MA: Harvard University Press, 1960) 13, 198.
104 Thomas Jefferson, *Thomas Jefferson: Autobiography*, 1821, ME 1:71.
105 Abraham Lincoln, as cited in, R. W. Johannsen, 162-63.

liberation of 3,000,000 negro slaves; a result which would not only be a total subversion of the Federal Union, but a revolution in the social organization of the Southern States, the immediate and remote, the present and far-reaching consequences of which to both races cannot be contemplated without the most dismal foreboding of horror and dismay. The proclamation invites servile insurrection as an element in this emancipation crusade — a means of warfare, the inhumanity and diabolism of which are without example in civilized warfare, and which we denounce, and which the civilized world will denounce, as an uneffaceable disgrace to the American people."[106] The statement of Emerson before the war and the resolutions of the state of Illinois during the war are evidence enough to prove that the North was not driven by high moral principles of human equality. By citing Northern wrongs, we are merely leveling the playing field for both sides in this discussion. Both Northerners and Southerners lived by the commonly held nineteenth-century philosophy of Negro inferiority. This concept was firmly held up unto the late twentieth century by people in both sections of the United States. We don't think it is fair to saddle the South with the total burden for these opinions.

Summary

These facts have had themselves recognized in the most decisive manner throughout the Northern States. No town, no city, or State encourages their immigration; many of them discourage it by legislation; some of the non-slaveholding states have prohibited their entry into their borders under any circumstances whatever. Thus it seems this great fact of 'inferiority' of the race is equally admitted everywhere in our country. The Northern states admit it, and, to rid themselves of the burden, inflict the most injuries upon an unhappy race; they expel them from their borders and drive them out of their boundaries, as wanderers and out-casts…. If the Negro was so much in just consideration of the North, his wretched plight in the North raises many questions. Why was he an alien, an outcast, in the North? Why in Illinois was he denied civil rights as we have seen? Why in August of 1834 did a race riot break forth in Philadelphia in which thirty Negro houses were sacked or destroyed, a Negro church demolished and many people killed? This was

---

106 Resolutions of Illinois State Legislature, January 7, 1863, as cited in, Henry S. Commager, ed., *Documents of American History*, Eighth Edition (New York: Appleton, Century, Croft, 1968) 1, 422.

followed by Negro mobbing at Trenton, and other towns in New Jersey.[107]
— Robert Toombs, 1856.

It's hard to dialogue with an individual who presents himself as a hypocrite. This is the point that Toombs, a partisan Southern Nationalist, was pointing out in Boston, Massachusetts, just four years before the outbreak of Southern secession. In our present politically correct world, Southerners still find themselves faced with opponents who see only evil and racism down South. During the years before the War for Southern Independence, while Northerners were condemning the South for slavery (while only about 6 percent of Southerners held a title to a slave), the North was doing all it could to protect its white society from contamination with African Americans. From the 19th century and into the 21st century, there seems to be a notion the North is the region that defended African Americans and the South was the region that oppressed African Americans. Yet, as Toombs pointed out in 1856 and we have demonstrated here, racism and evil is part of our sinful nature and is not confined or limited by geography. America has made great progress in promoting the rights and liberty of all its citizens. That progress needs to be encouraged. Hypocrisy will not promote the concept of liberty. Liberty is well served by a full and complete examination of the facts, including the facts about race-relations in the North and the South.

---

107 Robert Toombs as cited in, *Edgar Lee Masters, Lincoln The Man* (1931, The Foundation for American Education, Columbia, SC: 1997) 164-65.

History does not change: Attitudes do!

In modern 21st century America it is all too common to see monuments of Southern heroes and anything associated with Dixie to be scorned, ridiculed, and defamed. Yet as these photos above demonstrate, there was a time in America when symbols of the Confederacy were held in high esteem by all Americans. The coin above is an official United States commemorative one-half dollar. The Congressional Resolution to authorize the minting of this coin passed the US Houses of Representatives by unanimous consent March 6, 1924, and the US Senate six days later. President Calvin Coolidge signed the Resolution on March 17, 1924. The Resolution states in part that the coin was to assist in establishing "A monument to the valor of the soldiers of the South." The statement about Southern valor is clearly seen of the reverse of this coin.

This valor was also demonstrated by the 31st United States Army Infantry, known by its nickname, "Dixie Division." The photo above is of a shoulder patch worn by members of the United States Army's Dixie Division. Serving in the United States Army faithfully from 1917 through 1964, members of the Dixie Division announced their pride in their Southern roots every time they sang the Dixie Division's song which in part states: "In the days of sixty-one when Dixie took her stand … Lee and Jackson all fought for 'The dear lost Cause' for the Sunny Southland its customs and its law." Has history changed or is there an ulterior motive in the current attack upon Traditional American Values?

Chapter 5
History

What passes as standard American history is really Yankee history written by New Englanders or their puppets to glorify Yankee heroes and ideals.[108]
— Grady McWhiney

As the old truism states, "To the victor go the spoils," that is, the fruits. One of the "fruits" of victory in war is the ability to write and enforce the official version of the war. For the defeated, all that was lost on the field of battle is compounded by the loss of the ability to offer an alternate view to the one being enforced by the victor. Think about it, what would be the legacy of George Washington, Benjamin Franklin, or Patrick Henry if the British had won the War for American Independence? Would the British Broadcasting Corporation (BBC) do weeklong miniseries about the evil slave trading and slaveholding American rebels who tried to destroy the grand Union back in 1776? Would we routinely hear stories about the evil slaveholding general of the Continental Army, George Washington, and how he kept his slaves toiling away on his plantation until the king forced Washington to emancipate his poor downtrodden slaves? Would we hear about New England shippers who played the part of smugglers before the war and pirates during the rebellion? The way we view George Washington or Robert E. Lee, Benjamin Franklin or Jefferson Davis depends on the information we have about these people. The information we have all hinges on who won the war, because the victor will choose and enforce what type of information is told about the war. If we are to possess the complete truth of an event we must therefore look beyond the official view of history, i.e., the victor's view of any struggle, and examine the complete story of the conflict. In the following discussion we will answer questions by looking at the issues from the view of the defeated people, a view that has gone under-told or that has not been told at all.

1— Q. You have stated other issues were sources of conflict between the North and the South before slavery caused secession. I may not be too bright, although I did manage to get through college, but I don't

---

[108] Grady McWhiney, *Jefferson Davis the Unforgiven*, Journal of Mississippi History, XLII, May 1980, 124.

recall any issue other than slavery which was a point of conflict between the two sections. Other than slavery, what possibly could have caused problems between the two sections of America?

A. The North's attempt to give away the Mississippi River to Spain was an early point of conflict between the North and the South.[109] Early in the history of this nation the Northeastern ports were the center of commerce in the United States. With the expansion over the mountains to the west and the settlement of the vast areas drained by the Mississippi River, East Coast Northern merchants feared commerce which once flowed through their ports and was being carried by their ships would soon turn down the Mississippi River and exit to world markets via New Orleans. A shift of commerce away from the Northeastern ports and toward the port of New Orleans was such a threat that many leaders in the North, led by John Jay, approached Spain with a proposal to grant to Spain complete sovereignty over the Mississippi River. If this was done, American commerce on the Mississippi would have to pay a high tax to Spain, therefore making the markets in the Northeast more appealing. As for the South, such an arrangement would make the settlement of the area drained by the Mississippi very difficult and would hinder the growth of new Southern states. Another area of difficulty between the North and the South was the establishment of a national banking system. The commercial interests of the North desired such a system, since due to the nature of banking and commerce, the national bank would be located in New York and Philadelphia. The commercial interests of the North and East agitated for the national bank, whereas the agricultural interests of the South and West opposed such a system. President Thomas Jefferson of Virginia and President Andrew Jackson of Tennessee led the fight against such a bank, whereas Alexander Hamilton of New York led the fight for a national bank. And of course, the tariff issue, not just the one everyone knows about between South Carolina and the Federal government, but all such tariff issues, was a major point of conflict between the North and the South. Naturally, money was at the center of this issue. Even the issue of slavery was more about the North's attempt to keep the South from expanding and obtaining more votes in Congress than it was about any humanitarian issues.

---

109 Merrill Jensen, *The New Nation* (Boston: Northwestern University Press, 1981) 418.

2— Q. Isn't it true the South fired the first shot of the war at Fort Sumter? Doesn't this prove the South started the Civil War?

A. On December 7, 1941, the USS *Ward* fire upon and sunk a Japanese submarine well before any Japanese bomb was dropped on Pearl Harbor. Clearly, America 'fired the first shot" that fateful day. Does this mean America caused the war in the Pacific on that day? It is a recognized principle of international law that it is not the one who fires the first shot who "starts the war," but rather the one who makes the firing of the first shot necessary who is responsible for starting a war. To put it another way, if someone were to break into your home, gun in hand, would you have to wait for the intruder to "fire the first shot" before you would be authorized to shoot him? Simple reflection on the matter makes the charge of "you fired the first shot so it's all your fault" simply ridiculous. Now we must consider why the first shot was fired at Fort Sumter. South Carolina seceded from the Union in December of 1860. Fort Sumter was not fired upon until April of 1861, more than three months after the secession of South Carolina. Why didn't the people of South Carolina fire upon Fort Sumter in December of 1860 or in January, February, or March of 1861? By an agreement between the forces of South Carolina and the remaining Federal forces in Charleston, no surprise action would be taken against the other force until each side was properly notified. Before the secession of South Carolina, the Federal forces under the command of Major Robert Anderson were occupying Fort Moultrie, with work underway to strengthen Fort Sumter. Prior to his inauguration as president of the United States, Abraham Lincoln had already written General Winfield Scott, commanding general of the army, to "be as well prepared as he can to either hold or retake the forts, as the case may require, at and after the inauguration."[110] During the Christmas festivities in Charleston, Major Anderson ordered the abandonment of Fort Moultrie, the spiking of any guns left in the fort, and the removal of all men and equipment into Fort Sumter. This was seen by the people of South Carolina as an aggressive move by the Federal government to keep and maintain a fort in the heart of Charleston Harbor. This aggressive move by Anderson was the first overt act of war. The people of South Carolina attempted for several months to have the Federal forces removed from Fort Sumter. During this time no hostile actions were taken against the fort. Only after President

---

110 Robert McNutt McElroy, *Jefferson Davis: The Unreal and The Real* (New York: Harper and Brothers, 1937) I, 278.

Lincoln sent reinforcements, assisted by a fleet of United States naval vessels, did the people of the South "fire the first shot." Now, if this had happened in the same place with the exceptions of the forces being British rather than Yankees and the date being July 5, 1776, rather than April 12, 1861, how would you feel about Americans forcing the British out of Charleston Harbor? Once the seceding nation declared its independence, the mother country became a foreign invader. This was the case in 1776, and it was also the case in 1861. Lincoln's policy of military intimidation made war the only possibility. Lincoln and the North's aggressive action made the firing of the first shot necessary; thus, Lincoln and the North were responsible for "starting the war."

3— Q. Your reference to John Brown as a terrorist is somewhat off base. Wasn't he a freedom fighter? Didn't he make the ultimate sacrifice for human freedom?

A. Heroes are men who understand the ends do not justify the means. The barbaric notion of doing whatever is necessary to promote the "greater good" is a tool used by most twentieth-century tyrants and twenty-first-century jihadists. Joseph Stalin filled his gulags with innocent men and women; Adolph Hitler filled his gas chambers with helpless victims; and Mao Zedong slaughtered millions of his own countrymen, all in the name of what they considered the "greater good"— and they would stop at nothing in the pursuit of this objective. The men who took over the 9/11 jet planes and flew them into the World Trade Center buildings in New York were acting under the spell of "the ends justify the means." John Brown was years ahead of Al Qaeda in the pursuit of doing whatever is necessary to achieve a so-called "worthy objective." John Brown was a murderer who took pleasure in the slaughter of Southerners in Kansas. At Pottawatomie, Kansas, he and his sons hacked and shot to death five unarmed men within sight of their wives and children. This was done in the middle of the night without warning — a cowardly act of murder — and this is the man you want to call an American hero? President Washington warned Americans about the danger of using wrong policy as an "instrument of good." George Washington noted the desire to commit unjust acts in the pursuit of a worthy objective has dangerous consequences, "for though this, in one instance, may be the instrument of good, it is the customary weapon by which free governments are destroyed."[111] Yes, the pursuit of the elimination of slavery was indeed a noble undertaking, but even here the end does not justify the means. Murder and terrorism cannot be justified in the pursuit of eliminating slavery. By using unjust methods to promote a just cause a person merely sullies the cause he seeks to promote. John Brown, like the terrorist pilots of 9/11 infamy, cannot be justified in the taking of innocent lives in the pursuit of what is considered a worthy objective. John Brown was a terrorist, not a hero.

4— Q. You seem not to like Julia Ward Howe's *Battle Hymn of the Republic*. Aren't you a Christian? Why don't you like this beautiful Christian song?

A. Beautiful Christian songs are written by beautiful Christians, not by people like Julia Ward Howe who did not believe in the deity of Christ or the Trinity. Julia Ward Howe was a Unitarian, not a Christian. The *Battle Hymn of the Republic* was written as an encouragement to those who were going forth and "trampling out the vintage where the grapes of wrath are stored," which of course is in the South. Howe was a member of the radical abolition movement who saw the South as a stumbling block on the road of America's progress to final perfection. Howe and her Unitarian cohorts did not believe in the perfection of man by the work of Christ, but as secular humanists they believed in earthly perfection by the work of man. This work entailed ridding the United States of the evil of slavery, slaveholders, and the society which "protected" slavery, the South. This "Christian hymn" was actually a marching song for the army of man as it purged America of Southern influence and ultimately the South itself. As Southerners we find this concept by Howe and her fellow radical abolitionists as being arrogant, pompous, and foolhardily blind to the North's own guilt with the institution of slavery.

5— Q. Aren't you just pursuing revisionist history? After all, you keep calling the Civil War "the War for Southern Independence." You are just trying to revise the past by calling the Civil War by a name you like. No one ever used that term for the war.

A. A revisionist historian is one who attempts to change recognized historical facts. The Kennedy Twins on the other hand are merely telling the true story about Southern history, the history that

---

111 George Washington, as cited in, Clarence B. Carson, 561.

has been under-told or misrepresented. We do not want to change the history of the South; we would just like to have the South's history honestly reported, without bias or change. The war of 1861-65 has many names. The Civil War is the one that most people understand today, but it is not the most correct name for that war. A civil war is a war in which two contending parties fight for control of the same government. As you very well know, the South did not wish to rule the United States. All the South wanted was to be left alone. As for the government of the United States, it existed very well even after thirteen Southern states had left the Union. Southern secession did not spell the end of the United States, so there was no need to invade and conquer the Confederate States just to keep the United States alive. Other than the War for Southern Independence, other names used for that war are: The War Between the States, the War of the Rebellion, the War of Northern Aggression, Mr. Lincoln's War, the Secession War, and the War to Prevent Southern Independence. Various historians and authors have used the preceding names for the war, but the most descriptive and correct name is "The War for Southern Independence." The most often-used name, the Civil War, is the most incorrect because as stated, the South was not trying to take control of the government in Washington. Likewise, the War Between the States is grammatically incorrect because there were more than two states fighting the war. The War of the Rebellion is incorrect because, as the South noted, the Confederate States were not in rebellion against the United States; they had simply exercised their right as Americans to "alter or abolish" the form of government under which they were living. Exercising one's right is not an act of rebellion. The War for Southern Independence states why the South was fighting this war — for independence. Of course, partisan Yankees don't like this name because it puts them in a rather bad light. By sending armies into the seceded areas of America which had proclaimed their independence, the Yankees now look much like the British in 1776 — blue-coated rather than red-coated tyrants!

6— Q. How can you be proud of the South? Look at the way Southerners under the command of Major Henry Wirz treated Northern prisoners of war in the POW camp at Andersonville, Georgia. How can you defend what was done to American soldiers at Andersonville?

A. Have you ever heard of a place called Elmira, New York? There was a POW camp there during the war, and the death rate there was little or no different from the one at Andersonville. One can only speculate as to why more Americans don't know about this POW camp, but given the fact it was in New York and it was Southerners who were doing the dying, we do have our suspicions. It is one thing for prisoners to starve in a country where starvation is the common lot of the people, and something altogether different when it happens in a country of well-fed people who are exporting food. Unlike the besieged and blockaded South, the North had all the advantages of a modern society without any disruptions from invading armies, yet the North would not feed its prisoners of war. This was not the case in the South where an invading army destroyed the means of production and transportation so much so that many civilians were near starvation. If Andersonville represents an attempt by Southerners to torture or kill Northern soldiers, then why did an equal number of Southern soldiers die in Northern POW camps? After the war when the tally was completed on the numbers of deaths in Northern and Southern POW camps, many folks were shocked to realize an equal number from each side died in the camps. The fact is too many men died in both Northern and Southern POW camps; but one thing is for sure, the South did not have an equal capacity to house and feed its prisoners, as did the North. Time after time the South requested an exchange of prisoners, but following orders from General Ulysses Grant, the North refused an exchange. Who is at fault here, the South who sought an exchange of prisoners, or the North who refused to exchange these prisoners? As for Major Wirz and Andersonville, Lieutenant James M. Page of Company A, Sixth Michigan Cavalry, was a prisoner at Andersonville. He later wrote a book in which he defended both Major Wirz and the South against unjust charges. No such defense of any Northern POW commander was ever made by a Confederate POW.

7— **Q.** You like to hide from the fact the South fought the war to preserve and promote slavery. Really, I can't blame you there! Can't you even read? Each slave state who seceded from the Union made note of the fact it was seceding in defense of the institution of slavery. Why do you keep insisting Southerners were fighting in defense of freedom and not slavery?

A. Did the patriots in Boston throw tea into the harbor because they did not like the price of tea? Actually, the price of British tea, even with the added tax, was lower than other tea, yet the tea went into the harbor. There was a unique principle behind the issue of tea and taxes which was much more important than just price. The same is true with the issue of slavery. Up until the election of Abraham Lincoln, the elimination of slavery had been viewed as an issue to be dealt with by the states. With the election of a regional party, i.e., the Republican Party, Southerners no longer felt any of their property (slave or non-slave) was safe from the Yankee taxman. Even though slavery had several constitutional protections around it, Southerners felt with the election of Lincoln the North would use slavery as an excuse to tax the South for the benefit of the North. In other words, if slavery (with all of its constitutional safeguards) could not be protected, then no property or rights were any longer safe. Yes, there is some mention of the North's desire to destroy slavery in some of the secession documents, but the documents also speak of free government and government by the consent of the governed. These men of the Southern states in 1861 were no different from the men of the American colonies in 1776. At that time each colony had slaves, yet, Americans were not fighting for slavery — they were fighting for liberty. The same was true for the patriots of the South. The issue of slavery is nothing but a red herring drawn across the trail of history to throw off those who would know the truth about the real causes of the secession crisis.

8— Q. You claim that the North committed acts of "cultural genocide" against the South. Isn't this just a case of reciting the loser's propaganda?

A. General Sherman made the best case for genocide against the South when he stated, "There is a class of people [Southerners] men, women, and children, who must be killed or banished before you can hope for peace and order."[112] Sherman's plan to pacify the South was to put to death men, women, and children. By the destruction of homes, hospitals, and all means of food production, Sherman saw to it that his genocidal plan was carried out. Remember the words of Ralph Waldo Emerson (the man whose great-grandfather was a New England slave trader), "If it cost ten years and ten to recover the gen-

---

112 William T. Sherman, as cited in, *Official Records War of the Rebellion*, XXXIX, pt. II, 132.

eral prosperity, the destruction of the South is worth so much."[113] After the war, the North used its power to enforce its view of the causes and consequences of the war, so much so that in today's schools and universities the Northern myth is accepted as American history. The culture and heritage of the South is now nothing but the object of social scorn in the media, academia, and even the pulpit. It looks like the genocide of the South is well on its way to completion.

9— Q. The Confederate States Navy? Your so-called navy was nothing more than a bunch of pirates stealing from Northern merchants. The only notable war vessel of the Confederacy was the *Merrimac*, a vessel stolen from the North. What kind of navy was this?

A. The first sinking of an enemy vessel by a submarine, the first use of steam-powered commerce raiders, the destruction of an enemy's commercial fleet, the first use of electrical torpedoes, and the building of the second largest ironclad navy in the world; somehow this navy that you so flippantly speak of sounds rather impressive. When the Southern states seceded from the Union there was no Confederate Navy. For the most part the wood that would one day become the framework of the Confederate Navy was still growing in the forests of the South. With little industrial power at its disposal, the South created one of the largest navies in the world, and it did it while under attack by a foreign invader. The Confederate States Navy and Marine Corps performed their assigned tasks in such a manner as to impress and instruct navies of the future. Today's submarine forces owe much to the CSS *Hunley*, the first submarine to sink an enemy war vessel. During WWI and WWII both Allied and Axis forces studied the tactics of Captain Raphael Semmes of the CSS *Alabama* in the destruction of the commercial fleets of their enemies. By the end of WWII, the United States Navy had sunk virtually every commercial vessel of Japan, using tactics very similar to those used by Semmes. Now, as for your remark about the *Merrimac*: The USS *Merrimac* was a wooden naval vessel of the United States that was captured by the Confederates. It was completely overhauled, clad with iron, and christened the CSS *Virginia*. As the *Virginia* it became the first ironclad vessel to sink an enemy naval vessel (another first). This sounds like a pretty good record for a nation, which, according to you, didn't even have a navy.

---

113 Ralph W. Emerson, as cited in, Otto Scott, *The Secret Six* (New York: Times Books, 1979) 319-20.

10— Q. You condemn General Sherman and the North for the destruction of civilian property in the South, yet Captain Raphael Semmes of the Confederate Navy did the same thing to Northern commercial vessels. Why the double standard? If Sherman is to be condemned, why not Semmes?

A. Commercial vessels of an enemy nation have always been recognized as a legitimate target during time of war. Homes of women and children and other noncombatants (up until WWII) were not considered legitimate targets for destruction during war. After capturing an enemy vessel, Captain Semmes never left women, children, or military personnel to starve, nor did he allow personal property to be taken from civilians. Here is what Semmes said about his treatment of prisoners and private property, "No prisoner of mine was ever disturbed in the possession of his strictly personal effects. Under this head were included his watch, and his jewelry, as well as his wardrobe. Every boarding-officer had orders to respect these, nor do I believe that the orders were ever violated."[114] Did General Sherman give similar orders to his men? No, as a matter of fact looting personal belongings, burning homes, and making civilians suffer starvation were common policies for Sherman and his army. Many times, Captain Semmes refused to destroy an enemy ship in order to save the lives of passengers and/or prisoners. During WWII the United States Navy vigorously attacked and destroyed the commercial fleet of Japan. Unlike Captain Semmes of the Confederate States Navy, very seldom did the United States Navy rescue any enemy civilians or sailors before sinking an enemy vessel. The idea that Semmes's actions on the high seas and against commercial vessels are equivalent to the actions of Sherman on land and against the homes of innocent women and children is ridiculous.

11— Q. Everyone knows there were only eleven Confederate States, yet you keep saying the "thirteen" Confederate States. Can't you even count?

A. The question is not whether we can count but whether the Congress of the Confederate States could count. In both houses of the Confederate Congress representatives from Kentucky and Missouri were recognized and seated. When the Confederate Congress ap-

---

114 Raphael Semmes, *Memoirs of Service Afloat* (1868, Secaucus, NJ: The Blue and Grey Press, 1987) 270.

proved a national flag, it placed one star on the flag for each Confederate state. You will note the second national flag of the Confederacy, adopted at a time when both Kentucky and Missouri were member states, had thirteen stars on it. It is true both Kentucky and Missouri had areas of Union support within their borders, but each state did pass secession documents and joined the Confederacy. What confuses the question is the large numbers of Northerners who quickly moved into each state both as civilians and as Federal troops in an attempt to keep those states in the Union. Nevertheless, some of the most important battles fought by the Army of Tennessee and the Armies of the Trans-Mississippi included regiments from Kentucky and Missouri.

12— Q. You may not like President Lincoln, but you can't get around the fact he saved the Union. Why try to dispute history?

A. Saved the Union? Are you talking about geography or principles of free government? Nowhere in the Declaration of Independence do we find a statement that the colonies were fighting to maintain the geographical integrity of America. There are some very significant and relevant principles which are announced in the Declaration of Independence. Here are some of those principles: the right of a people to alter or abolish their government at their pleasure, government by the consent of the governed, the fact that governments that do not recognize these rights are illegitimate governments, and these rights are unalienable rights. What kind of Union did Lincoln save? Lincoln did not recognize the right of the people of the Southern states to live under a government of their own choice — exit the principle of consent; Lincoln did not recognize the right of the people of the Southern states to alter or abolish the government under which they lived — scratch another worthy principle; Lincoln did not believe the rights announced in the Declaration of Independence still applied to the people of the Southern states — exit the principle of unalienable rights. By refusing to recognize these rights, Lincoln, according to the Declaration of Independence, turned the Union into an illegitimate government — the death knell of free government in these United States. The words of John C. Calhoun correctly define the place of the Union in America: "The Union: Next to our liberty, the most dear; may we all remember that it can only be preserved by respecting the rights of the States and distributing equally the benefits and burdens of the Union."[115] Without liberty, Union is worse than meaningless. What would free men call a place in which they were held against their will, a place where they were shot if they attempted to leave? Such a place would be a prison — free men do not live in prison. Lincoln has reduced this once great Federal Union, a union of free men in sovereign states, into a Federal prison — once again we must insist that free men do not live in a prison!

13—Q. If the colonies became sovereign states before the Federal government was formed, why was the "United States," that is, the Federal government, the one who fought the British in our war for independence?

A. It would be just as impossible for someone born in 1950 to have fought the Japanese in World War II as it would be for the Federal government to have fought the British in the War for American Independence. The present Federal government did not come into existence until 1788, which were several years after the War for American Independence was won. Well before the signing of the Declaration of Independence, the people of each colony, acting independently of each other, had eliminated British control within their colony. At that time each colony assumed control of its own political destiny and by the nature of that act became a *de facto* sovereign state. With the signing of the Treaty of Paris at the close of the War for American Independence, the government of Great Britain was forced to recognize, *de jure*, the independence of each state of these United States of American. A reading of the Treaty of Paris will demonstrate that Great Britain recognized each state by name as a free and independent state. These free and independent states thereafter formed a central government at their pleasure, a government which ultimately became the present Federal government. This Federal government was called into being by the act of nine sovereign states, which were later joined by four more states, well after the hostilities with Great Britain had ended.

14— Q. Supreme Court Justice Joseph Story informed us that in pursuing independence the colonies acted as one people or nation and

---

115 John C. Calhoun, as cited in, Clyde N. Wilson, ed., *The Essential Calhoun: Selections from Writings, Speeches, and Letters* (New Brunswick, NJ: Transaction Publishers, 1992) 393.

not as independent states. Can't you see you are wrong in maintaining the false notion the thirteen colonies were thirteen independent states?

A. In WWII many allied nations worked together to be free of Nazism — did that fact make these nations "one people?" The thirteen colonies had one and only one common connection, their common desire to be independent from Great Britain. Common language did not make them one people; if that were the case, they would have been one people with all English-speaking people in the world including the subjects of King George. Living on the same continent did not make them one people; if that were the case, they would have been common people with the English, French, and Spanish people of this continent. Having a common allegiance to the King of England did not make them a common people; if so, then the people of Canada and the islands of the Caribbean would have been one people with them. The only thing that can make free people "one people" is the free and unfettered choice of those free people. Anything less than the free choice, or anything that would demand a "oneness" at the point of a bloody bayonet, smacks of tyranny — the very thing the people of the colonies were fighting against. Story was wrong, the South was right!

15— Q. You have stated that Lincoln was elected by only 39 percent of the vote in 1860. Yet after four years of war he got more than 55 percent of the vote for reelection. Doesn't this prove that Lincoln had a mandate to save the Union?

A. Yes, Lincoln did get 55 percent of the 1864 vote in the states where elections for president of the United States were held. Only by removing the Southern states from the process could Lincoln get a majority! If we add the Southern vote, those people who were voting against Lincoln with blood and bullets instead of ballots, to the anti-Lincoln vote, he is still elected by a minority vote of Americans. We know of no well-known historian who will maintain that Lincoln's second election was a fair election. During this time, and for the first time in American history, the Federal government monitored and censored the telegraph and mail service in the United States.[116] More than three hundred newspapers in the North as well as the South

---

116 Jeffery R. Hummel, *Emancipating Slaves, Enslaving Free Men* (Peru, IL: Open Court Trade and Academic Books, 1996) 256.

were shut down by the Lincoln administration.[117] Political rivals such as Representative Clement L. Vallandigham (Democrat Ohio) were harassed, jailed without due process, or, as in the case of Vallandigham, banished from the United States. Here is what Vallandigham, a duly elected Democratic Ohio Representative had to say about his military arrest and imprisonment: "I am here in a military bastile for no other offense than my political opinions and the defense of them, and of the rights of the people, and of your Constitutional liberties."[118] Is this type of political atmosphere conducive to fair and impartial elections, or does it resemble the "elections" held in the Soviet Bloc countries during the Cold War?

16— Q. When you say "history as interpreted by the North" has misrepresented the Southern contributions to American history, aren't you just talking about Civil War history?

A. Ask any group of college freshmen to name the most important events or battles in the War for American Independence, and how many of these young people will include battles and/or events which took place in the South? Perhaps some will remember the Battle of Yorktown took place in Virginia, but not many. Most students will talk about the Boston Tea Party, Bunker Hill, Saratoga, Washington crossing the Delaware River, and the subsequent Battle of Trenton, New Jersey; perhaps they will talk about July 4, 1776, and Philadelphia, Pennsylvania. Notice nothing about the South is mentioned. At or about the time that the Battle of Bunker Hill in Boston was taking place, the patriots of North Carolina met and defeated British loyalists at the Battle of Moore's Creek Bridge. If the American patriots had lost this battle, everything south of North Carolina could have remained in league with the British. The Battle of Moore's Creek Bridge was a very important battle for America. In fact, more battles of the War for American Independence took place in South Carolina (more than 250 battles and engagements) than in any other state.[119] This is just one piece of evidence to demonstrate how Southern history is under-told in today's world. Another example of how the South's history is distorted is seen when the history of the civil rights struggle is told. Most Americans have the idea that before the civil rights move-

---

117 Ibid.
118 Clement L. Vallandigham, *The Record of Hon. C. L. Vallandigham on Abolition, the Union, and the Civil War* (Columbus, OH: J. Walter & Co., 1863) 253.
119 Barbour, 7.

ment black people in the South had little or no educational opportunities and that most black people in the pre-civil rights movement era were restricted in property and business ownership. Yet, when compared to Africans anywhere outside of the United States, black people in the South before the civil rights movement enjoyed better education, more real property ownership, and a longer life span than black people anywhere else in the world.[120] Yes, people in the North had more wealth, better education, and a longer life span than people in the South, black or white. But nowhere in the world outside of the United States did black people have as many educational or economic opportunities as they did in the pre-civil rights movement in the South. Now, this is not to be taken as a defense of laws which discriminated against people of color; after all, it was a Southerner, St. George Tucker in 1808, who first condemned such laws.[121] While the Northern-controlled media and academia condemns the South for its history of laws that discriminated against black people, few take time to chronicle the equally egregious laws passed by Northern states. In reality the first states that passed laws which discriminated against people of color were Northern states; the court that made discrimination against people of color the "law of the land" was not a Southern court but the Federal Supreme Court in its infamous Plessy v. Ferguson decision.[122] In rendering its decision in the Plessy v. Ferguson case, the Federal Supreme Court based its decision on the state of Massachusetts' law that segregated black and white school children in 1848.[123] This and many other points about race in America are seldom discussed. Only those points which will paint the South as America's homeland of racism are freely discussed. Yes, the South's entire history, not just its "Civil War" history, has been and is being misrepresented.

17— Q. The Confederate flag has an invisible motto written all over it. That motto is one of eternal hatred of African Americans. In reality the Confederate flag is a racist symbol. How can any decent person, especially one who calls himself a Christian, respect such a rag?

---

120 Walter D. Kennedy, *Myths of American Slavery*, 214-18.
121 Ibid., 239.
122 Forrest McDonald, *A Constitutional History of the United States* (Malabar, FL: Robert E. Krieger Publishing Co., 1986) 154-55.
123 Ibid.

The Confederate Myth-Buster

A. Superman could see through stone, but even he could not read something that is invisible. You must have remarkable eyesight! Some hate groups have misused the Confederate flag, but they also have misused the United States flag and the Holy Bible: does that mean we must have no respect for the Bible or the United States flag? When one thinks of the great Christian leaders of the South — Generals Robert E. Lee, Thomas Jonathan "Stonewall" Jackson, Leonidas Polk, and great theologians such as R. L. Dabney, Benjamin Morgan Palmer, and Fr. Abram J. Ryan — one has to respect the Christian nature of the men and the cause they held dear. Contrast the Christian generals of the South with the likes of Yankee generals such as Joseph "Fighting Joe" Hooker, whom legend says gave prostitutes their nickname — the hard-drinking and often drunk Ulysses S. Grant — called a "butcher" by his own countrymen — and the thieving rogue Benjamin "Beast" Butler — who earned another one of his nicknames, "spoons," because of all the Southern silverware he stole and sent back to Massachusetts. As Christians we find it hard to understand why anyone would rather praise the not-so-Christian Yankee leaders instead of Christian Southern leaders. The Southern leaders and their flag should be respected.

18— Q. I have heard some Southerners complain about the North breaking "international" law in its conduct of the Civil War. How could this be true? After all, the war was a civil war.

A. As has already been discussed, the so-called Civil War was not a civil war at all. As a matter of fact, there was nothing civil about the way the Yankees prosecuted the war. A civil war is a war between two contending groups vying for control of the same government. The South had its own government and was well pleased with it; it didn't need another one. As for the breaking of international law, everything from stopping, searching, and removing persons from foreign vessels by the United States Navy;[124] to attacking a Confederate States naval ship in the harbor of a neutral nation;[125] to enforcing a blockade

---

124 Jefferson Davis, I, 470.
125 J. Thomas Sharf, *History of the Confederate States Navy* (1887, New York: The Fairfax Press, 1996) 793. The CSS *Florida* was attacked and captured while docked in Bahia, Brazil, by the USS *Wachusett*. As the *Wachusett* was towing its prize out of the Brazilian harbor it was fired upon by both a Brazilian naval vessel and a harbor fort. This act of war inside a neutral port by the United States Navy is no less a breach of international law than the bombing of Pearl Harbor without a declaration of war seventy-eight years later.

against what the Federal government said was its own harbors;[126] all of these are major breaches of international law. The civilized nations had trouble understanding why the United States would so flagrantly breach international law; nevertheless, Southerners understood if the people who were in charge of the Federal government did not respect the limits of a written constitution, there was little hope of them abiding by international law.

19— Q. The Civil War had to be fought. Don't you remember what Lincoln had to say about our nation not being able to live half slave and half free? After all, didn't this war make us "one nation?"

A. Why is it this nation lived very well with both slave and free states for more than seventy-two years before Lincoln became president? Why all of a sudden could it no longer do so? What made such a great difference? Were the slaveholding states demanding every state become a slave state? No, the change was not with the nation but with Lincoln, the Republican Party, and their radical abolitionist allies. In 1776 slavery and the African slave trade existed in every state of the Union. By 1808 the slave trade had been eliminated, at least two states had begun a system of gradual emancipation of their slaves, and several organizations both in the North and the South were encouraging ending slavery. By the mid-1800s few of the leading people in the South believed slavery would last forever. Men as diverse as Jefferson Davis and Robert E. Lee had spoken up for the gradual elimination of slavery. With the advantages of modern farming equipment and the internal combustion engine, slavery was soon to be doomed. It is a sad commentary on the elimination of slavery in this nation to note the only other nation in the Western Hemisphere who ended slavery by warfare was Haiti. Lincoln did not have to fight a war to end slavery. One thing is for certain, Lincoln did turn this republic of republics into "one nation." The republic of republics became a Federal empire after Lincoln had finished with his war. Lincoln trampled upon every principle of free government announced in the Declaration of Independence. Today it is said Abraham Lincoln freed the slaves; the truth is, Abraham Lincoln made slaves out of free

---

126 Ibid., 430. A nation may close its own harbors and ports, but a blockade is an act of war between belligerents in a conflict. By imposing a blockade, Lincoln's government was sending an unintended message to Europe that the United States was recognizing the Confederate States as a sovereign nation.

men. Warning America of the dangers of the loss of States' Rights and the consolidation of all power in the central government in Washington, General Lee stated, "I fear for my country when all the powers that once resided with the States are consolidated in Washington for at that time, America will become aggressive at home and despotic abroad."[127]

20— Q. You make reference to the South's effort in the Civil War as a "conservative" struggle or war. Secession, rebellion, and waging war on your country's flag, how can this be a "conservative" movement?

A. Have you ever wondered why the South is called the "conservative" region of America? Yes, the South does elect more conservatives than liberals, but that has been going on during the entire history of the South. It all started back during the time of the colonies. Our founding fathers did not wake up one morning in America and just decide to "revolt" against the mother country. For several years before the famous July Fourth declaration, the people of the colonies petitioned the king to force the English Parliament to recognize their "rights as Englishmen." It was only after it became obvious to all of the colonies that their constitutional rights, i.e., their rights as guaranteed in the English Constitution, were not being respected they chose the course of independence. Notice nothing in the colonies changed other than a break in their allegiance. Society was not turned upside down as would later happen during the French Revolution. All the people of America were fighting for was their constitutional rights, nothing new or exotic. The only point that was remotely "revolutionary" was the republican principle of equality, i.e., that no natural-born ruler or aristocracy was recognized and government existed for the benefit of the people and not the people for the government. Even these two principles did not cause a great change in the day-to-day life of the colonies because they were already organized along those principles. It should be noted here the very same thing could be said about the Confederacy. There was no great upheaval when a state seceded from the Union; after all, the day-to-day work of the citizens of each state was not under the control of the Federal government

---

127 Robert E. Lee, from letter to Lord Acton, original on file, Washington and Lee University, Lexington, VA. For more information on the despotic at home and aggressive abroad concept of the post-Lincoln USA, see Kennedy and Kennedy, *Yankee Empire: Aggressive Abroad and Despotic at Home* (Shotwell Publishing Co., Columbia, SC: 2018).

(unlike today's society). Remember the words of General Lee, "All the South ever desired was that the Constitution as given to us by our fathers be honored and respected."[128] Many scholars have recognized the conservative nature of the Confederacy and the people of the South. In his work on the Confederate Constitution, Dr. Marshall DeRosa stated, "The Southerners did not abandon constitutional government; to the contrary, they reaffirmed their commitment to constitutional government under the auspices of the Confederate Constitution."[129] Maintaining constitutional rights, as Englishmen or as Americans, were and still are a conservative effort.

21— Q. Yankee atrocities is an often-cited theme in *The South Was Right!* Why don't we read about Lawrence, Kansas, William Quantrill, or Jesse James?

A. Comparing the destruction of Lawrence, Kansas, by Quantrill to the burning of Atlanta, Georgia, by Sherman would be like comparing the St. Valentine Day's massacre by gangsters to the Holocaust by the Nazi government. Both are reprehensible, but in the one case, Lawrence, Kansas, the act was committed by a rogue group without the sanction and support of their government; whereas, in the case of the Holocaust, not only did the act have the sanction of the government, but the government did everything in its power to make sure the perpetrators were successful in their efforts. The Confederate government never ordered nor did it approve of the actions carried out by some guerrilla groups; whereas, the Federal government, including Lincoln himself, approved and encouraged attacks upon civilians and the destruction of civilian property — including the killing of women and children. Notice again the words of General Sherman on this subject, "There is a class of people men, women, and children, who must be killed or banished before you can hope for peace and order."[130] Upon reading about Sherman's suggestion to exterminate Southern men, women, and children, Federal Secretary of War Edwin Stanton replied, "Your letter of the 21st of June has just reached me and **meets my approval**"[131] (emphasis added). Jefferson Davis's government

---

128 Robert E. Lee, as cited in, Gamaliel Bradford, Jr., 739
129 Marshall L. DeRosa, *The Confederate Constitution of 1861* (Columbia: University of Missouri Press, 1991) 1.
130 William T. Sherman, as cited in, *Official Records War of the Rebellion*, XXXIX, pt. II, 132.
131 Edwin Stanton, ibid., 157.

never encouraged such a policy even in the face of some in the South who demanded the adoption of a similar war policy as the one pursued by the North.

22— Q. In your book you complain about the actions of Federal General Benjamin Butler in New Orleans after the rebels were driven out of the city. Why not mention some of the positive things General Butler did for New Orleans?

A. No one has ever said tyrants don't do positive things. Let's look at a few examples: Adolph Hitler ended runaway inflation and joblessness in Germany; Benito Mussolini did something few leaders in Italy up until his time could do, he made the trains run on time; Joseph Stalin changed Russia from a weak provincial power into a world-class powerhouse. The list could go on for a long time, but you get the message; the good a tyrant does in no wise makes up for the damage to life, property, and liberty that is achieved by tyrants. No man in American military history has a more loathsome and repugnant record than General Benjamin "Beast" or "Spoons" Butler. The "good" Butler did in no wise makes up for his beastly actions against the people of New Orleans.

23— Q. The Confederate States of America was an illegitimate government. You say you believe in government by the consent of the governed, yet, the people of the South were never allowed to vote on whether they desired to secede from the Union. How can such a government be a legitimate government?

A. How many Americans were allowed to "vote" for independence on July 4, 1776, or better yet, how many Americans were allowed to "vote" on the adoption of the Constitution? The answer is none — that is, no ordinary citizen of any state ever got a chance to vote yes or no on independence or the adoption of the Constitution. The only people who voted for independence were the delegates sent to Philadelphia by the legislatures of the various states. As for the Constitution, there were about forty delegates at the constitutional convention who voted for the Constitution by state, i.e., each state had one vote regardless of how many delegates they sent. After the forty delegates agreed on the Constitution it was sent to the states where a constitutional convention for that state was called, and only the delegates at that convention were allowed to vote for the Constitution. So far, we don't see any great democratic process of mass voting in the establishment of the United States government. Yet you seem willing to condemn the Confederacy because, as you seem to think, "the people were not allowed to vote on secession." Even if this was true, and it is not, the Confederate States of America followed the American plan; the same plan used by the American colonies when seceding from Great Britain was used by the Southern states when seceding from the Union. Also, many of the Southern states, after passing an ordinance of secession by a convention of the people of that state, referred the issue to a vote of the people. In each case the vote was overwhelmingly positive for secession. Nevertheless, it is plain the South followed in the footsteps of the Patriots of 1776 when they seceded from the Union, as well as actually having the citizens of many Southern states vote directly for secession. As pointed out earlier, this is something never done by the colonies when seceding from the union with Great Britain or in adopting the Constitution. Using your measure of illegitimate government, the Confederate government is much more legitimate than the United States government!

24— Q. Your glowing remarks about the valor of your rebel soldiers are impressive. But why not make a few such remarks about the men who defended the glory of the Union?

A. What is the glory of the Union? Is it the massive force it can apply to anyone who disagrees with it? Where is the glory in brute force? The true glory of the Union is in its ability to promote and defend the rights as announced in the Declaration of Independence and codified in the Constitution. John C. Calhoun said it very succinctly, "We are told that the Union must be preserved, without regard to the means. And how is it proposed to preserve the Union? By force! Does any man in his senses believe that this beautiful structure — this harmonious aggregate of States, produced by the joint consent of all — can be preserved by force? You cannot keep the States united in their constitutional and federal bonds by force. Force may, indeed, hold the parts together, but such union would be the bond between master and slave: a union of exaction on one side, and of unqualified obedience on the other.... Disguise it as you may, the controversy is one between power and liberty."[132] Bloody bayonets cannot maintain a union of free people. With the application of force, liberty must

---

132 John C. Calhoun, as cited in, Clyde N. Wilson, ed., *The Essential Calhoun*, 371-72.

retreat. Bloody bayonets are the implements of tyrants. Free people cease to be free when they are forced to agree to any proposition which runs counter to their desires. Therefore, the glory of the Union died when the North invaded the South. There is no glory in tyranny!

25— Q. The South complained about paying tariffs to the Federal government. So what? Nobody likes paying taxes, but we don't attack IRS agents in protest. Tariff revenues were needed to run the government and execute the constitutional mandate to promote the "general welfare" of the United States. Why should the rest of America allow first South Carolina and then all the other Southern states to get away with not paying their fair share of taxes?

A. If the tariff, i.e., taxes, had been fair, there would not have been any problems. It was the very unfair nature of the tax system which was the source of problems between the South and the North. During the antebellum period the revenues from Southern ports were the source of two-thirds of the Federal government's budget. That would not have been as much of a problem, but the South complained that most of the monies spent by the Federal government went for improvement in Northern infrastructure. Even moderate Southerners from Border States noted this discrepancy. Senator Thomas Hart Benton of Missouri stated the South had defrayed three-fourths of the expenses of the Federal government.[133] In a speech to the Senate in 1828, Senator Benton noted, "Virginia, the two Carolinas, and Georgia, may be said to defray three-fourths of the annual expense of supporting the Federal Government; and of this great sum, annually furnished by them, nothing, or next to nothing is returned to them, in the shape of Government expenditures. That expenditure flows in an opposite direction — it flows northwardly, in one uniform, uninterrupted, and perennial stream. This is the reason why wealth disappears from the South and rises up in the North.... It does it by the simple process of eternally taking from the South, and returning nothing to it."[134] These are the words of a moderate border state senator who had a record of voting with the North on many slavery-related issues. Fairness in the taxation and expenditures of the Federal government is what the South was seeking; Northern plundering of Southern resources is what it got.

---

133 Semmes, 80.
134 Ibid., 58.

26— Q. How do you justify the claim a huge national debt with a soaring interest rate is "just one more consequence of a Northern victory in the War for Southern Independence"?

A. Before Mr. Lincoln's war the total expenditures of the Federal government were around two percent of the national economic output, whereas during Lincoln's administration the Federal government gobbled up more than 20 percent of the national economic output.[135] This gargantuan surge in Federal tax and spending power has not decreased since the time of Lincoln's war; it has only increased. From a nation in which citizens seldom came into contact with the national government, Americans digressed to a nation in which the national government extracted taxes directly from the citizens, subjected the citizens to drafts, paid subsidies to favored businesses, and snooped into the private activities of the citizens, and all of this was in the nineteenth century. Is it any wonder that in 1882 Rev. R. L. Dabney, a noted Presbyterian theologian and former member of General Stonewall Jackson's staff, had this to say about the loss of liberty, "The heritage of freedom which our fathers left us, we have not been able to bequeath to you."[136] As we have progressed into the twenty-first century things have gone from bad to worse. For example, the per capita tax paid by each citizen in America has increased from $151 in 1900 — this in itself was more than a hundred times more than was paid by a citizen in 1800 — to more than $7,000 in 2000.[137] This was made possible because there is no way, as in the good old days before Lincoln, for "we the people" at the local level to rein in a runaway Federal government. Yes, thanks to Lincoln and the Northern victory in the War for Southern Independence, real States' Rights are dead, and the Federal government is the sole judge of its own authority. As sole judge it has "judged" for itself to continue its growth and its tax and spend authority.

27— Q. I am a young Southerner. When I look at the history of the South, I see a section of the United States that was at one time loved and respected. For example, in 1961 the United States celebrated the

---

135 Hummel, 328.
136 Robert L. Dabney, *Discussions, Secular* (1897, Harrisonburg, VA: Sprinkle Publications, 1979) 1.
137 James R. Kennedy, *Reclaiming Liberty* (Gretna, LA: Pelican Publishing Co., 2005) 169. For a more complete study of the reason governmental taxing policy is anti-liberty, see, *Reclaiming Liberty*, chapter 10.

centennial of the Civil War. The US Post Office issued stamps honoring numerous Confederate generals, positive news articles were written about the South's struggle, and President Dwight D. Eisenhower made statements honoring Robert E. Lee as a great American. Today, no one in Washington wants to say anything that even comes close to being fair to the South. What happened?

A. The South lost the war! Up until about a hundred years after the War for Southern Independence most Americans viewed the South's struggle in the "Civil War" as a foolish and incorrect effort but one nevertheless full of honorable men and many heroes. This was the view President Eisenhower held of General Robert E. Lee and the Southern war effort in general. Just before the Civil War Centennial and with the advent of the modern civil rights movement, a budding political correctness movement began which did all in its power to denigrate the South. Gaining control of the media and academia, the agents of political correctness began to attack everything Southern. Today many Southern icons which were recognized and respected by all Americans prior to the age of political correctness are "gone with the wind." Nevertheless, there are still many Americans who are willing to stand up and defend the cause of the South, a growing number of whom are from the North as well as the South. A great Presbyterian theologian and friend of General Stonewall Jackson, Rev. Robert Lewis Dabney, in 1882, told a group of young Southerners, "There is still life in the old land yet!"[138] This is something the Kennedy Twins of Louisiana also believe today. Although weak and desperately ill, the "life" of liberty is still alive in these United States.

28— Q. Okay, so the South was not treated completely fair, but you have to admit the South was somewhat to blame for most of these problems. All of that was in the past. Today we are one nation and have done so much for the world, why keep complaining? How can the United States be so bad when it is the freest country in the world?

A. Yes, the United States is the freest and best nation to live in when compared to any other nation in the world. That is not something to brag about; in fact, it is rather sad. Just think how little freedom exists in the rest of the world. But what is the condition of liberty and freedom in the United States? If we compare America to other nations of the world, we can see we are freer and better off than

---

138 Dabney, 24.

the citizens of those other nations, whether they live in France or in Somalia. But as patriotic Americans, we do not judge our freedom by what other people do not have but by what we don't have as compared to the freedom that our founding fathers had! For Americans the benchmark of good government and a liberty-based society is not the amount of liberty exercised in some foreign nation but the amount of liberty that was won for us by our founding fathers. Americans of today are much like an old hunchback man who gets great pleasure in seeing another hunchback man with a greater hunchback than his own. Just because Mr. Hunchback number one has a smaller hunchback than Mr. Hunchback number two, that does not relieve him of the problems associated with his condition. Furthermore, Mr. Hunchback number one may very well be doing himself a great disservice by taking a small measure of pleasure in seeing someone in a worse condition than himself. He may not feel the need to do those things that would improve his condition. Today most Americans, like Mr. Hunchback number one, take great pleasure in reassuring themselves how much better off they are than all those other people in the world. Yet, when judged by what our forefathers gave us — a free republic of republics in which total taxes that were paid to all governments amounted to no more than one percent of a citizen's income and little to no Federal regulation was ever felt by the average citizen — present-day Americans are at best serfs of the government and, at worse, tax slaves of the government. Think about all the Federal rules and regulations in education, environment, crime, land use, travel, income acquisition and dispersal, and the list could go on seemingly forever. Now ask yourself, did Patrick Henry have to put up with this (or better yet, would Patrick Henry have put up with this)?[139] It is true we are freer than the citizens of most other nations, but as Americans we should always judge ourselves by this benchmark: "How free were our founding fathers?" Then we need to ask ourselves, "How free are we today?" This is the true measure of freedom and liberty in America. Now that we have established that the freedom and liberty of our founding fathers is to be the only benchmark to judge our society, we need to look at your point about America being "one nation now." Our forefathers had the right to consent to the form of government they lived under — do we? Lincoln and his army of invasion and conquest answered that question many years ago. Lincoln's bloody

---

[139] James R. Kennedy, *Reclaiming Liberty*, 163-83.

bayonets destroyed government by the consent of the governed and many attending freedoms. Lincoln successfully canceled these freedoms our forefathers established as an American birthright. Yes, we are "one nation," but that nation is not a nation based upon the freedom and the liberty our forefathers enjoyed, but upon the ability of a tyrant to abuse an otherwise free people. Your "one nation" is based upon conquest, not consent. As painful as it is to say, we must insist that, according to our forefather's Declaration of Independence, your "one nation" is an illegitimate government.[140]

Summary

With all the astute activity of their race, our conquerors strain every nerve to pre-occupy the ears of all America with the false version of affairs which suits the purposes of their usurpation. With a gigantic sweep of mendacity, this [Northern] literature aims to falsify or misrepresent everything; the very facts of history, the principles of the former Constitution as admitted in the days of freedom by all statesmen of all parties.... The whole sway of their commercial and political ascendancy is exerted to fill the South with this false literature. Its sheets come up, like the frogs of Egypt, into our houses, our bed chambers, our very kneading troughs. Now, against this deluge of perversions I solemnly warn young men of the South, not for our sakes, but for their own.[141]
— Robert Lewis Dabney, 1882

In the above citation Dabney, a noted Presbyterian theologian and General Stonewall Jackson's chief of staff during the Valley campaign, is speaking at the Annual Commencement of Hampton Sidney College June 15, 1882. Notice this was seventeen years after the defeat of the South and six years after the end of Reconstruction. Nevertheless, Dabney is warning these young Southerners concerning "false literature" about the War for Southern Independence which was even then flooding the South and America. Dabney points out that this false information about the South's struggle for independence was so pervasive that it could be compared to the plague of frogs in Biblical Egypt.

That which Dabney warned young Southerners about, just a few

---

140 The Declaration of Independence states any government not based on the consent of the governed is illegitimate.
141 Dabney, 21.

years after the conquest of the South, has grown into an even greater problem today when trying to give a "fair and balanced" account of Southern history. In his speech given at Hampton Sidney College, Dabney noted the form of government he had inherited from his fathers was not the same form of government his generation was bequeathing to the young people of the "New" South. As has been pointed out in this and other books by the Kennedy Twins, Appomattox changed America. More than General Robert E. Lee's army was surrendered there. The Constitution as given to us by America's Founding Fathers was turned upside down and the Republic of Republics was replaced by a unitary, indivisible, all-powerful, supreme Federal Empire. This new (post-Appomattox) government exercises the exclusive authority to judge how much power it can exercise and what "rights" the states can exercise. This new government allows no one other than itself to be the judge of its power is completely opposite of that government described by Jefferson and Madison in the Kentucky and Virginia Resolves.

It is often asserted at the surrender of the British Army at Yorktown, Virginia, the British Band played a song titled, *The World Turned Upside Down*. When viewing the Federal Empire today, an empire of Federal supremacy and state inferiority, one must acknowledge that indeed, constitutionally speaking, the world has been turned upside down.

Jefferson Davis

Davis, a graduate of the United States Military Academy, US Representative and US Senator from Mississippi, veteran of the Black Hawk War and the Mexican War, Secretary of War in President Franklin Peirce's administration, and President of the Confederate States of America. Named in honor of Thomas Jefferson, Davis followed the Jeffersonian tradition of strong States' Rights including the right of the people of each state to determine how they would be governed.

Chapter 6
Lincoln v. Davis

The idea of freedom is captivating, that of slavery repellent to the moral sense of mankind in general.[142] — Jefferson Davis

Free them, and make them politically and socially our equals? My own feelings will not admit of this.[143] — Abraham Lincoln

No two men in American history represent two more contrasting views of America than the sixteenth president of the United States, Abraham Lincoln, and the first president of the Confederate States of America, Jefferson Davis. For most Americans, one man is a national hero who suffered the horrors of war to keep his country united and free, while the other man is the archenemy of an indivisible nation and a defender of slavery. Yet, as the Kennedy Twins of Louisiana so often pointed out in their first book, the myth of American history and the reality of American history often are at odds with each other. To speak of the "myth of history" is not to say a particular historical account is a falsehood as much as it is to acknowledge there are always two sides in any conflict. When that conflict degenerates into warfare, the victor wins the ability to write and enforce the victor's opinion, concept, and view of that conflict. At the close of the War for Southern Independence all official channels of the reporting of that conflict passed into the hands of the United States. The only means of reporting the Southern view of the war resided with the defeated people of the Confederacy. After the living memory of the war passed from the scene of daily Southern life, that is, after the passing of those who had firsthand experience of the conflict, Americans in general and Southerners in particular were left with only the official United States view of that conflict. Although Southerners are still likely to express some lingering doubts about the "accepted" view of the war, they, like their Northern counterparts, are prone to parrot the Northern view of American and Southern history. The simple act of walking into any public or private school down

---

142 Jefferson Davis, I, 6.
143 Abraham Lincoln, as cited in *Abraham Lincoln From His Own Words and Contemporary Accounts*, Roy E. Appleman, ed. (National Park Service Source Book Two, Washington, DC: 1956) 19.

South provides proof the Southern view of its history and culture has been virtually muted. Walk the halls, classrooms, and offices of the schools of the South, and you will find photographs of Abraham Lincoln prominently displayed. Yet in 99 percent of those same Southern schools you will never find a photograph of Jefferson Davis. Check out the library of those schools and you will find many books and publications about the so-called Civil War offering up the "accepted," that is, the Northern, view of Southern history and culture. In most public schools the Confederate flag has been officially prohibited or informally removed from display on school property. Taking the cause of cultural cleansing even further, students who wear clothing with a Confederate flag or Confederate leader displayed upon it are ejected from the school or otherwise punished. While the singing of the *Battle Hymn of the Republic* is not unusual in these schools, the playing or singing of *Dixie* merits the strongest punishment. Given this reality of history as enforced by the victors of the War for Southern Independence, is it any wonder American students, even Southern students, have little knowledge of the complete history of Abraham Lincoln and Jefferson Davis? The following questions are some of the more commonly fielded questions about these two remarkable individuals in American history the Kennedy Twins of Louisiana have dealt with while defending the cause of the South.

1— Q. History has proven Abraham Lincoln was right. After all, where would America be today if the South had been allowed to break up our country? Now, how can you say Jefferson Davis was an American patriot in light of the fact of Lincoln saving the American nation?

A. Remember, liberty and not geography, is the foundation of a truly free nation. By following in the footsteps of our founding fathers, who believed any people had the right to consent to the form of government under which they live, America would be truly a free nation. Neither the government nor the landmass which belonged to the other states of the United States was under attack by Jefferson Davis and the Confederate States of America. Even if all thirteen Confederate States had been allowed to go free, the government and national integrity of the United States would still be intact and functioning. Just as Canada to the north and Mexico to the south of the United States do not decrease the ability of this country to function, so the existence of the Confederate States of America to the south of the United States would not irreparably harm the United States. But let's look at what has been harmed by Abraham Lincoln and his war against the South. Before the war the government of these United States was held to the limits of the power delegated to it from the states as described in the Constitution. "We the people" of each sovereign state used the undelegated power (remember the Ninth and Tenth Amendments to the Constitution) to check any abuse of power by the central government. Every action of the Federal government had to flow from a delegated power found in the Constitution. The end result of this type of limited constitutional government was a central government which had little power over the lives and property of its citizens. Today, after Lincoln's victory and conversely Davis's defeat, every conceivable act of an American citizen is regulated, supervised, and taxed by the Federal government. In a nutshell, Davis and company fought for limited government, that is, small government; whereas, Lincoln and company fought and succeeded in implementing a strong, indivisible, and absolute big government. This indivisible and all-powerful government is more akin to an empire than it is to the republic of republics our founding fathers gave us after 1776.

2— Q. Everything about Jefferson Davis and the Confederacy reminds me of Adolph Hitler and Nazism. I am sure Hitler would have admired the slaveholding Davis. How can anybody honor Davis when he sounds like a man Hitler would admire?

A. I agree with you any person whom Adolph Hitler would have admired should be the subject of suspicion, but it was Lincoln and not Davis Adolph Hitler admiringly wrote about. In his book, *Mein Kampf*, Hitler praised the efforts of Lincoln and the North as they enforced the will of the Federal government over the will of the state governments of the South. Even when describing the theory of American government, Hitler parroted the very ideas, if not the very words, of Lincoln. Here is the way Lincoln described the formation of the America Union: "The Union is older than the States and, in fact created them as States. The Union, and not themselves separately, procured their independence and their liberty. The Union threw off their old dependence for them and made them States, such as they are."[144] Note here Lincoln stated the Union existed before the states

---

[144] Abraham Lincoln, July 4th Message to Congress, July 4, 1861.

and the states owe their "liberty" and all other rights to the Union which created them (all of which is completely wrong). Discussing the nature of the American government, this is how Hitler described the American Union: "The states that make up the American Union are merely in the nature of territories ... formed for technical administrative purposes. These states did not and could not possess sovereign rights of their own. Because it was the Union that created most of the so-called states."[145] You will notice Hitler made two points about the nature of the American Union which parallel the views of Lincoln: (1) The states owe their existence to the Union, and (2) no state of the American Union possesses sovereignty. Compare the words of Lincoln and Hitler. Lincoln stated the Union is older than the states and in fact created the states; whereas, Hitler stated the Union created the states and they existed only for administrative purposes. Also notice that Hitler said these states were not sovereign. A sovereign state has the right to control its destiny. When we refer to States' Rights, we are talking about the innate rights that flow from a sovereign political body. In the American tradition, states have rights because these states are sovereign. It must be noted here the state government is not sovereign, but in reality, the people of the state are sovereign. The agent of these people is said to be sovereign, but we understand it is "we the people" who hold the final, ultimate, and complete right to judge how we are to be governed. Notice Hitler did not believe in States' Rights. Just as Lincoln before him, Hitler believed the central government had the ultimate right to control the government of a nation. When the Southern states seceded from the Union, Lincoln stated those states were not sovereign and therefore the act of secession was an act of rebellion against the central government. When faced with many independent states within the Federal Republic of Germany, Hitler asserted the same right Lincoln asserted and destroyed any power within the nation that posed a threat to the actions of the central government. Remember, Fascists, Nazis, socialists, and surely communists will *NOT* like States' Rights because States' Rights puts a limit on their ability to control the national government. Lincoln and his government fit quite nicely into this group of big government advocates.

3— Q. Lincoln was a man of the downtrodden and common peoples not the rich and powerful. Jefferson Davis was a rich man living on

---

145 Adolph Hitler, *Mein Kampf* (New York: Hurst and Blackett, LTD., 1942) 312.

a big plantation and owning many slaves. How can you say Davis should be honored like Lincoln?

A. Lincoln was not some backwoods country bumpkin daily rubbing shoulders with the common man. Lincoln was a prominent Illinois lawyer serving the interests of one of the largest corporations of his day, the Illinois Central Railroad. Before Lincoln joined the Republican Party, he was a member of the Whig Party. The Whig Party represented the interests of big business and was a supporter of the so-called American System. The American System advocated the use of Federal money and policy to advance the interests of various businesses and corporations. Furthermore, the American System promoted the creation of government controlled central banking, which the States' Rights Party, that is, the Democratic Party, had resisted from the beginning of the Union. With the formation of the Republican Party these big government measures were adopted and supported by the Republican Party. Supporting the interests of central banking and big business was a founding principle of the Republican Party that led to its becoming known as the party of the rich. The advocacy of big government policies is one of the main reasons that European socialists and communists, as well as homegrown socialists and communists, supported the formation of the Republican Party, the election of Lincoln, and Lincoln's war on States' Rights.[146] A well-heeled, high-powered lawyer with strong connections with large corporations and big banking interests does not fit the model of a "man of the common people."

Now let's look at Jefferson Davis. Yes, Davis was a plantation owner, but his plantation was a middle-class establishment; his house was relatively simple, not one of the large colonnaded homes of millionaire plantation owners. Rich, large slaveholding plantation owners lived in the archetypical "Gone With the Wind" Southern-style plantation homes. Davis was a typical small plantation owner who managed a much smaller land and labor force. More than likely, the "Gone With the Wind" type of Southern plantation owner was a member of the Whig Party (not unlike Lincoln); whereas, Davis was a member of the Democratic Party, the party of the common man. As for your suggestion that Davis was an evil slaveholder, it should be remembered that both Jefferson Davis and his older brother were advocates of education for their slaves and making slaves "Fit for

---

146 Al Benson and Walter D. Kennedy, *Lincoln's Marxists* (Pelican Publishing Co., Gretna, LA: 2011) 13-17.

freedom and unfit for slavery."[147] These and other "liberal" views of slavery did not endear the Davis Brothers to their better-heeled Whig neighbors. Davis held the view slavery had a natural end and it was the responsibility of slaveholders to equip their slaves for freedom, and it was America's responsibility to allow these free people of color to move into the commonly held territories of these United States — something Northerners fought against.[148] These facts about Jefferson Davis and the fact Abraham Lincoln did not free the slaves, as well as his being a strong supporter of white racial superiority, proves your statement to be more than just a little incorrect.

4— Q. Your suggestion that communists supported Lincoln and what you are calling "Lincoln's war" is absurd. Anyone with even the simplest understanding of history knows communism did not exist until after the 1917 communist revolution in Russia. This was fifty-seven years after the Civil War. How can you believe that these communists fought in the American Civil War?

A. The Russians did not invent communism. Karl Marx, a German, proposed what we call modern communism in his 1848 work, *The Communist Manifesto*. Long before the 1917 Bolshevik, that is, communist, revolution in Russia, communism was alive and well. Communism and its twin brother socialism are utopian political ideologies which promote big government solutions for any real or imagined problems of mankind. Whether it is socialist nations such as Fascist Italy, Nazi Germany (remember, the term Nazi stands for National Socialist German Workers Party), or any of the numerous communist nations of the twentieth century, the one notable common denominator of these totalitarian regimes is their devotion to big government and their loathing of what Americans would call "States' Rights." When Abraham Lincoln led the United States into a war with the Confederate States of America, none other than Karl Marx began to write articles for European newspapers promoting Lincoln's war against the South. Not only did he write articles condemning the South's struggle for independence, he also led demonstrations demanding that England and other European nations refuse to recognize the Confederacy as a legitimate nation. While Karl Marx was acting the part of Lincoln's unofficial minister of propaganda in Europe, radical socialists and communists who had fled Europe

---

147 Jefferson Davis, as cited in, Kennedy and Kennedy, *Was Jefferson Davis Right?* 14.
148 Walter D. Kennedy, *Myths of American Slavery*, 212-13.

after various unsuccessful socialist revolutions in their European homeland and had made America their new home, became vigorous supporters of Lincoln, the Republican Party, and Lincoln's war against the South. Men such as Joseph Weydemeyer, a close friend of Karl Marx and a fellow member of the London Communist Club along with Marx, became strong supporters of both the new Republican Party and Abraham Lincoln. When Lincoln began his invasion of the South, Weydemeyer joined the Union Army, rising to the rank of brigadier general. The friendship between Marx and Weydemeyer is demonstrated by Marx's description of Weydemeyer as "My friend Joseph Weydemeyer."[149] In a letter to Weydemeyer, Fredrick Engels, Marx's co-founder of modern communism, points out in order to promote communism, a republic consisting of many sovereign states had to be reduced to "a single and *indivisible* republic"[150] (emphasis added). Notice that the co-founder of modern communism was telling a fellow communist and future Union general the foundation of communism is laid when small independent republics (as seen in these United States before Appomattox) are reduced to one single and indivisible republic. By waging war upon the seceded states of the South and forcing them to comply with the dictates of the Federal government, Lincoln was doing what Engels pointed out as the "preliminaries of the proletarian revolution."[151] General Weydemeyer is only one of many communist or socialist generals and officers in the Union Army. These same men were strong supporters of the Republican Party and the election of Lincoln. This is why we say communists and radical socialists fought for the Union cause during the War for Southern Independence.

5— Q. Your suggestion Karl Marx admired Lincoln is ridiculous. Marx was a communist! Communists don't believe in freedom. Jefferson Davis led a government that promoted slavery, and Davis was a slaveholder. Can't you see that Davis, and not Lincoln, would be admired by Marx?

A. Facts can be somewhat disturbing, but the fact is Marx was an admirer of Lincoln. From the beginning of the War for Southern Independence Marx wrote articles and assisted in demonstrations to

---

149 Karl Marx and Fredrick Engels, *Letters to Americans* (New York: International Publishers Co., Inc., 1953) 23.
150 Fredrick Engels, as cited in, ibid., 57.
151 Ibid.

assist the North's effort against the South. After Lincoln's 1864 reelection, Marx wrote a memorandum for the International Workingmen's Association congratulating Lincoln on his electoral victory. Marx began his memorandum by stating, "We congratulate the American people upon your re-election by a large majority."[152] In articles published in various European newspapers Marx attacked the effort of the South to win its independence and referred to Jefferson Davis as a dictator. Marx stated "Mississippi, which has given the Southern Confederacy its dictator, Jefferson Davis...."[153] The chief executive of the Confederate States of America had less power than any American president up until that time — which is not the type of president that can rightfully be described as a dictator. One great stumbling block to the formation of a dictator in the Confederate government was the right of secession. If Davis (or any other Confederate president who might have succeeded him) began to exercise dictatorial powers, the states of the Southern Confederacy could have done as their forefathers had done in 1776 and 1861 to the "dictators" of first England and then the Federal government, that is, secede from the unhealthy union and live as free men. Secession is indeed a great bulwark against the tyranny of the central government, and this is one reason socialists and communists did not and do not like the idea of secession. Not only was Marx incorrect about Davis being a dictator, but he also failed to understand Lincoln did not win his 1864 election by a majority vote of the American people. Yes, in the most corrupt presidential election in the history of the United States up to that date, Lincoln won more votes than his Democratic opponent. Yet when one factors in the numbers of Southerners who were opposing Lincoln with not just votes but their blood, sweat, and tears, then you will notice that Lincoln was still a minority president, just as he was in his first election victory.

6— Q. Why did you say that Abraham Lincoln was the first American president to have a communist in his cabinet?

A. Actually we said Lincoln was the first American president to have a communist sympathizer or perhaps a communist in his cabinet. The individual we were referring to was a man by the name

---

[152] Karl Marx, Address of the International Workingmen's Association to Abraham Lincoln, as cited in, ibid., 65.
[153] Karl Marx, as cited in, *Karl Marx and Fredrick Engels, The Civil War in the United States* (New York: International Publishers, Co., Inc., 1953) 76.

of Charles A. Dana. In the mid-1840s, Dana struck up a friendly relationship with Karl Marx, Fredrick Engels, and other European communists. This relationship proved to be a godsend for several of Marx's disciples who were fleeing Europe. One such man was Joseph Weydemeyer, the future Republican Party operative and Union general. When Weydemeyer came to New York, he had in his possession letters from two communists, Karl Marx and Ferdinand Freiligrath, a German revolutionary poet and editor. As we have pointed out, Marx and Weydemeyer were close friends. As Weydemeyer was departing London for New York, Marx gave his good friend the following advice: "When you are in New York, go to A Dana [Charles A. Dana] of the *New York Tribune* and give him my regards and regards from Freiligrath. Perhaps he may be of some use to you."[154] In another letter to Weydemeyer, Marx noted: "I wrote to A. Charles Dana [Charles A. Dana], one of the editors of the *New York Tribune*, and also enclosed a letter from Freiligrath, in which he recommends you. Hence, all you have to do is to go to him and mention our names."[155] With Dana's assistance Weydemeyer was able to have published in the United States the first American copies of Marx's *Communist Manifesto*. It was with Dana's assistance Marx was given a job as a contributing editor for the *New York Tribune*. It should be remembered Dana was a member of the quasi-communist association of New England known as Brook Farm, a communal association of radical New England socialists.[156] By the time of the War for Southern Independence, Dana had made a large enough impression on people within the Republican Party to be appointed assistant secretary of war. Without a doubt no American prior to the communist revolution in Russia did more to promote the ideas of communism and socialism in the United States than Charles A. Dana.

7— Q. Where did the so-called radical socialists and communists that you say were part of the Republican Party and Lincoln's war effort against the South come from?

A. The communists and radical socialists, commonly known as the "Forty-Eighters," came from Europe. But the question which should be asked is not so much where did they come from, but why did they embrace the Republican Party, Abraham Lincoln, and the

---

154 Karl Marx, as cited in, *Marx and Engels, Letters to Americans*, 65-66
155 Ibid.
156 Benson and Kennedy, 43-47.

war against the South. As we have stated, these radicals were collectively known as Forty-Eighters. This name came from the numerous socialists and communists who led revolutions in various Europe nations that began around 1848. Many of the revolutions were temporarily successful, but ultimately crushed. Many factors were driving these revolutions, not the least of which was the liberal demand of the middle class for a voice in running their country. Unfortunately, these demands for a more republican form of government were hijacked by radical socialists and communists, which ultimately led to the crushing of these revolutions. With the defeat of the revolutions, many revolutionaries were jailed and otherwise punished. To protect themselves from being punished as traitors, many of these radicals began to flee their homeland and seek asylum in the United States. They may have left their homeland in Europe, but they did not leave their proclivity for radical politics in Europe. In a letter to a close friend and fellow communist, Karl Marx explained to Joseph Weydemeyer that the scattering of radical thinkers could be a healthy thing for the cause of the communist revolution. In this letter to Weydemeyer (the future Republican, supporter of Lincoln, and Union general), Marx took note of the advantages that presented themselves, "But once you are going to America, you can't be doing so at a more opportune moment, both to find a means of existence over there as well as to be ***useful to our party***"[157] (emphasis added.) The list of nations that provided so many radical socialists and communists to the United States after the 1848 revolts would read like a travel map of Europe. Germany or at least the various German republics we know today as Germany, France, several Italian states, Poland, Hungary, and to a lesser extent, England, all were more than happy to rid themselves of these revolutionaries, at the peril of the United States. Let's not forget these European radical socialists and communists did not come to the United States without finding home-grown friends and fellow radicals here. Throughout the North, especially New England, there were many communistic and socialistic societies attempting to reshape society into a utopian dream world. These kindred spirits began forming groups such as the New York Communist Club. Major Robert Rosa of the Union Army and a Forty-Eighter was a prominent member of this New York communist association. The preamble of the Communist Club of New York states it "rejects every religious belief," "recognizes the perfect equality of all men regardless of color

---

[157] Karl Marx, as cited in, *Marx and Engels, Letters to Americans*, 23.

or sex," "strives ... to abolish all private property," and "to inaugurate in its place the participation of all in the material and intellectual enjoyments of the earth."[158] The estimated number of Forty-Eighters who served both in the Union Army and in the Republican Party range from a few hundred to tens of thousands. While these numbers are impressive by themselves, the fact virtually none of these radicals served in the Confederate Army, nor did any friend of Karl Marx and Fredrick Engels serve in Jefferson Davis's cabinet, should make anyone with an open mind question the legacy of Abraham Lincoln as a defender of freedom.

8— Q. You condemn President Lincoln for not abiding by a ruling of the United States Supreme Court. You somehow forget to mention the chief justice of the Supreme Court at that time was a slaveholding justice from Maryland. Like Jefferson Davis from Mississippi, this justice was defending slavery. Why should Lincoln be condemned for resisting a slaveholding justice just as he was resisting a slaveholding traitor like Jefferson Davis?

A. Your attack upon a so-called slaveholding Supreme Court justice, and Karl Marx's attack upon the "slaveholding" Supreme Court justices sound almost like identical statements. You are correct by stating during the latter half of the 1850s and until the advent of the war, five of the nine justices on the United States Supreme Court were indeed slaveholders. Chief Justice Robert Brooke Taney of Maryland was undeniably a slaveholding justice. It was Justice Taney who wrote the seven-to-two majority opinion in the famous Dred Scott case. After rendering this decision Taney was forever vilified by members of the radical abolitionist movement and is still being vilified by today's politically correct (p.c.) pundits. While Marx and modern p.c. pundits denounce this decision as a victory for Southern slaveholders, the truth is somewhat different. Yes, five of the United States Supreme Court justices were from the South and were slaveholders, but the decision was seven to two, not five (Southerners) to four (Northerners). Furthermore, to portray the five Southern justices as promoters of slavery does not correspond to the facts. Two of the Southern justices, Robert Brooke Taney from Maryland and John Archibald Campbell from Alabama, were practicing abolition-

---

158 Morris Hillquit, *History of Socialism in the United States* (New York and London: Funk and Wagnalls Company, 1910) 97.

ists. (It must be pointed out not all abolitionists in the United States were from the North, and these Southern justices were not agents of the extremist group known as radical abolitionists.) Both Taney and Campbell had freed all their slaves with the exception of those too old to care for themselves. These older slaves were maintained at the personal expense of these two Southern abolitionists. It should also be pointed out these so-called evil Southern slaveholders bore the cost of freeing their slaves. Which people can truly be said to support the ending of slavery in America — those who demand the owners of slaves give up their investment in their slave property, much of which was purchased from the families of rich Northern abolitionists, or those who at their own personal expense take it upon themselves to free their slaves? Not only did Justice Taney at his own expense free his slaves, he made sure they had the job skills needed to provide for themselves and their families and they were established in a home before being freed. Justice Taney and his brother-in-law, Francis Scott Key (the author of *The Star-Spangled Banner*) were very active in the abolition movement in Maryland. It may come as a surprise to those who believe Southerners were fighting to promote slavery to learn some of the first abolition societies in America were founded by Southern slaveholders.[159] This is just one more bit of evidence to prove the true or at least complete history of slavery in America has been grossly under told. Lincoln refused to abide with an order from the United States Supreme Court and acted as if he and his party were the only true judges of his power. As has been pointed out, only five of the nine justices of the Supreme Court were slaveholders, leaving four Northern justices who were non-slaveholders; add to this number the two Southern abolitionists on the Court, and we are left with only three slaveholders on the Supreme Court. Three out of nine is a distinct minority. Given the numbers of abolitionists on the Supreme Court, four Northerners and two Southerners, why should Lincoln be allowed to disregard an order from the Supreme Court? Now who is the real traitor, a man who refused to abide by the Constitution, such as Lincoln, or a man who was willing to turn his back on a lifetime of work for these United States to protect true American liberty? Remember the words of Patrick Henry: "The first thing I have at heart is American liberty; the second thing is American union."[160] Notice according to Patrick Henry, liberty always trumps union, that is,

---

159 Walter D. Kennedy, *Myths of American Slavery*, 28.
160 Patrick Henry, as cited in, William Wirt Henry, III, 449.

government. Abraham Lincoln was the man who was willing to go to any length, including waging war upon civilians, trampling upon the Constitution, and breaking international law, to hold the Union together; whereas, Jefferson Davis was the man who held to a strict construction interpretation of the Constitution and State's Rights, a man who helped establish a new government more to the liking of the people, just as the Declaration of Independence says free men have a right to do, and a man who resisted by an executive veto a bill which transgressed the spirit of the Confederate Constitution's ban on the importation of new slaves into the South. In light of the previously mentioned facts, let us now ask the question: Which man was following in the footsteps of Patrick Henry, Lincoln or Davis? If liberty comes before union, then it must be admitted Jefferson Davis and not Abraham Lincoln more closely followed in the footsteps of Patrick Henry. By using bloody bayonets to force people into a union they did not wish to be in, Lincoln turned a formerly free Federal government into a Federal prison. Remember, a prison is a place where one is shot if he attempts to escape or leave! This being the case, Davis was right, Lincoln was wrong, and of course, the South was right!

Summary
Lest any foreigner should read this article let me say for his benefit that there are two Jefferson Davises in American history — one is a conspirator, a rebel, a traitor, and the 'fiend of Andersonville' — he is a myth evolved from the hell smoke of cruel war — as purely imaginary a personage as Mephistopheles or the Hebrew devil; the other was a statesman with clean hands and pure heart, who served his people faithfully from budding manhood to hoary age, without thought of self, with unbending integrity and to the best of his great ability: he was a man of whom all his countrymen who knew him personally, without distinction of creed political, are proud, and proud that he was their countryman. I never met any man in public who reverenced the Constitution as Mr. Davis reverenced it.... If the Constitution had been lost, I think Mr. Davis could have rendered it from memory.[161]

— James Redpath, 1888

The preceding rather glowing defense of Jefferson Davis was not made by a fellow Southerner or a partisan supporter of the so-called

---

161 James Redpath, as cited in, Joseph McElroy, *Jefferson Davis: The Unreal and the Real* (Konecky & Konecky, NY: 1937) 693.

"Lost Cause." James Redpath was a firebrand Radical Abolitionist before the war and a well-established late nineteenth century progressive spokesman. After meeting Jefferson Davis in 1888 at Beauvoir, on the Mississippi Gulf Coast, Redpath and Davis became steadfast friends. During this time and up until Davis' death Redpath became so impressed with the character of the former Confederate President that he later wrote a book titled, *Neither Traitor nor Rebel* in which he described Davis as a noble man of strong Constitutional convictions.

Unfortunately, in today's politically correct world, Davis is either totally ignored or derided as the arch villain of American history second only to Benedict Arnold. Today even the most extreme "Tea Party" conservative will view Lincoln as second only to Washington, while ridiculing Davis as an enemy of America. Yet as we have pointed out, it was Lincoln who made big government (Federal supremacy) not only possible but also inevitable. Going one step further, as Redpath points out, it was Jefferson Davis who "reverenced the Constitution" and it was Jefferson Davis who defended the America given to us by our founding fathers.

President Dwight D. Eisenhower

President Dwight D. Eisenhower, 34th president of the United States and Supreme Commander of Allied forces in Europe during WWII. In 1960 Eisenhower warned Americans about the danger of the Military-Industrial Complex, which could lead to an American foreign policy of war for profit. Eisenhower kept a photograph of Confederate General Robert E. Lee in his office, the same Lee who, after having seen the death of real States' Rights, warned Americans of the danger of the United States becoming "aggressive abroad and despotic at home." The past 100 years of conservative failure to control the growth of big government proves both Lee and Eisenhower were correct.

Chapter 7
100 Years of Failure

The twentieth century in America witnessed glorious victories for those who believed in extreme federalism, big government, central control, liberalism, and socialism. Conservatives, on the other hand, can look back with shame at one humiliating defeat after another.[162]

— James R. Kennedy

After electing more "conservative" Republicans to Congress and the White House than at any time in the past hundred years, Southerners who still believe in limited government are faced with the painful reality of a Federal government which still continues to grow in power and taxing authority. Why, after the success of so many "conservative" election victories, are we still faced with a central government that few if any of our founding fathers would have found to their liking? The answer is one that few conservative leaders are willing to address: Our system of government with its original system of checks and balances on political power no longer exists. The republic of republics founded by the Patriots of 1776-88 has been overthrown and replaced with a unitary, indivisible, and all-powerful Federal government — a government that looks and acts like an empire, a Yankee Empire! Since Appomattox no state of the Union dares to stand against the will of Washington, DC, with any hope of success. Washington calls the shots and sets the limits on what powers "we the people" of each state in the Union are allowed to exercise. The system was broken before the War for Southern Independence; its demise was finalized at Appomattox. After the fall of the Confederate States of America, Confederate Vice President Alexander Stephens noted that one day all Americans would understand "the Cause of the South is the Cause of us all!" With the death of real States' Rights, the Federal government became the "king of the hill" in the United States. The abuse of Federal power is displayed in many acts of Congress from issuing unfunded Federal mandates to forcing state governments to enforce Federal speed limits on state highways. These and numerous other examples of Federal domination over the will of "we the people" of the various state governments prove Alexander Stephens was correct. The end result of the loss of real States' Rights is today the

---

[162] James R. Kennedy, *Reclaiming Liberty*, 15.

average citizen stands unprotected from the abuse of an all-powerful central government. Today the average citizen feels overtaxed, over regulated, and underserved by a Federal government which acts more like an empire than a republic of free people. That same citizen feels he cannot withstand the weight of that government, nor does he feel secure about his ability to force the Federal government to respect his rights and property. Thus, we see the prediction of the Confederate vice president coming true more than 150 years after the beginning of hostilities between the North and the South.

1— Q. Why don't you Southerners just get over it — you lost the war. Aren't there more important things to worry about these days?

A. There is nothing more important than the protection and expansion of liberty. The unspoken message in your statement is the so-called *Civil War* has nothing to do with the problems faced by Americans today. Exposure of your premise to historical fact and the reality of today's events demonstrate when it comes to defending liberty, there were many deleterious effects caused by the defeat of the South in 1865. When considering the establishment of a truly liberty-based society, one must not overlook the one thing which has made the growth of big government within the United States both possible and inevitable; that is, the defeat of the States' Rights Party during the War for Southern Independence.

True States' Rights serve as the counterbalance to the growth of big government. The emasculation of States' Rights after the defeat of the South left Americans with a system of States' Rights which is a mere shadow of the vigorous opponent to the growth of big government that once protected our liberty. If you are an advocate of big government, then of course you will view this effort to restore real States' Rights as a dangerous and foolhardy effort. Today, more and more people are beginning to understand something has gone wrong with the efforts to conserve our liberty and traditional values. In the past one hundred years many people have complained about the growth of the scope and power of big government; nevertheless, that growth continues. As many Southerners have noted, the political philosophy of twentieth century American conservatism contains a fatal flaw: "it had no real means to defend itself from the attacks of those wanting to expand the powers of the federal government."[163] Failure

---

163 Ibid, 17

to recognize this flaw in their philosophy set the stage for one hundred years "of conservative defeat, retreat, and retrenchment."[164]

As you can see, this failure to recognize an inherent flaw in its strategy has left the conservative movement with one hand tied behind its back as conservatives fight the advocates of big government. Restoring real States' Rights in the American political forum will sound the death knell for big government. But how can people find that which they do not know is lost or restore that which they do not appreciate being absent? Herein is the great dilemma for modern neo-conservatives. Today neo-conservatives fully embrace Abraham Lincoln's view of Federal supremacy within the Union. Lincoln's view of the Federal government paralleled the views of Alexander Hamilton and other High Federalists; that is, states of the Union must be subservient to the Federal will. A subservient state cannot block any unconstitutional act of the Federal government and therefore is just what an advocate of big government desires. Most conservatives began the twentieth century believing that States' Rights in the post-Appomattox era were alive and well. For one hundred years they fought the growth of big government, and lost the vast majority of the time.

At the beginning of the twenty-first century neo-conservatives gave lip service to the cause of limited government and States' Rights, but in reality, only complained about big government when neo-conservatives were not in control of the power of government. When Hurricane Katrina hit the Gulf Coast (August 2005), it was none other than Newt Gingrich (a Republican neo-conservative) and George Bush (another Republican neo-conservative) who vied for bragging rights on who was advocating the largest expenditures of Federal monies and Federal control of the disaster-struck area. Obviously, the neo-conservative club has jettisoned the traditional conservative value of limited government. Neo-conservatives, just like their socialist/liberal associates, are advocates of big government. Neo-conservatives have as little use for real States' Rights as their socialist competitors. Each desire to win enough votes in order to stay in control of the massive power of the Federal government. The only difference between neo-conservatives and socialists is who gets the perks of victory. As you can see, the so-called *Civil War* is not some arcane past event with little relevance to modern times. No, we Southerners won't "get over it." We will continue the struggle to restore the original

---

164 Ibid.

constitutional republic of republics and realize our American birthright of living in a liberty-based society — the fight is not over until Freedom is won.

2— Q. Being taught by some very patriotic people that the United States Constitution is the most perfect document for organizing a democratic society; I find it difficult to believe your concept of a fatally flawed Constitution. Do you really think the United States Constitution is flawed?

A. The Constitution is not so much flawed as the people who hold power under the Constitution are flawed. Most orthodox Christians believe that since the fall of man in the Garden of Eden, every man has been born flawed. This flaw is intensified when man is given authority over other men, and the more authority he holds, the more obvious is this flaw. The old truism "power corrupts, and absolute power corrupts absolutely" still holds true. If you don't believe in this concept of fallen man, you will no doubt agree most people choose things that will help them personally even if what they choose may not be the best for society. Therefore, governments which can use force to compel people to surrender their income and rights, will eventually find itself controlled by people who use those governments for their own benefit. The founding fathers of this nation understood this concept and therefore established a republic of republics in which the Federal government was given strict limits on its powers. These limitations of power were placed in a written constitution so as to be easily recognized by everyone. Early in the history of the republic, one means by which "we the people" could force the Federal government to abide by the limitations imposed on it by the Constitution was by the threat or actual exercise of the right of nullification or secession.

Even though these rights were not prohibited to the states, and even though states had exercised the right of nullification and secession in the past, when the South exercised this right in 1861, the North rose *en masse* and denied the Southern people this basic American right: the right to live under a government ordered on the free and unfettered consent of the governed. This throttling of freedom could have been prevented if the original Constitution had clearly and precisely acknowledged these rights; thus, we see a fatal flaw in the Constitution.

3— Q. You are very critical of conservative efforts during the twentieth century. But what about conservative victories such as electing Ronald Reagan, winning the Cold War, and regaining control of Congress?

A. The point is not that conservatives have won some victories, but rather the point is despite many opportunities (victories), conservatives have never rolled back the victories of the left. We have been an effective army at times, but our leaders have never figured out what to do with our hard-won victories. They have never followed these victories by pursing their political enemies and destroying their strong positions. Once our leaders get themselves elected, their primary goal from that time onward seems to be to remain in office — sometimes at any cost. Yes, we won the Cold War. But what has happened to our liberty during that time? Would you prefer to pay income tax at the pre-Cold War rate or at the present rate? Big taxes go hand in hand with big government. Do you think unconstitutional governmental intrusion is less today than it was at the beginning of the Cold War? Do you think that the men who died in World War I, World War II, Korea, Vietnam, and numerous other subsequent conflicts sacrificed their lives so that government could order the Ten Commandments out of public view, support so-called gay rights, federalize the definition of pornography, and enforce racial quotas? Our few conservative victories are overwhelmed by our leaders' failure to envision a strategic plan to destroy the liberal/socialist political system which has been foisted upon the people of the United States and to return us to a land of real American liberty. It is easy to understand why our leaders have reacted as they have for the past century. Conservatives have been playing the role assigned to them by the proponents of Federal supremacy ever since 1865. As long as we play their game, by their rules (the Federal supremacist) and refereed by their (Federal supremacist) agents, we will always end up losing the contest. The time has come for "we the people" of the sovereign states to change the rules of the game if not the game itself!

4— Q. You seem to think no one believes in limited government anymore. Yet, look at what happened with Ron Paul's presidential campaign for the Republican nomination for president of the United States. Why don't you just get behind someone like Congressman Paul and reclaim the Constitution?

A. Get behind Ron Paul? I (Walter D. Kennedy) voted for Ron Paul, placed my name on the Republican ballot in Louisiana twice, 2008 and 2012, as a delegate pledged to Ron Paul, gave money to Ron Paul's presidential campaign, and after his defeat sent money to his congressional reelection campaign — just how much more can one person do for Ron Paul? Yes, I know what you are asking is why I tried to get into the Republican primary of 2008 when a man such as Ron Paul had already announced his candidacy for the Republican presidential nomination. Ron Paul is a good Republican, one of the best, but as pointed out early in the Kennedy presidential exploratory effort, good Republicans won't do. Now let me explain why I don't think Ron Paul has the correct answer to the problem facing Americans in general and Southerners in particular. Also, I hope you will understand why I did support Ron Paul during the 2008 Republican presidential primary. The Kennedy Twins of Louisiana are Southern Nationalists who believe in strict constitutional government and liberty, but we are not American Nationalists. Ron Paul is an American Nationalist who believes in strict constitutional government and liberty, but he is not a Southern Nationalist. The Kennedy Twins of Louisiana hold to the view that there has been and continues to be a great gulf between the people of the South and the people of the rest of America. In other words, Southerners are different from other Americans. As Ron Kennedy pointed out in his article "Dixie's Unwelcomed Presence in Rosie O'Donnell's America," there is more than accent or geography that divides Dixie and the rest of America. Even if we elected a Ron Paul as president of these United States the vast cultural difference between the two sections would remain. Given that fact, regardless of who is president, the South will remain a minority section within these United States, and Southerners' values and mores will be held hostage to the Northern majority. Traditional values such as our biblical world view on matters such as sanctity of life, one-man-one-woman marriage, respect for the Ten Commandments, full and complete punishment of sexual perverts and murderers are just a few things which have come under attack by forces outside of the South. We understand many people outside of the South hold these same values, but as the Pew Report[165] has shown, it is in the South these values are held much stronger than anywhere else in America. Yes, it is true the South would be better served by the elec-

---

[165] The Pew Research Center, *Trends in Political Values and Core Attitudes: 1987-2007*, www.people-press.org, reviewed March 28, 2007.

tion of a candidate such as Ron Paul, but the problem of "those people" always attempting to remake the South into something more to the liking of the North would have continuous deleterious social and political consequences for Southerners. Note, even though Ron Paul ran on a platform advocating a strict construction view of the Constitution, he never addressed the one issue which separates American Nationalists from Southern Nationalists; that is, the right of secession. Advocating secession does not make a person a Southern Nationalist. Advocating the right of secession wherein "we the people" at the state level exercise the American right, as announced in the Declaration of Independence, to live under a government to which we freely consent is the cornerstone of Southern Nationalism. Advocating the right of "we the people" of each sovereign state to be the judge of how we are governed is the antidote to Federal tyranny. When the Federal government understands it must abide by the limitations of the Constitution, our lives, our property, and our rights will be secured from abuse by the central government. A true Southern Nationalist is not one who seeks to destroy the Federal government, but rather one who seeks to compel the Federal government to abide by the Constitution. If the Federal government refuses to abide by the Constitution, Southern Nationalists understand secession is a reasonable alternative, because we love liberty more than we love government. An American Nationalist, even one with the credentials of a Ron Paul, will seek to control the Federal government by electing enough good people to the Federal government to keep it under control and restricted by the Constitution. While this is something that should be done, it still places in the hands of the Federal government the means whereby it can at its own volition violate any of the rights and liberties of the citizens of the states. What will happen to our rights when a Ron Paul is defeated and a big government Republican or Democrat is elected president? By allowing the Federal government to be the sole guardian of our rights and liberty, we establish the very mechanism for the destruction of our rights and liberty. The old and simple question is still relevant today: "Who shall guard the guards?" When we allow the Federal government to be the sole guardian of our liberty, the heavy hand of tyranny is firmly established, even if every representative and senator in Congress, every justice on the Supreme Court, and every inhabitant of the White House is a Ron Paul. Herein is the demarcation between the Kennedy Twins of Louisiana and Ron Paul: The Kennedy Twins understand the Federal government can never be trusted to safeguard our liberty even if good Republicans such as Ron Paul occupy the White House. Ron Paul is a good man, but he is not wiser than Thomas Jefferson and James Madison, authors of the Kentucky and Virginia Resolves. Jefferson and Madison both stated our rights and liberty cannot be safe from Federal abuse unless "we the people" of the sovereign states have the power to judge for ourselves whether the Federal government is acting within the limits of the Constitution. As Jefferson and Madison pointed out, not only must "we the people" of the states judge the actions of the Federal government, we must also have the power to resist Federal tyranny. Southern Nationalists understand the acts of nullification and secession to be the ultimate weapon of "we the people" for the defense of our dearest interests from being abused by the Federal government.

5.— Q. You moan and complain about big government, and yet it is this same big government that offers hope to so many poor Americans. How can you be so uncaring for the underprivileged of our country? Did we not strike a blow at poor education for these underprivileged Americans by the efforts of our so-called big government?

A. Yes, a blow was struck, but it fell upon America's poor and underprivileged, and it was big government that threw the punch. In the mid-1960s President Lyndon Johnson established the Great Society's social programs ostensibly for the benefit of the poor and underprivileged. From that time to now, we, as a nation, have spent more than one trillion dollars fighting poverty without winning that fight. Also, during that time the Federal government has spent more than $125 billion on education for the poor and underprivileged, and what has been the result of that effort? The SAT scores have fallen from a high of approximately 980 in 1960 to approximately 900 in 1990. During this time of falling SAT scores the expenditures in constant dollars rose from around $60 billion in 1960 to $250 billion in 1990. What did we get for the expenditure of all those billions of dollars, other than a decrease in the quality of education? One thing we got was more government intrusion into the education process which should have remained in the hands of parents and local school administrators. But the bad news does not stop there, because we got one more thing from this gargantuan expenditure of tax dollars, the fleecing of the American taxpayer. By removing money from the hands of private citizens, the government disrupts the normal activity of the free market, the only true generator of wealth, and reduces that ability of society, that is, the free market system, to provide jobs to the poor and underprivileged. In response to the failure of public education to improve the education of the poor and underprivileged after the expenditure of so many tax dollars, in 2001 Roderick Paige, then Secretary of Education, stated: "After spending $125 billion of Title I money over 25 years, we have virtually nothing to show for it."[166] No improvement in the education of the poor is bad enough, but coupled with decreasing SAT scores and the detrimental effect the increased tax burden has had on the creation of jobs for the poor, the result is a real and deleterious blow struck upon the very people big government says it is trying to help. If the Kennedy Twins were among these poor folks, we would tell the government, "Please stop; you are helping us to death!" Beyond the fact of decreasing SAT scores and increasing tax burdens, there is one more fact to consider when thinking about big government solutions to local problems. When any problem becomes a Federal problem, local citizens must abide with Federal rules and regulations. In other words, with every increase in Federal control, "we the people" lose the right to control our own lives. As always, more government equals less freedom. The Kennedy Twins fail to see how the loss of freedom and the creation of a massive and uncontrollable Federal government helps the poor and underprivileged.

Summary

The great vital question now is: Shall the Federal Government be arrested in its progress, and be brought back to original principles, or shall it be permitted to go on in its present tendencies and rapid strides, until it reaches complete Consolidation?

Depend upon it, there is no difference between Consolidation and Empire; no difference between Centralism and Imperialism. The consummation of either must necessarily end in the overthrow of Liberty and the establishment of Despotism. To speak of any Rights as belonging to the States, without the innate and inalienable Sovereign power to maintain them, is but to deal in the shadow of language without the substance. Nominal Rights without Securities are but Mockeries![167]

— Alexander H. Stephens, 1870.

---

166 Roderick Paige, as cited in, Bill O'Reilly, *Racism in Public Education*, www.worldnetdaily.com, reviewed May 30, 2001.
167 Alexander H. Stephens, *A Constitutional View Of The Late War Between The States; its Causes, Character, Conduct and Results* (1870: Sprinkle Publications, Harrisonburg, VA: 1994) II, 668.

The statement "Nominal Rights without Securities are but Mockeries!" hits at the core of the issue of why America needs *REAL* States' Rights. As has been demonstrated in the past 100 years of conservative failure, what good does it do to speak of our Constitutional Rights if the Federal government is the sole agent which determines what Constitutional Rights are allowed to be exercised? As a result of now living under the system of Federal supremacy, all Americans now must kowtow to their masters in Washington. The reality of Americans kowtowing to Federal masters is not something discovered in the 21st century. "The only hope, in my view, now left for its [Constitutional Liberty] preservation and maintenance on this Continent, is, that another like cry shall hereafter be raised, and go forth from hill-top to valley, from the Coast to the Lakes, from the Atlantic to the Pacific; The Cause of the South is the Cause of us all!"[168] Just five years after the defeat of the South and the ascendancy of Federal supremacy to dominance in Washington, the former vice president of the Confederate States of American foretold what was going to happen and what needed to be done to correct the problem. With the warning, "… there is no difference between Consolidation and Empire," Stephens is pointing out the dire results of putting all political power into the hands of the Federal government. Empires do not exist for the benefit of "we the people," but rather the people exist for the benefit of the empire. Civil liberty is the first victim when a once free republic of republics morphs into an empire.

The result of this un-Constitutional metamorphosis of our republic of republics into an all-powerful, indivisible, sovereign empire has two deadly results for Americans: First, the loss of the ability of "we the people" at the local level to force the central government, i.e., the now supreme Federal empire, to respect our civil liberty under the Constitution; and second, placing the American people in a no-win political situation, where no matter how many "conservatives" we send to Washington, no real change in the nature of the Federal empire takes place. Washington is the seat of power for the Federal empire. Two things every empire has in common are money and power. Ron Paul is an excellent example of what happens to an individual who attempts to dismantle the Federal empire from within. No matter how diligent a Paul or a group of statesmen like Ron Paul are in their efforts to replace the all-powerful Federal empire with a government based upon the principles of 1776, all the money and

168 Ibid, 666.

power of the empire will crush the effort. Thus, as a result we see what has happened in the past one hundred years of conservative efforts to dismantle the empire. President Trump's struggle with Deep State Republicans and Democrats is an example of the power of "those people." Yes, we have had some very impressive tactical victories but has the Federal empire been changed by those victories? After Reagan's victory, after Newt Gingrich's congressional victory, after many "conservative" appointed Federal judges (such as Chief Justice Roberts), has the size and power of the Federal empire been reduced? Do "we the people" at the local level have the tools necessary to force the Federal government to respect our Constitutional rights? As will be pointed out in chapter 8, until the right of nullification and secession are firmly in the hands of "we the people" of the sovereign states, we remain nothing but serfs of the Federal empire. Alexander Stephens hit a home run when he noted, ***Nominal Rights without Securities are but Mockeries!***

Thomas Jefferson   **James Madison**

Thomas Jefferson, the virtual author of the Declaration of Independence, and James Madison, often referred to as the "Father of the Constitution," were strong defenders of the concept of state sovereignty and States' Rights. This concept of the states as sovereign members of a federal republic guided every American president until the election of Lincoln. Lincoln viewed the Federal government as the sovereign government and the states as being created by the Union and therefore, submissive to the will of the Federal government. In their famous Kentucky and Virginia Resolves (Jefferson authored the Kentucky Resolves and Madison the Virginia Resolves) these founding fathers proclaimed four points Lincoln denied ever existed: (1) the states were sovereign, (2) the Constitution was a compact among the states, (3) the states and not the Federal government were the final judge of the actions of the Federal government, and, (4) the states had every right to take whatever action they deemed necessary against un-Constitutional actions of the Federal government. Is it not strange that the States' Rights theory held by Jefferson, the "author" of the Declaration of Independence, the third president of the United States, and Madison, the "Father of the Constitution" and fourth president of the United States, was nullified and declared to be treason by the 16th President, Lincoln, who was elected by only 39 percent of the popular vote? Lincoln, who had not even been born at the time of the writing of the Kentucky and Virginia Resolves, presumes to lecture Jefferson and Madison on the true nature of American government — said lecture resulted in more than one million deaths and the enslavement of all Americans to big government!

Chapter 8
The Shield and Sword of Liberty

Nullification is a remedy which it is sought to apply within the Union, and against the agent of the States. It is only to be justified when the agent has violated his constitutional obligation.[169]
— Jefferson Davis

The rules of engagement are set by those who have a vested interest in maintaining "we the people" in a subservient position as vassals of America's ruling elite.[170]
— James R. Kennedy

When knights of medieval Europe were sent out to defend their lord's rights and property, they were always equipped with two very important articles of armament: a shield and a sword. In the founding and establishment of these United States our founding fathers were likewise eager to provide "we the people of the sovereign states" sufficient "armaments" to protect our Rights from being infringed by the newly formed central government. As Patrick Henry, a representative of the Anti-Federalist class of patriots, so correctly pointed out, "The first thing I have at heart is American liberty, the second is American union."[171] Even mild Federalists such as James Madison noted, "… the safety and happiness of society are the objects at which all political institutions aim, and to which all such institutions must be sacrificed."[172] As our founding fathers demonstrated in the Declaration of Independence, they also did in the adopting the Constitution when they pointed out that in these United States of America, liberty always trumps government. This principle has great historical significance but it has more importance as it is applied or not applied to modern events.

The great struggle for American Independence was not centered on the promotion of newly gained "Rights" but was centered on a

---

169 Jefferson Davis, 143 Farewell Address to the US Senate, January 21, 1861.
170 James R. Kennedy, *Nullification! Why And How*, Free downloadable book at www.kennedytwins.com pulled June 17, 2012, 6.
171 Patrick Henry, as cited in William Wirt Henry, *Patrick Henry: Life, Correspondence and Speeches*, (1891: reprint, Harrisonburg: Sprinkle Publications, 1993) III, 449.
172 James Madison, as cited in, 143 *The Federalists Number 43*, George W. Carey and McClellan, 228.

struggle against an all-powerful central government. But more importantly the struggle was against a central government which had become unresponsive to the needs and desires of the citizens of 13 individual colonies. Unlike the French Revolution where the people were discovering rights unknown to them, the War for American Independence was a "conservative" struggle to preserve and maintain their "Rights as Englishmen." It was the action of an abusive central government that forced the American colonies to join together to defend their rights from being infringed by an all-powerful central government.

This fear of an all-powerful central government was displayed in the first "Federal" government that existed among the states under the Articles of Confederation. So fearful were the people of the states of establishing a government that would become a runaway government that would expand into another all-powerful central government, that in Article II of the Articles of Confederation it is clearly stated "Each state retains its sovereignty, freedom, and independence and every Power Jurisdiction and right, which is not by this confederation expressly delegated to the United States, in Congress assembled."[173] Likewise, the new Federal government under the Constitution was established under the watchful eye of Americans fearful of an all-powerful central government. The ratification of the Constitution was not possible until the Anti-Federalists were assured that "The powers not delegated to the United States by the Constitution, nor prohibited by it to the States, are reserved to the States respectively, or to the people." The States ratified the Constitution on the condition that the Bill of Rights would be added to the Constitution. It should be noted here at that time the Bill of Rights *ONLY* applied to the acts and actions of the newly formed Federal government. Obviously, the founding fathers wanted to assure themselves the newly formed central government would be under the control of the people of the states and not control the people of the states. Also note many states proclaimed upon ratification they reserved the right to judge for themselves how they would be governed. In other words these founding fathers in their ratification document noted if they so desired they and they alone would judge if they stayed in the newly formed Federal government.

The ninth and tenth amendments to the Constitution demon-

---

173 Article II, Articles of Confederation, as cited in, John H. Ferguson and McHenry, *The American Government* (McGraw-Hill Book Co., NY: 1969) A3.

strate our founding fathers understood that with a means to *FORCE* the newly formed Federal government to abide by the Constitution, their rights or the rights of their children would not be held hostage to an all-powerful central government. Thomas Jefferson and James Madison, authors of the Kentucky and Virginia Resolves made this point clear only ten years after the adoption of the Constitution. It is these resolves that clearly point out "we the people" of the sovereign states have the final say on how we are to be governed. As Jefferson and Madison point out, it is not government that is the most important entity in these United States, rather it is liberty that holds the highest status for free men.

The Kentucky and Virginia Resolves point out the meaning of *REAL* States' Rights and American liberty. *REAL* States' Rights, as opposed to the milk-toast, weak-kneed, spineless States' Privileges Americans are accustomed to exercising, boldly directs our agent, the Federal government, to live within its natural boundaries and do the will of "we the people." Compare that with States' Privileges such as in California (2008) when it passed an ordinance that marriage is between one man and one woman, the Federal government told California it could not enforce that act. When Arizona (2010) passed a law to enforce existing Federal laws on immigration, the Federal government told Arizona to "cease and desist" from such action. When, during Hurricane Katrina, Louisiana (2005) attempted to protect its wetlands from oil, it was the Federal government which told Louisiana only the Federal government could act on this matter. In Alabama (2003) the Federal government ordered the removal of the Ten Commandments from Alabama Courthouses giving us one more example of the actions of the Federal empire's dictatorial rule over the states. This is what happens when one lives under an all-powerful central government, something we call "Federal Supremacy." Where once "we the people" of the states were supreme in all matters not delegated to the Federal government nor prohibited to the states by the Constitution (and these were few and clearly stated in the Constitution) today we live under the very type of government that our founding fathers fought so hard to defeat and prohibit in these United States. An all-powerful central government, that is, Federal Supremacy via the Federal Empire, is now the law of the land. The question is how do "we the people" force that all-powerful central government back into the mold that our founding fathers envisioned?

The reality of Federalism in post-Appomattox America is one

of indivisible Federal supremacy. Today there are no places in life where the Federal government does not intrude with some form of rule, regulation, edict, guideline, or law. In all these areas, it is the will of the Federal government that is supreme, making the Ninth and Tenth Amendments a complete nullity. Under Federal supremacy the Ninth and Tenth Amendments are nothing more than a Constitutional anachronism. Two fundamental changes must take place before the evils of Federal supremacy can be removed from the American political landscape: 1. Americans must understand the government of the founding fathers is *NOT* the government we live with today. Under the original intent of the founding fathers, "we the people of sovereign States" held the ultimate voice on how we are to be governed. Under Federal supremacy, the Federal government determines how we are to be governed. Once Americans understand the people of each state have the right to determine for themselves if the Federal government's acts are legitimate or how long they shall remain a part of the Federal government, 90 percent of the work of bringing the Federal government under control will have been accomplished. Unfortunately, even Tea Party patriots, some of America's most politically active and knowledgeable citizens, don't understand the difference between the Federal government of the founding fathers (where *REAL* States' Rights existed) and the Federal government of today (where Federal supremacy rules the day). 2. The Constitution must be amended so as to acknowledge the innate and inherent right of "we the people" of each state of the Federal Union to judge for itself if the acts of its agent, that is, the Federal government, are Constitutional. Such an amendment must clearly state that the right to judge how "we the people" of each sovereign state are to be governed resides in the hands of the people of each state, acting under no compulsion from their agent, the Federal government.

Once the Federal government has been put on notice it is no longer the sole judge of its actions and the people of the states are not held hostage to an all-powerful central government, a new form of government will spring forth reflecting the original intent of the founding fathers. Liberty will be "born again!" It should be noted here that said change cannot take place by merely amending the Constitution. There must be a change of attitude by the people of these United States as to what is and is not the function of their state and the Federal government. Once Americans no longer accept the un-Constitutional and illegitimate actions of the Federal government as legal, the end of Federal supremacy will be at hand. In *Nullification! Why and How*,[174] Ron Kennedy explains in some detail why this type of amendment is needed. What is being attempted is to "put the genie" back into the bottle. The "genie" here is big, out of control, government or what we call the "Federal Empire." In 1991 with the publication of the first edition of *The South Was Right!* and restated in the 1994 in the second edition, the Kennedy Twins noted the struggle for liberty was ongoing. That either these United States would be called back to the original intent of the founding fathers or absent that, the people of the South had every right to seek a better government of their own choosing. Subsequently every book written by the Kennedy Twins has pointed out that liberty always trumps government. If we are to be a free people then we must do those things which will end Federal tyranny and reinvent *REAL* American liberty. What was written in 1991 and 1994 is still true today: "The rising of the moon will see a return of government as established by the Original Constitution or if we cannot convince our Northern neighbors to reform this current overgrown, and unresponsive government of their making, then we shall work for the re-establishment of a Constitutional Republic known as the Confederate States of America."[175]

1— Q. Nullification is just a dead horse from the Calhoun area. Why do you think Americans in this modern age would want to embrace that old concept?

A. Nullification well preceded John C. Calhoun. As a matter of fact, the first amendment added to the new Constitution (Eleventh Amendment, 1798) was in response to the nullification of a Federal Supreme court action by the State of Georgia. But nullification goes back to before the signing of the Declaration of Independence. When the English Parliament attempted to legislate for the American Colonies, an act the colonists stated Parliament had no right to do, the legislatures of various colonies would pass laws that tended to nullify acts of Parliament. When these actions were not enough to secure their rights, our founding fathers performed the ultimate act of nullification by seceding from the union with Great Britain on July 4th 1776. Prior to the secession of the Southern States in the mid to late 1850s with the passage of "Personal Liberty Laws" that prevented

---

174 James R. Kennedy, ibid.
175 James R. Kennedy and Walter D. Kennedy, *The South Was Right!* (Pelican Publishing Co., Gretna, La: 1994) 10-11.

the Federal government from fulfilling its obligation under Article IV, Section 2 of the Constitution, many Northern States nullified part of the Constitution of these United States. Article IV, Section 2 of the Constitution (The Fugitive Slave Act) demands the return of any runaway slave who escapes into another state. Even though this article is a direct descendant of America's first "Fugitive Slave Act" by the United Colonies of New England[176] (1643) and even though many Northern States had taken advantage of this part of the Constitution, many people of the North no longer felt they should be bound by this part of the Constitution and nullified it within their state. Obviously, this "old" concept of nullification is a very American concept. This American concept of nullification by "we the people" of sovereign states is one which tends to place the power of the people between our liberty and a central government who is attempting to trample upon our rights. When the American people no longer "want to embrace that old concept," we truly will become the serfs of an all-powerful central government and no longer will we be free.

2— Q. By allowing the States to nullify any action of the Federal government you will be creating a very weak central government and establishing national political anarchy. How can solving one problem, an all-powerful central government, be a positive step if you are thereby creating national political anarchy?

A. Your question shows keen insight into what our founding fathers were struggling with during the Constitutional ratification debates, that is, how do we balance national security and commercial freedom (free trade among the states) with the security for the liberty of the individual of each state? Remember, protecting the individuals of sovereign states from an abusive central government was the flash point in the War for American Independence. Being mindful of the recent history and having played a major part in those historical events, our founding fathers' desire was to give us a nation where we would be safe from foreign attacks, have a free trade zone among the states, and yet be able to control the actions of the Federal government. Today in post-Appomattox America, we see that the first part of this concept, i.e., national security and a free trade zone among the states is a reality. But the second part of the founding fathers' equation, security of the rights of the people of each sovereign state from

---

[176] George H. Moore, *Notes on the History of Slavery in Massachusetts* (D. Appleton and Company, NY: 1866) 27-28.

an abusive central government is non-existent. As everyone understands, in modern America, the Federal government's wishes and desires trumps the rights of the states and the people thereof. So, the question now is "how shall we solve the problem of an out of control Federal government?" If one or more states quickly nullify every act of the Federal government, we would have a very weak central government; one that I contend would be too weak. Unfortunately, our founding fathers, even Jefferson and Madison, nor even Calhoun, ever codified the act of nullification. As you will notice in *Nullification: Why and How*,[177] the suggested Constitutional Amendment does codify and explains how and under what circumstances nullification would take place. For example, if your state feels it has been wronged it can only nullify said act, law, or judicial edict by a convention of its people. Although the governor and/or legislature will call the convention, it is the act of the people in convention which must nullify a perceived Federal injustice, not the sitting legislature. If three-fourths of the states also nullify said action, it is no longer law in any state. But if three-fourths of the states refuse to accept your state's nullification, said action is to be considered Constitutional in every state of the Union. So, you see there is little chance of national political anarchy. What we do see is the Federal government being chastised and directed to act according to the will of "we the people" of sovereign states.

3— Q. Nullification is one thing but I also noticed in your proposed Constitutional Amendment that you are giving the states the right of secession. What can cause more national political mayhem than states seceding from the Union?

A. What do you think should be of more value in America, liberty or government? Patrick Henry stated it very well when he noted, "The first thing I have at heart is American liberty, the second is American union." After a long struggle with an all-powerful central government, our founding fathers understood that in a liberty-based society, liberty always trumps government. When government becomes more important than liberty, there is tyranny. The old slogan "If you can't leave you are not free" is just as true today as it was when our founding fathers were contending with King George's all-powerful central government. What do you call a place where you are shot if you try to leave? Whether it is called a gulag, a concentration camp, a jail, or a prison, if you can't leave you are not free. If "we the people"

---
177 James R. Kennedy, Ibid, 93-96.

of sovereign states are not allowed to leave the Federal Union but are forced to abide by laws or edicts that "we the people" find immoral, unjust, and/or decadent, are we really free? How far removed are we from the words of the Declaration of Independence which states that the only "just government" is that government based upon the consent of the governed? Our founding fathers boldly affirmed "we the people" have the right to "alter or abolish" any government we do not like and to replace it with one more to our liking. You see secession is the ultimate defense of our rights against an otherwise unresponsive central government. There seems to be one point most people overlook when talking about secession of a state from the Federal Union. In a free association whether that be states of the Union or people in a civic club, the forces that hold people together are always stronger than those tending to divide people. What are the forces that tend to hold people together in a free association? Simply put it is respect for the individual's person and Rights which hold free associations together, not bloody bayonets. Anytime a "free" government employs the instruments of bloody bayonets to force its will upon its citizens, liberty dies and tyranny is born. By possessing the right of secession, "we the people" put the Federal government on notice that it is "we the people" and not the Federal politicians, judges, and bureaucrats who hold ultimate power in this nation.

4— Q. What chance do you have in getting Americans to embrace such a radical idea as nullification and secession?

A. As of today, very little chance at all! As is pointed out in both *Nullifying Tyranny: Creating Moral Communities in an Immoral Society*,[178] and *Nullification: Why and How*, putting the genie of Federal supremacy back into the bottle of limited government is not going to be an easy project. What we are talking about here is something akin to the Tea Party Movement where two objectives must be pursued. First, we must educate our fellow citizens about the danger of Federal supremacy and the necessity of "we the people" at the local level having the Constitutional tools to force the Federal government to abide by the Constitution. Second, we must use that "educational" organization of the people, once sufficient education has been accomplished, to push for two political objectives: (1) Passing of a resolution

---

178 James R. Kennedy and Walter D. Kennedy, *Nullifying Tyranny: Creating Moral Communities in an Immoral Society* (Pelican Publishing Co., Gretna, La.: 2010) 167-174.

by the state calling for a Constitutional Convention for the purpose of amending the Constitution to force the Federal government to recognize the right of nullification and/or secession; (2) Placing the said Constitutional amendment before Congress and requiring Congress to pass the amendment or face a state called Constitutional Convention. Again, it must be pointed out why this Constitutional Convention is being called. The purpose of the Constitutional Convention is for amending the Constitution recognizing the right of "we the people" of each sovereign state to nullify odious acts of the Federal government and/or the right of secession.

With an ever-growing number of "educational" or Tea Party type of organizations pushing the goal of reclaiming our right to control the Federal government, the number of states needed to call forth a Constitutional Convention will begin to grow. The magic number of states needed to call said convention is thirty-four or two-thirds of the states. As of today, there is no chance of the United States Congress considering alone passing an amendment that would neuter the power-elite in Washington and make *THEM* submissive to the will of "we the people." Just stop and think what would have happened to President Obama's vaunted National Health Care Initiative (since we did not have *REAL* States' Rights back then we got Obama's Health Care fiasco) if "we the people" at the state level had the power to nullify acts of the Federal government which "we the people" do not approve or desire. So, it should be obvious that the power elite in Washington both Democrats and Republicans will not easily surrender their power. But if forced by the people of each state (or at least two-thirds) to either pass our amendment or face a Constitutional Convention called for that very purpose, they then can be forced to act according to our wishes and not their desire.

All of this and more is explained in *Nullification: Why and How*. Our purpose here is to point out we must have a plan that will force the genie of Federal supremacy back in its Constitutional "bottle" and execute that plan in such a manner as to favor our strengths and take advantage of our opponent's weaknesses. Nationwide Congressional approval at this time is at an all-time low of around 20 percent. People trust government the closer it is to them and distrust government the further it is removed from them. This is their weakness and our strength. To accomplish this we must educate locally, organize locally, and stay involved locally. The only way Washington will ever relinquish its strangle hold on its power, perks, and privileges is when "we the people" at the local level, united with our fellows in their local level, place the power elite in a no-win position.

5— Q. You keep talking about States' Rights as if it would solve all of America's problems. Was it not under States' Rights that slavery and racial discrimination existed?

A. States 'Rights is not a panacea for all of America's problems. It is *THE* bulwark behind which our individual rights can be protected from an abusive federal government. In *The Federalist* No. 51, James Madison, points out under the Constitution Americans live in a "compound republic." As he points out, the new nation exists as a compound governmental unit. The power of government is divided into "two distinct governments," state and federal. Madison assures us that "The different governments will CONTROL EACH OTHER; at the same time that each will be controlled by itself."[179] The Founding Fathers gave us a nation where the states were sovereign; the states delegated certain powers to the Federal government in order said government would act in accordance to the will of the people of the states. The people of each state would organize their society as they deem necessary and proper, while depending upon their agent, the Federal government, to provide for the common defense and maintain a free trade zone among the states of the Union. Remember, the one great reason the patriots of 1776 issued the Declaration of Independence was their fear of an all-powerful big government who would not respond to their desires. The patriots of 1776 viewed the central government in London much like the Confederates of 1861, and many, if not a vast majority of Americans do today: A government that does not respect the interests and desires of "we the people" but tyrannically follows its own desires. As explained by Madison, the "compound" nature of the American government was a defense against the tyranny of the majority. The people of each sovereign state could not be compelled to act against their will by a simple majority because a sovereign entity cannot be compelled to act against its will. Madison clearly warns us about the danger of the tyranny of numbers: "If a majority be united by a common interest, the rights of the minority will be insecure."[180] A purely democratic government can be likened to two wolves and a lamb voting on what to have for

---
179 James Madison, as cited in, 152 *The Federalists Number 51*, George W. Carey and McClellan, 268.
180 Ibid.

supper! Everybody gets a vote but it only takes two to determine if hay or mutton will be served. Under the compound republic system, the lamb has ultimate veto (nullification) or escape (secession) powers at the supper table. This is why we have States' Rights, so "we the people" of a sovereign state will not be eaten by the Federal wolf! It is up to each citizen of each state to organize their state government in such a manner that their rights and liberties are protected from the abuse of the local government. If we say this job should be in the hands of an all-powerful Federal government then we are left with the old dilemma of "Who shall guard the guards?" Do you want the IRS to be the guardian of your interests? In essence the question is who is the best guardian of your rights and liberties, the millionaire professional politicians in the Federal Congress, five unelected and virtually un-removable judges (five is a majority of the Supreme Court) of the Supreme Court, or any number of faceless Federal bureaucrats? Our Founding Fathers feared this type of government, that is why they gave us a compound government where the Federal government could be controlled by "we the people" and not a government where "we the people" are controlled by the Federal government.

6— **Q**. States' Rights are not the shield and sword to defend America; Christianity and our religious beliefs are the real shield and sword. Also, Lincoln was a great Christian president. How can you say such things about a good Christian president?

A. If Lincoln was a great Christian this fact was totally missed by his wife, personal secretary, body guard, and law partner and life-long friend. Lincoln was not a member of any church, never tithed to a church, was never baptized, and did not take communion in a Christian Church. One can Google "Religious affiliations of American Presidents" and you will find only one president that does not have a church affiliation, Abraham Lincoln. But as a fellow Christian, I must agree with you that Christianity is the most important aspect of our national identity.

7— **Q**. All my life I have been told it would be a disaster for America if we ever allowed a Constitutional Convention to be called. What in the world would "they" give us in place of our founding fathers' Constitution?

A. "They" are not the ones calling forth this Constitutional Convention, "they" are not the ones stating why it is being called and "they" are not the ones who will be organized to the point of controlling the outcome of the amendment process. The effort to amend the Constitution to restore *REAL* States' Rights cannot proceed to the point of an actual Constitutional Convention if we are not organized and powerful enough to do what this amendment is suggesting, i.e., putting the genie of Federal supremacy back into its bottle.

Yes, this effort is a very different approach to the problem of how "we the people" can control our agent, the Federal government. Yet look at the past one hundred years of conservative efforts to control the growth and power of the Federal government.[181] Has any effort been successful in controlling the power of the Federal government? Has FDR's big government programs been placed under the control of "we the people"? Has LBJ's Great Society boondoggles such as the War on Poverty, an ongoing project which has been an utter failure if one judges by the level of poverty today as compared to when it was enacted, been recalled? Did electing one of America's greatest conservative presidents, Ronald Reagan, decrease the size and power of the Federal government? No, Reagan only managed to slow down the growth of the Federal government. Look at how much more intrusive and larger the Federal government is today as compared to when we elected Mr. Conservative as our president. Did Newt Gingrich's vaunted 1994 conservative takeover of Congress make America less of a Federal supremacy dictatorship? Yes, conservatives gained a remarkable victory but in the long view of history the Federal government proved it could still grow and exercise more power not less power than before Mr. Gingrich and his associates took control of Congress. Remember, it was *AFTER* Reagan's election and *AFTER* Gingrich's successful takeover of Congress that Alabama was told by the Federal government it could not display the Ten Commandments in its supreme court; Arizona was told by the Federal government it could not enforce the laws on immigration; California was told by the Federal government that the people of California could not define marriage as the union of one man and one woman. Groping and taking nude photographs of Americans (TSA) took place after Reagan and Gingrich's tactical victories. All of this points out why the Ken-

---

181 For more information on the subject of one hundred years of conservative failure, see, James R. Kennedy, *Reclaiming Liberty* (Pelican Publishing Company, Gretna, LA: 2005) 15-43.

nedy Twins believe we are now at that point where something other than just electing good conservatives will be sufficient to solve the problem of an out of control Federal government — what we call the Federal Empire.

One should note unless we are strong enough to get two-thirds of the states to pass our resolution calling for a Constitutional Amendment to restore *REAL* States' Rights, your worry of what "they" will do to us is moot. But if we are strong enough to pass through the legislatures of two-thirds of the states said resolution, don't you think we will be very well placed to control anything which comes out of that process? Also, the whole process of pushing our States' Rights resolution (resolution recognizing the State Right of nullification and secession) will be the greatest educational event for our fellow citizens. They will come away from the process with a clearer view of what actions are and are not right and proper for the Federal government to perform. The death knell of Federal supremacy will be sounded once our fellow citizens have a clear view of the proper relationship between themselves and the Federal government. Once they become aware the Federal government should fear "we the people" and not "we the people" stand in fear of the Federal government, victory for real American liberty is assured.

Once this process has begun, we can then push for a "radical reformation" of the Federal government. If reformation cannot be accomplished, we can then use our power and elect pro-States' Rights members to Congress. Once we have enough members in Congress, we then can use our power at the local level, in Congress, and in the business community to demand Independence for those people in states who desire to live under a Constitution where "we the people" at the local level can control the central government. At this point Southern Independence will become the new political hot potato throughout America.

Summary

We the people can accept our current status as subjects of an illegitimate, all-powerful, supreme federal government or we can organize and begin the movement to allow the people to vote to change our status to that of citizens in a constitutionally limited Republic of Republics.[182]

— James R. Kennedy

---

182 James R. Kennedy and Walter D. Kennedy, *Punished with Poverty: The Suffering South* (Shotwell Publishing Co., Columbia, SC: 2016) 172.

Every book written by the Kennedy Twins has pointed out that real American liberty belongs to all Americans and was the product of Americans in 1776, both the North and the South. This is why we have always asserted that yes indeed, the South was right but the South was right in 1861 because America was right in 1776. The concept that "we the people" at the local level are the ultimate arbitrator of how we are to be governed is a very unique American idea. The clash between the colonies and London, which led to the establishment of these United States, was a conflict between each colony and the central government in London. Americans demanded a central government that could be controlled by "we the people" at the local level and London believed that, within the British Union, it was supreme in all matters of government. London's argument in favor of London's supremacy is the very same argument Lincoln and the Republican Party used to defend their belief in Federal supremacy. Today, when any state law runs counter to that which the Federal government approves, it is the argument of London, Lincoln, and modern liberals and neo-conservatives which props up the notion of Federal supremacy. As the Kennedy Twins pointed out in *The South Was Right!*, "There must be a radical reformation in the current, overgrown, unresponsive, tax-and-spend federal government.... [or] the Southern people ... demand the right of self-determination." This may sound too radical but remember the words of Patrick Henry, "The first thing I have at heart is American liberty, the second thing is American union." Our forefathers viewed liberty as the *sine qua non* (something absolutely indispensable or essential) of American government. Without this essential element of liberty, government or union became not only dangerous but also ultimately tyrannical. The question for Americans in general and Southerners in particular is a simple but a shocking question: Do you agree with Patrick Henry or do you agree with the agents of Federal supremacy? If Federal supremacy is your idea of good government then laugh at what is written and do nothing for surely Federal supremacy will continue to reign in America. But if you agree with Patrick Henry and believe that liberty always trumps government, you now have a challenge. You must get involved in either restoring *REAL* American liberty or the establishment of a nation where those principles of 1776 are not just verbally recognized on July the Fourth but are a real and living part (*sine qua non*) in the daily life of our new government. For as an eminent nineteenth century American patriot, John Randolph of Roanoke, observed, "This is a state of things that cannot last.... [W]e must combine to resist, and that effectually, these encroachments, or that little upon which we now barely subsist will be taken from us."[183]

A few years past, Americans were given the news about the Supreme Court's decisions that the National Health Care was constitutional and at the same time the State of Arizona was forbidden to enforce existing Federal immigration laws. Once again this proves Federal supremacy and not the will of the people is the "law of the land." Even though a majority of Americans do not approve of the nationalization of health care and even though Arizona only passed laws which supported existing Federal immigration law, Federal supremacy trumps the rights and will of "we the people." It is of interest to note that in his minority dissent on the Arizona immigration law, Justice Antonia Scalia noted if Arizona is a sovereign state it has every right to protect its borders. Scalia also noted if the states had known they would not be allowed to protect their borders if they interred the union, they would have never joined the union. In his dissenting opinion, Scalia questioned if the State of Arizona was even sovereign if it could not control its border. Scalia, not unlike the vast majority of Tea Party conservatives, seems to think that in this age states in the Federal Union are sovereign. As the Kennedy Twins of Louisiana have so often pointed out, "state sovereignty died at Appomattox." No Justice Scalia, neither Arizona nor any other state in the union today is sovereign — sovereignty, under the system of Federal supremacy, resides with the Federal government. As Justice Scalia noted, this is not the type of government our founding fathers intended to establish, nor would the Constitution have ever been ratified if they had understood that this type of action by the Federal government would become a reality.

Ask yourself this question: What would Patrick Henry think of a government which would send American military personnel all over the world to defend a foreign nation's borders while refusing to defend its own borders and at the same time denying a state of the union the right to protect its borders? What would Patrick Henry think of a government who forced its citizens to buy a product (healthcare insurance) and take legal action against those citizens

---

183 John Randolph of Roanoke as cited in, Russell Kirk, *John Randolph of Roanoke* (Liberty Press, Indianapolis, ID: 1978) 439.

if they refused to do so? Would Patrick Henry stand up and wave the United States flag, pledge allegiance to the flag, sing *God Bless America*, and otherwise support that government? Remember we are talking about a man who believed liberty was more important than his life — "Give me liberty or give me death." Also note we are talking about a government which has more control over American citizens than the government of King George III ever hoped to exercise. If Patrick Henry was faced with the choice of being a citizen of the current Federal government with its multitude of rules, edicts, regulations, and laws that intrude into virtually every aspect of human endeavor, or a citizen under the government of King George III, which do you think he would choose? As odious as it is to admit, the government of King George III was much less intrusive and demanded many fewer taxes from its citizens than the current Federal government. Again, please remember the words of Patrick Henry: "The first thing I have at heart is American liberty, the second is American union."[184] This message about the true nature of American government as stated by one of our foremost founding fathers must be repeated until Americans in general and Southerners in particular understand what Henry was describing. Henry was describing a Federal government that understood it had only a few delegated powers and those powers must be used for the benefit of the people. He also is informing his fellow Americans that this Federal government was not more important than the liberty of the people. As already stated, the current Federal government, armored in the impervious and unyielding armor of Federal supremacy, is the polar opposite of the type of government handed down to this nation by America's Founding Fathers.

How long will America blindly follow the seductive and deceitful Siren's call for bigger and more intrusive government? If America does not turn a deaf ear to the allure of cradle to grave "free" government security and provision, this once free ship of state will surely crash upon the rocks of tyranny. The song of the Sirens may be sweet to the ear but the result of following that sound is death to the soul of America because the soul of American is (*sine qua non*) liberty. "[W]e must combine to resist, and that effectually, these encroachments, or that little upon which we now barely subsist will be taken from us."[185]

---

184 Patrick Henry, III, 449.
185 Randolph, 439.

Captain Raphael Semmes, CSN

As the terror of their merchant shipping, is it any wonder Yankees would refer to Semmes as a "pirate"? Nevertheless, during WWII the United States Navy deployed Semmes tactics to destroy Japan's merchant fleet. In his post-War memoirs Semmes noted the real issue in the War: "The slavery question was the issue which finally tore them [North and South] asunder, but, ... this question was a mere means, to an end. The end was empire ... a more powerful nation crushing out a weaker [nation]."[186] Semmes closing remarks in his post-War memoirs reflects his belief that the ultimate struggle is not yet completed: "The form of government having been changed by the revolution, *there are still other acts of the drama to be performed.* [emphasis added]."[187]

---

186 Raphael Semmes, *Memoirs of Service Afloat* (1868, The Blue and Grey Press, Secaucus, NJ: 1987), 69.
187 Ibid, 833.

Chapter 9
Consequences of Conquest

Impoverishing the South
*It is not humanity, that influences you in the position that you now occupy before the country.... It is that you may have a majority in the Congress of the United States and convert the government into an engine of Northern aggrandizement. It is that your section may grow in power and prosperity upon **treasures unjustly taken from the South**. [emphasis added].*[188]
— Jefferson Davis

It is not uncommon to hear a well pacified Southerner (one who has imbibed too deeply in the foul and polluted waters of modern-day political correctness) say, "We are better off because the South lost the War." Only if one segregates and refuses to consider the lot of the average post-War Southerner can this most offensive statement be said to be true. Most Americans fully accept the false assumption that poverty has always been the lot of the common Southerner. Yet, this assumption falls apart when considered under the light of historical truth.

How we define wealth and poverty is not something that is written in stone for the entire world to see. In a society of dollar worshipers, poverty would be accounted as the absence of a large accumulation of money. In a society which values the spiritual over the material, the absence of leisure time spent with family and friends would make an individual poverty ridden. In both societies money and leisure time is important but the status each holds on members of their society will be inverted. Therefore, what looks like poverty or wealth in one society is very different in the other society. As pointed out in Punished with Poverty: The Suffering South, Northern society and Southern society held not just opposite views about money and leisure but they held antagonistic views of these matters.[189] Noted Southern historian, Dr. Grady McWhiney points out Northerners and Southerners held values which were more than just "different, they

---

[188] Jefferson Davis, as cited by Simkins, Francis Butler, *A History of the South* (Alfred A. Knopf, NY: 1959) 190.
[189] Kennedy, James R. and Kennedy, Walter D., *Punished with Poverty: The Suffering South* (Shotwell Publishing, Columbia, SC: 2016) 21-24.

were antagonistic."[190] As noted in the above citation, Jefferson Davis understood that the North's vaunted anti-slavery/anti-South movement was not based upon altruism or "humanity" but upon the desire of the industrial, commercial, and financial elites of the North to gain unlimited control and maintain that control of the government in Washington. This cabal of moneyed elites was attempting to form a close relationship between their interests and a powerful Federal government. With the Federal government under their control, all manner of special deals could be made to increase their profits at the expense of Southerners and Northerners who were not a part of their cabal, i.e., Northern Democrats. Lincoln and the Republican Party brought to Washington and the Federal government the first crony capitalists which would from that day forward plague the nation. These crony capitalists were the antecedents of today's "to big to fail" plutocrats who dominate the donor class of each political party and finance the campaigns of both major political parties.

Speaking of these early Yankee crony capitalists, historian Francis B. Simkins states that, "Northern capitalism was eagerly imperialistic."[191] Additionally Simkins notes that these Northerners were "creating a nation of dollar-worshipers…who regarded themselves as the lords of creation. They tore down in order that they might rebuild. To tear down the civilization that lay to their south was but a chapter in their history."[192] When Northerners looked to the South, they saw a society where people were not driven to work just to accumulate money. From their "dollar-worshiping" world-view they interpreted the leisure-oriented society of Dixie as a society of slothful and lazy people. To Northern minds these people needed to be remade into the image of hard working and industrious Yankees. This evangelical zeal of the dollar-worshipers was interpreted by Southerners as an arrogant, pushy, and "know it all" Yankee fanaticism. Southerners, who worked fewer hours each year than Yankees, were responsible for over two-thirds of the nation's exports.[193] In addition to this, 75 percent of the revenues for running the Federal government were collected, via tariffs, in Southern ports. In other words, most of the money to run the Federal government was being provided by Southerners and most

---

190 Grady McWhiney, *Cracker Culture: Celtic Ways in the Old South* (University of Alabama Press, Tuscaloosa, AL: 1988), 245.
191 Simkins, 191.
192 Ibid.
193 Ibid, 130.

of this money was being spent on "internal improvement" projects in the North.[194] The small farmers and ranchers of the South, which made up the largest portion of non-plantation owners, each year produced livestock and grain products that equaled the total output of all plantation crops.[195] This production and its leisurely lifestyle were made possible by the open range herding of swine, cattle and other farm animals. According to McWhiney, "the open range method of herding and the leisure ethic were integral parts of…antebellum southern culture."[196] From colonial times through the antebellum era, this open range herding, plantations, and limited industrial and commercial activity in the South produced the wealthiest section of the United States.[197] In a study of colonial and antebellum income, investigators from the University of California, University of Wisconsin, and Harvard University noted that Southerners had average incomes well "above those of New England."[198] This increased wealth and income for Southerners did not reside only in large plantation families but "even average free labor earnings were higher in the South."[199] The advantages of living in a society where incomes were higher than in the North and where leisure time to be spent with family and friends was an everyday experience, was something Southerners did not feel the need to change. This "need to change" was especially odious when it was being demanded by what was perceived as pushy, self-righteous, evangelizing dollar-worshiping Yankees.

Indeed, the loss of the War for Southern Independence impoverished the South. Unfortunately, the only Southern "cost" of this war that most Northern observers ever discuss is the monetary loss. The sudden loss of wealth was and is to this day very important to the life of Southerners. But there were other losses that adversely impacted the South such as cultural losses, infection of the South with New England-style racism, and loss of civil liberties.

The Southern financial and human losses incurred during the War have been estimated by various students of the War. In his book,

---

194 Kennedy and Kennedy, *Punished with Poverty: The Suffering South*, 38.
195 Ibid., 22.
196 McWhiney, 62.
197 Lindert, Peter H., (University of California Davis) and Williamson, Jeffery G., (Harvard University and the University of Wisconsin), *American Income 1774-1860*, 14, http://emi.berkeley.edu~/webfac/cromer/e211_f12Lindert Williamson.pdf (Accessed 3/21/2019).
198 Ibid.
199 Ibid.

It Wasn't About Slavery, historian Dr. Sandy Mitcham notes the following: one out of four young men of the South die as a result of the War; one out of four remaining young men suffered debilitating wounds as a result of the War; 60 percent of Southern capital investments were lost; the property value of the South in 1870 (five years after the defeat of the Confederate States of America) as compared to property value in 1860 was down 41 percent if one excludes slave property and down 63 percent if one includes investment in slaves. At the same time the North's property value increased 100 percent![200] As explained in *Yankee Empire: Aggressive Abroad and Despotic at Home,* more Southern men died fighting the Yankee invader than died in all modern wars conducted by the United States.[201] Consider this fact, more Southern men died at the hands of the Yankee invader of the South than were killed by Germans in two world wars, Japanese in the Pacific War, North Koreans in the Korean War, Vietnamese in the Vietnam War, and Muslims in the War on Terror all combined. As shocking as these statistics are it must also be noted that none of the just mentioned enemies of the USA ever burned even ONE Southern city, raped one Southerner woman, starved and brutalized old men, women, and children to the point of death, or imposed a government upon the defeated and starving people in total disregard of the free and unfettered consent of the governed.

If the preceding facts were the only negative consequences of the defeat of the Confederate States of America this alone would be enough to damn the Yankee Empire as an imperialist tyranny, but there is more. Another act of impoverishment committed by the subjugator of the South was the instigation of Southern cultural genocide. The word "culture" has its roots in the Latin "*cultus*," meaning to cultivate, grow, reverence, or worship. The attack upon Southern culture is an attack upon those elements in society that maintain a proper reverence for those who helped shape our lives and made our society more civilized. This attack is more than just an attempt to remove Confederate monuments, flags, and heroes. These are merely the obvious symbols of a deeper culture which stands in the way of a hedonistic money-worshiping society. As the well-respected Southern scholar, Richard Weaver, noted, it is the South that stands

---

200 Sandy Mitcham, p 214 publication date, 2019.
201 James R. Kennedy and Walter D. Kennedy, *Yankee Empire: Aggressive Abroad and Despotic at Home* (Columbia, SC, Shotwell Publishing Co., 2018)

alone as the "last non-materialist civilization in the Western World."[202] This "non-materialist civilization" has deep roots in the South which extend all the way back to Colonial America. It was and still is, even after the defeat of the Confederate States of America, a culture which places high value upon chivalry, honor, and a "reverence for symbolism, whose existence haunts the nation."[203] The South's remaining attachment to the Ole South's code of chivalry is demonstrated in its willingness to donate from its meager purse the highest per capita donations to charity in America. While living in the most poverty-ridden section of the United States, Southerners give more freely of their time and money to assist other people. In contrast to the nation's highest charitable giving by Southerners, the North holds the record for the lowest charitable giving in the nation. This is just one example of the innate difference between these two societies: one founded upon chivalry and leisure and the other based upon the worship of the "Almighty Dollar." Once again it must be pointed out that leisure does not mean "lazy." True leisure time is that time spent with family and friends to assist them in some needed task (not to gain money from said task) or to strengthen the bonds of kinship and friendship — the building blocks of "community." In the Old South and in much of the present South, community begins to form with the gathering of people around church, family, and friends. Religious faith, while not demanded for community membership, is respected and embraced even if one is not an active member of a church group. Thus, we see in a recent study of America's church attendance, it is the South that leads the nation in regular church attendance while the North has the lowest rates of church attendance.[204]

The stark difference between the North and the South as it relates to church attendance and charity exposes why the two sections are usually seen on opposite side of political battles. When votes are cast in the Federal Congress on issues such as voluntary prayer in school, public display of Christian symbols, abortion, illegal immigration, and gun control; the majority of Southern delegates vote one way while the majority of Northern delegates vote the opposite way.[205] On these "social issue" votes the vast majority of the time the South and

---

202 Richard W. Weaver, *The Southern Tradition At Bay* (Arlington House, New Rochelle, NY: 1968) 391.
203 Ibid.
204 Kennedy and Kennedy, *Punished with Poverty*, 104 F,H.
205 Kennedy and Kennedy, *Was Jefferson Davis Right?* (Pelican Publishing Co., Gretna, LA: 1998), 274.

its cultural heritage are the losers. While debating the adoption of the Constitution in 1787, Patrick Henry warned the South about the danger of being in a government where Northern control of Congress would be used to force the South to accept domination from the North. Henry warned that as soon as the South became a minority in the Federal government the North would impose taxes and controls on commerce beneficial to the North but detrimental to the South. He closed his remarks about Northern domination of the South with these words: "Sir, this is a picture so horrid, so dreadful, that I need no longer dwell upon it."[206]

The poverty of poor race relations in the South in particular and in the North in general is a "gift" from America's original racists in New England. The concept of New England being the original racist society in America is explained by New Englander, Joan Pope Melish.[207] Of course this idea of New England racism runs counter to "accepted" American history — history as told and enforced by the victory of the War to Prevent Southern Independence! This concept of New England and Northern racism during the Antebellum Era is supported by not only Northerners but also foreign visitors to the United States. James S. Buckingham a British author, journalist, and traveler upon visiting the United States (1837-40), made this observation on race relations in the United States: "The prejudice of race in not nearly so strong in the South as in the North."[208] During this same time a Frenchman, Alex de Tocqueville, made a similar observation: "The prejudice of the race appears to be stronger in the States which have abolished slavery [the North], than in those where it still exists" [the South].[209] These are but a representative sample of numerous observers of American society as it existed at that time who report on the unique race-relationship in America. By no means do these authors assert that slaves were happy with slavery but it does point out that they were not enemies of those people in the South with whom they enjoyed a close relationship. After the defeat of the South, General Carl Schurz, a Union Officer, made a survey of conditions in the South. One of the more shocking (shocking to him and many Northerners) facts that he discovered was the close relation between

---

206 Patrick Henry: *Life, Correspondence and Speeches*, III, 520.
207 Joan P. Melish, *Disowning Slavery: Gradual Emancipation and Race in New England 1780-1860* (Cornell University Press, Ithaca, London: 1998) 221-37.
208 James S. Buckingham, *The Slave States of America* (Negro University Press, NY: 1968) II, 112.
209 Alexis de Tocqueville, *Democracy in America* (1838, NY: 1945) I, 339.

the races in the South. Schurz noted that in the South, "Centuries of slavery have not been sufficient to make them [former slaves] the enemies of the white man."[210] This close relationship was damaged almost to the point of being beyond repair due to the greed and vindictiveness of the conquering Yankee.

The loss of real American freedom is the forth form of poverty inflicted upon the South after its defeat — and that loss weighs heavily on all Americans, not just Southerners. Most Americans brag about being "citizens of a free country." They become incredulous when told that they are not a "free people." They often will reply that they are the freest people in the world today. That statement may be true, "mores the pity!" The Declaration of Independence is the only true yardstick to measure real American Freedom. This document announced to the world that from that day forward the only way to judge a free government was by ascertaining does it exist by the "consent of the governed"? This document clearly states that free people have the right to sit in judgment of their government and if that government is found wanting, they, the people, had not only the right but the duty to "alter or abolish" that government. In simple modern-day terms, our founding fathers understood that "If you can't leave, you are not free." With the defeat of the South, government in the United States nullified the Declaration of Independence and from that day to this, Americans are held captive by their big, all-powerful, indivisible, government.

1— Q. How can you say that he South was robbed of its wealth when everyone knows that it has always been the land of a few super rich slaveholders and the rest just poor white trash?

A. According to research done by a Nobel Prize-winning economist Southerners had the fourth highest income in the world by 1860, ahead of every European country except Great Britain. As a matter of fact the richest section of the United States at that time was the Southwestern section of the US[211] A study of the economic conditions of the South from colonial through antebellum times by University of California-Davis and Harvard University demonstrated that "Even average free labor earnings were higher in the South"[212] than in the

---

210 Carl Schultz, *Report of Carl Schurz, A Just and Lasting Peace* (Signet Classics, NY: 2013) 140.
211 Robert W. Fogel and Stanley L. Engerman, *Time on the Cross* (Little, Brown, and Co., Boston: 1974) 248-50.
212 Lindert and Williamson.

North. Yes, the highest number of millionaires per capita lived south of the Ohio River during the antebellum era but wealth in dollars existed even among the non-slaveholding population of the South. It was the wealth of the South which paid almost three-quarters of the taxes (tariffs) which financed the Federal government from approximately 1815 until 1860. The dire consequences of losing this stable and lucrative flow of cash into the treasury of the United States and more importantly the loss of Southern markets to European merchants was the reason the Republican Party was willing to wage war upon the Confederate States of America.

2— Q. Even if the South had a lot of rich people before the War, didn't they get their wealth by abusing slaves in the cotton fields of the South?

A. Although cotton was a major source of wealth in the South, it was not the largest source of wealth. As a matter of fact the income created by livestock production of the non-plantation-owning class of Southerners surpassed the wealth created by cotton, sugar, rice, and tobacco products combined in the late antebellum South. But addressing your notion that slaves were routinely abused by their masters in the South, that too, is a cherished myth of those who hate the South. When the United States was a mere 25 years old, slavery had existed in the New World (Western Hemisphere) for more than 300 years. At that time slavery had existed in the United States for around 175 years. During this time the conditions in the non-United States areas of the New World, slavery was so harsh that slaves had to be replaced because of deaths and injuries. Yet, at the same time slaves in the United States, mostly in the Southern States, were living longer and reproducing at a rate far in excess to their death rate. As the Nobel Prize winning economists Robert W. Fogel and Stanley L. Engerman noted, the food, housing, and shelter for slaves was high by both American and European standards. The life expectancy for slaves in the South was higher than the life expectancy of industrial workers in New York, Boston, Philadelphia, and Manchester, England.[213] Dr. Grady McWhiney states the average slave worked around 1,470[214] hours per year and Fogel/Engerman give the hours worked by slaves at 2,160[215] per year. The higher number represents what the

---

213 Fogel and Engerman, 123-24.
214 McWhiney, 47.
215 Fogel and Engerman, 208.

average industrial worker in modern America works. The average worker today works five days a week, has sick time, holidays, and vacation time — just like the slaves in the South. It's hard to make the argument these slaves were being "worked to death" any more than modern industrial workers are being "worked to death."

3— Q. Even if there was a great loss of Southern wealth because of the South's defeat in the Civil War, don't you think it was worth it in order to end slavery?

A. The so-called *Civil War* did not end slavery, it merely morphed it or changed it into a different form of slavery, sharecropping. If at the end of the War for Southern Independence the North had provided land, which it held in abundance, to the newly freed slaves and provided education and civil rights to these new landowners, that would have been a great benefit to both the nation and the freed slaves. Also, if the United States had ended slavery like the British had done by compensating the slaveholders, there would have been money enough for owners to hire and pay free workers on their plantations. None of this was done. The South suffered total destruction of its economy, its fields were untended, most of the valuables, gold, silver, libraries, churches, homes, and public property were destroyed, stolen, or looted by the invader. Under these conditions no one in the South, especially the newly freed slaves, had a chance to build a brighter future. As one Southerner noted after the War the most they could do was just stay alive. To add insult to injury, Republicans imposed the horror of Reconstruction upon the South and passed tax schemes which plundered the remaining wealth of the South and for the advantage of Republican politicians set black and white Southerners at war among themselves. None of these measures aided anyone in the South, black or white, but it surely advanced the cause of the conquering Yankee.

4— Q. The South is booming today, how can you complain about poverty when the South is in a boom economy?

A. Booming economy? The ten states with the lowest per capita income are all in the South, whereas the ten states with the highest income are in the North — now where is your so-called booming Southern economy? A 2016 survey reveals the five states where children are living in homes with the lowest household income are in the

South and the five states where children are living in homes with the highest household income are in the North. A 2014 study of median household income in the United States shows that only two Southern States have incomes above the median US household income, Maryland and Virginia. These two states' median household income is artificially inflated due to a vast influx of "foreign," that is, non-Southern, residents who work and live in counties around the Empire's capital in Washington. Remove those counties from Maryland and Virginia and those states too will fall near or below the national US median household income. The truth is that a child born south of the Mason Dixon Line will have a much lower lifetime income than one born north of the Mason Dixon Line. This economic fact is directly due to the South being forced to live in this "one nation indivisible."

5— Q. We Americans are all free members of "one nation indivisible," why do you insist on trying to divide Americans into groups?

A. Please point to where in the Constitution this nation is declared to be "one nation indivisible." Or let's look at the Articles of Confederation, the first form of government of these United States; or perhaps the Declaration of Independence and see if we can find any evidence of the United States being founded upon the idea of being "one nation indivisible." Yes, the preamble of the Constitution does state, "We the people" but it does not read, "We the people are one people" nor does it proclaim, "We the people of 'one nation indivisible.'" The preamble of a document cannot be used to change the meaning of any article of that document. Therefore, we must look to the document, in this case the Constitution, to find what type of nation or union it is creating. In Article I Section I of the Constitution it clearly states "all powers herein granted," which tells us the union or nation being created has a creator, that is, a "grantor" of powers. To answer the question of who is "granting" this power one only has to look at Article VII which clearly points out it is the states who are authorizing and therefore granting said powers to the newly created Federal government. Nine states acting in their sovereign capacity empowered the Federal government thereby creating a FEDERAL republic. This "federal" republic is made up of a federation of sovereign states, after all, they had the authority to grant power to their agent so it cannot be denied that they (the states) existed before the union or nation was formed. To further protect their sovereignty, these states conditionally ratified this Constitution by stating they had the right to recall any power they had delegated to the new government and they demanded a Bill of Rights with two amendments (9th and 10th) which announced to the world that any power not delegated to the Federal government remained with the people of the states. These measures clearly void any argument that the United States was created as "one nation indivisible." But how about your argument about dividing Americans into groups. Again, nowhere in the Constitution is there a positive affirmation that the Federal government, aka the Union, would be indivisible, that is, non-divided. On the contrary, the Declaration of Independence clearly voids that notion by stating unequivocally that the people have an unalienable right and duty to "alter or abolish" any government which did not suit the needs of the people. These United States were not created as "one nation indivisible" nor is it "divisive" to proclaim the truth about American history.

6— Q. Since most Americans, North or South, believe in God, how can it be maintained there is a great difference in the religious values of the North and the South?

A. It's not a question of do you believe in God or not but rather what type of god do you believe in. A recent Gallup poll on regular church attendance demonstrated this deep religious divide between the United States and the Confederate States. The Gallup Poll identified thirteen states with the highest regular church attendance; all but one state was a Southern State (Utah being the only non-Southern State making the list). On the flip side of the issue of the thirteen states with the lowest rates of regular church attendance all were Northern states with New England leading the pack and states of the West Coast states rounding out the thirteen. This difference is not just a one-time oddity but is reflected in how each section votes on social issues such as public prayer, display of religious symbols such as the Cross and the Ten Commandments, abortion, and traditional marriage. The sad fact is that the religious South will vote one way on most of these issues only to be outvoted by its liberal Northern nemesis. Southern culture, which is based upon a Biblical worldview, is given a sharp blow to the head while the secular humanist North goes marching on — "glory glory hallelujah!"

7— Q. The First Amendment is an American safeguard on the exercise of religion, isn't this enough to protect the religious values held by Southerners?

A. No, if the Ninth and Tenth Amendments are not enough to protect the reserved rights of the states from federal abuse, why should we have overwhelming faith in the protection offered by the First Amendment? The problem is that neither the Ninth, Tenth, nor the First Amendments are self-enforcing. A power superior to parchment must be available to command respect for what is written upon the parchment document or its limits will never be respected. If the Federal government is infringing upon any of these Amendments, who do we call upon for redress? The Supreme Court of the United States cannot be an impartial judge because it is part of the Federal government. As Thomas Jefferson and James Madison pointed out in the Kentucky and Virginia Resolves of '98, the only real judge of the actions of the Federal government resides with the people of the sovereign state. "We the people" of the sovereign states created the Federal government as our agent, not as an agent to sit in judgment of us or the document we drew up to create that government.

8— Q. Even if there is a big difference in the culture between the North and South, what difference does that matter?

A. If you are a member of the majority culture it matters very little because your viewpoint will always win in a democratic vote. On the other hand, if you are a member of the minority culture you can only sit back and watch the values you hold dear slowly disappear as your children are indoctrinated with the ideas of the majority culture. A good example of this is the Irish during their long domination by the British Empire. The dominate culture was the English while the Irish were looked upon as an inferior culture. As such the Irish became second class citizens of not only the British Empire but also in their Irish homeland. Under pressure the British Empire finally allowed the Irish to elect members to the British Parliament. What good did this do the Irish? Very little! Every time an Irish issue was brought up in the Empire's Parliament, the Irish got voted down. While doing little good for the Irish this deception worked wonders in pacifying the Irish people who were being used by the British Empire, after all, you can vote and elect Irish members to the Empire's Parliament — you now have a voice in your government. But what good is the voice of the minority when the majority is hell-bent on taking advantage of the minority? This is the very reason Patrick Henry opposed the adoption of the Constitution. Henry feared that as the minority in the new government the South would become the Milch (milk) Cow of the Union.

9— Q. How can you say racism is something injected into the South by Yankees?

A. During the antebellum era, European (British and French) and Northern authors and journalists all went on record stating the sense of racial prejudice and bigotry was much stronger in the North than the South. In 1998 a New Englander, Joanne P. Melish wrote a book which was very critical of New England's role in promoting the African slave-trade, slavery in New England, and racism. Melish was simply following in the steps of other notable Northerners such as Leon P. Litwack, *North of Slavery: The Negro in the Free States, 1790-1860*; Lorenzo J. Green, *The Negro in Colonial New England*; and Edgar J. McManus, *Black Bondage in the North*. After the War Yankee General Carl Schurz noted that even after 300 years of slavery the black and white people in the South were not enemies.[216] To keep the South under its control, the Republican Party embarked on a campaign to divide the Southern population into warring camps. After 300 years of slavery old friends were taught to fear and hate each other which resulted in the horrors of Reconstruction. After the Republican Party no longer needed the black vote in the South (it had gained good white voters in the West, which had been purged of the Native American residents and Asian voters) they abandoned African Americans in the South. At this point the Democrats gained control of the South and using the old fear of the "Black voter" and Reconstruction, instituted laws that openly discriminated against African Americans. For the following 100 years the Democrats could count on a "Solid South" to help keep the National Democrat Party in power. Both the Republicans and Democrats used and abused Southerners, black and white for their own selfish reason. But always remember the use of racial hate between the races in the South is not something that was a natural relationship. Southern racial animosity is an unnatural racial relationship created by outsiders for the purpose of keeping the South under the control of the newly created Federal, i.e., Yankee Empire.

10— Q. It's not hard to understand why racism existed in the South. African Americans naturally hated those who misused and abused them for hundreds of years, so why not admit how racist Southern society was and is?

---

216 Carl Schurz, as cited in Kennedy and Kennedy, *Punished with Poverty: The Suffering South*, 28.

The Confederate Myth-Buster

A. African-American slaves never loved slavery but they never hated their white neighbors and friends. When most people think of slavery they visualize the large, impersonal plantations which were common in the Caribbean Islands or in South America. Most of these plantations were so large that few if any of the slaves ever had many dealings with their masters. It is easy to hate someone you never see. But in the South almost half of the slaves lived with or next to their master and his family. In many such cases one white family lived with one black family for generations. Most of the plantations of the South were small in comparison to those in the Caribbean Islands and South America. In such situations it is easy to understand how a close relationship would exist. Also, the laid back, leisure-oriented society in the South lends itself to promoting activities such as hunting, fishing, and festivals which ameliorate some of the harsh conditions of slavery. This is one of the main reasons even with the announcement of Lincoln's Emancipation Proclamation there was no slave uprising in the South. This in no ways means slaves enjoyed slavery but they did not hate white people to the point of doing them harm. Even Yankee General Schurz noted this when just after the defeat of the South he stated: "Centuries of slavery have not been sufficient to make them the enemies of the white man."[217]

11— Q. With all the Jim Crow, that is, racists, laws enacted by Southern States, how can you say that the South is not responsible for racial discrimination?

A. As I have pointed out already, many Europeans and Northerners testified there was less racial bigotry in Southern society than in Northern society. Racial discrimination occurred, then and now, in every part of the world, not just in the South. Even though races in the South seemed to "get along" better than in the North that does not mean that discrimination did not happen down South — slavery is the ultimate form discrimination. What I have said is that it was not the South, or more correctly, the Confederate States of America, which was responsible for the introduction of segregation, that is, Jim Crow laws that discriminate against people based upon skin color in America. Here are the facts about segregation (Jim Crow) laws in the United States. It was the United States Supreme Court that made discrimination by race (segregation) the law-of-the-land with its 1896

---

[217] Ibid.

Plessy v. Ferguson decision.[218] In this case the Supreme Court in an eight to one majority (wasn't even close) established racial discrimination as the law-of-the-land. The court ruled that if a person was 7/8 Caucasian and 1/8 African blood, that person would be legally classified as African. The court further ruled laws that discriminate against people by race were Constitutional as long as "separate but equal" accommodations were provided. The majority opinion for this case was written by a Federal Judge from Michigan, citing an 1849 Massachusetts law that segregated (Jim Crow) Black and White school children[219] — please note here that I said Michigan and Massachusetts NOT Mississippi or Missouri! There was only one Southerner on the United States Supreme Court at this time and he was the only judge to vote against the establishment of segregation (racial discrimination) in the United States. The concept of discrimination based upon race was further enhanced by the Supreme Court in subsequent court cases such as *Cumming v. County Board of Education*, and *Berea College v. Kentucky*. In these cases the Federal Supreme Court (again, I must point out this is not being done by a Southern State Court or the Supreme Court of the Confederate States of America) upheld laws to prevent racial mixing in private schools. In defending its decision, the court often pointed out the schools in Washington, D.C., had been segregated by the action of the Federal government itself.[220] This is why I insist on saying (of course with a little hyperbole) that the South is not responsible for laws which discriminate against people based upon skin color. The truth is that all Americans are equally culpable in this matter, yet it seems to be the South who is daily tarred and feathered because of Jim Crow laws.

12— Q. You say that there were many African-Americans who fought for the South during the Civil War. Isn't it true that if they did fight for the South, they were made to do so because they were slaves?

A. Nathan Bedford Forrest, the most maligned Confederate officer of the War, provides us with proof beyond refutation that the premise of your question is incorrect. Forrest, a wealthy slaveholder, took as many as forty-three slaves with him to the War. He made a deal with his slaves, if they fought and the South won the War, he

---

218 Forrest McDonald, *A Constitutional History of the United States* (Robert E. Krieger Publishing Company, Malabar, FL: 1986) 153.
219 Ibid.
220 Ibid.

would free them, if the South lost the war they would be free anyway. These men stood with Forrest, many fighting alongside of Forrest's white troops. Of the forty-three he took with him only one deserted. Speaking about these men's courage and devotion, Forrest noted, "Those boys stuck with me.... Better Confederates never lived."[221] After three years of war, Forrest realized the South was unlikely to be able to maintain its independence and therefore he freed all his slaves. Once freed, these men stayed in the Confederate Army until the end of the War. At the end of the War, twenty of these former slaves returned with Forrest to his home and remained in his service for several years.[222] If Forrest is believed, these hard-fighting Confederate soldiers that Forrest described as "Better Confederates never lived" were not wimpy spineless men that could be intimidated into fighting for something they did not believe in. There is a Confederate Memorial in Jackson, Mississippi, that stands there today because of a speech given by an African American Representative from Washington County, Mississippi. In his speech before the Mississippi Legislature, Rep. John Harris, stated, "I too, wore the gray, the same color my master wore…if that war had gone on till now I would have been there yet."[223] Rep. Harris praised the valor of his fellow Confederates and insisted funds be found to erect this monument. Rep. Harris and all other African-American Mississippi legislators voted to erect this monument to the Confederate Soldiers. Does this sound like men who were being forced to fight for the Confederacy and some twenty-five years later vote to erect a memorial to those soldiers?

13— Q. Your statement that the Civil War "enslaved free men rather than freeing enslaved men" sounds like a bad case of "sour grapes." How can freeing the slaves cause the enslavement of men?

A. Let's review what I said earlier about the war not ending slavery. Before the War there were 4.5 million slaves working the fields of the South. After "freedom" a new system of labor was instituted often referred to as "sharecropping." Sharecropping or tenant farming was a system of debt peonage in which the "field hands" were tied via debts to the owner of the land. The tenant farmer had to provide his food,

---

[221] Nathan B. Forrest, as cited in, Samuel W. Mitcham, *Bust Hell Wide Open: The life of Nathan Bedford Forrest* (Regnery Publishing, Washington, D.C.: 2016) 73.
[222] Ibid.
[223] John Harris, 176 *Daily Clarion-Ledger*, as cited in, Kennedy and Kennedy, *The South Was Right!*, 108.

clothing, medical care and care of his sick or injured family. This system was just another system of slavery using debt accumulation to hold the tenant to the master's farm as securely and chattel slavery. As already noted, before the War the South was a very wealth society exporting food, cotton, sugar, tobacco, rice and other commodities. During this time the slave population of the South was provided with a larger and more diverse food source than most industrial workers of the North. According to one study the dietary intake for slaves "actually exceeded" that of the average population of America in 1964.[224] Franklin Roosevelt's Secretary of Agriculture noted in 1933 the "extremely low standard of living"[225] that existed in the South, especially among sharecroppers.[226] Before the War malnutrition was virtually unheard of in the South but after the war and "freeing" of the slaves, all types of diseases associated with poor diet plagued Southerners. One such disease that haunted the South was pellagra, a disease caused by a dietary deficiency of protein. Before the war the Southern farmers and ranchers produced livestock which was valued at more than all the crops produced by large plantations. After the War, they could not feed themselves. What is surprising to many non-Southerners is more than 60 percent of the sharecropper slaves were white[227]—people who before the War were living a life of plenty. After "freeing the slaves" we now see a people, white as well as black, living in rank poverty, suffering from malnutrition, living in a government forced upon them at the point of a bloody bayonet (there goes the American principle of legitimate government being one of the "consent of the governed") and you don't understand how I can say Lincoln and the North "did not free enslaved men but rather enslaved free men."

14— Q. The concept of States' Rights you advocate was used to prevent men like Martin Luther King from ending racial discrimination. Why should anyone, especially a minority citizen, agree with your concept of returning States' Rights to America's government?

A. One hundred and twenty-six years before Martin Luther King was born, St. George Tucker, a founding father of this nation was speaking out against not only slavery but also against laws which

---

224 Fogel and Engerman, 115.
225 Henry A. Wallace, as cited in, *Kennedy and Kennedy, Punished with Poverty*, 95.
226 Ibid.
227 Clark & Kirwan, *The South Since Appomattox* (Oxford University Press, NY: 1967) 205.

discriminate against free people of color. Tucker was a Southerner from Virginia and a strong advocate of real States' Rights. In his 1803 essay on slavery, he identified three forms of slavery: domestic slavery, the ownership of one individual including his labor by another individual, civil slavery, the polar opposite of civil liberty or civil rights, and political slavery, the condition where the citizens of a nation cannot "alter or abolish" a government that has ceased to be a desirable government. Civil slavery (as in racial discrimination) is the infringement of those rights each individual hold as a grant from the Creator. When a government prohibits or infringes upon the free exercise of an individual's civil rights, government is acting in such a manner as to make slaves of its citizens. In Tucker's view of States' Rights, which included the right of a sovereign state to secede from the Federal union, people at the local level, that is, the state level had a secure defense against an abusive federal government. Tucker understood the real reason Americans need to understand and embrace real States' Rights. If a people create a government powerful enough to defend the nation from foreign invaders and provide needed services, how can the people have confidence that those powers will not be turned against the people who created the government? This is not a new problem when dealing with government or personal concerns. Almost two thousand years ago the Roman poet, Juvenal, made these words famous: "*Quis custodiet ipsos custodes?*" (Who shall guard the guards themselves?). How do we the people of this republic have any assurance that the "guards," that is, elected officials and government workers, are acting for our benefit and not acting for the benefit of themselves or an outside group? Real States' Rights is the answer! Using the power reserved to the states and not delegated to the central government, the people of the states, one or any number collectively, can nullify any unconstitutional law or act of the central government. If that fails to reverse the growth of big government, the people of the state or states can withdraw their consent to be governed and form a new government — just like it is stated in the Declaration of Independence. States' Rights do not attack civil rights nor is it designed to be a defense of civil rights. States' Rights are designed to defend the civil right and/or civil liberties of the people of sovereign states from an abusive federal government. It is the job of "we the people" of each state to ensure that no laws are passed that establish civil slavery in the state in which we reside.

15— Q. The Constitution states that it is creating a "more perfect" union. How can breaking this more perfect union apart promote civil liberties?

A. Hitler's concept of a "more perfect" government was one which would last 1,000 years and whose authority could not be questioned. The first question to answer here is, "What is your definition of a more perfect union."? According to Lincoln, a more perfect union was one in which the Federal government's will was beyond question and whose life would be everlasting. Patrick Henry noted liberty always trumps union, that is, government.[228] The Declaration of Independence speaks in no uncertain language about the right and duty of free men to "alter or abolish" any government that no longer meets the needs and desires of the people. If the patriots of 1776 had embraced your concept of not breaking a union someone had declared to be "more perfect," we would all be subjects of the British Crown today. For those who place liberty above government, a "more perfect union" is one that the people respect while the government respects the peoples' right to alter or abolish it if it strays from its founding principles. Always remember that in a truly free society, liberty always trumps government.

16— Q. If we don't have a strong Federal government, who will guard and protect the civil rights of our citizens?

A. John Locke, a very famous scholar and political theorist whose writings our founding fathers consulted often in the early days of this republic, stated, "Men can never be secure from Tyranny, if there be no means to escape it."[229] In Locke's book, chapter XIX which is titled, 'Of the Dissolution of Government,' Locke makes it clear that man's freedom and liberty is of greater importance than government. Notice that in the Declaration of Independence America's founding fathers stress the same principle when they say that the only legitimate government is one that is based upon the "consent of the governed." They go further and proclaim that it is the right and duty of free men to "alter or abolish" any government that does not meet their concept of a good government. The great American patriot, Patrick Henry,

---

228 William W. Henry, ed., *Patrick Henry: Life, Correspondence and Speeches*, (1891, Sprinkle Publications, Harrisonburg, VA: 1993) III, 449.
229 John Locke, *Two Treatises of Government* (1698, The Classics of Liberty Library, NY: 1992) 336

offers us an insight into where our true loyalty should reside when he said, "The first thing I have at heart is American liberty, the second is American union."[230] As has been discussed (see answer for question number 14) the old conundrum of "Who shall guard the guards themselves?" is something every society has struggle with for ages. Nothing can be more abusive to the rights of people, including the right to life, than a government which cannot be held accountable to its citizens. Consider the lives lost in the twentieth century as a result of numerous big all-powerful indivisible governments. Hitler killed his millions but was out done by Stalin. Both Hitler and Stalin were surpassed in millions of people killed by Mao Zedong in China. These are but three examples of tyrants too numerous to count who have plagued the world because of the power of an uncontrollable big government. Understanding the dangers of big government, is it any wonder many people embrace the notion "That which governs less, governs best"? Even those of us who follow this logic understand that even a small government can become abusive but it is easier to influence and deal with an abusive small government than an abusive big government. Locke was right!

Summary

The preceding questions and answers demonstrate there are serious and long-lasting consequences for Americans in general and Southerners in particular resulting from the South's defeat in the War for Southern Independence. Today the average American worker will work four to five months in order to earn enough money to pay his family's taxes. America's founding fathers were enraged by the application of a small tax on tea by the British Parliament; what would they think about modern Americans' lack of response to current heavy taxation? Before Abraham Lincoln there was no such thing as the IRS or an income tax. Before the invasion, conquest, and occupation of the Confederate States of America, Americans were safe from Federal interference in their mail, papers, and private business. Today all Americans are subject to Federal rules and regulations which impact every aspect of their lives from conception to burial. Before the South was reduced to political impotence in the affairs of Washington, there were no American worldwide military interventions

---

230 Henry, William W., ed., ibid.

and a US foreign policy aimed at making other nations kowtow to American policy. In 1860 the United States had no military bases in foreign lands but today there are more than 50 major American military bases and more than 700 smaller support bases spread around the world. This projection of military power by the United States is greater than that projected by either the Roman Empire or the British Empire at the height of their imperial dominance. One year after the defeat of the Confederate Army, Robert E. Lee predicted that with the loss of States' Rights, America would become "aggressive abroad and despotic at home."[231] Is it any wonder after the defeat of the Confederate States of America, its Vice President, Alexander Stephens, opined that one day all Americans would understand that "The Cause of the South is the Cause of all."[232]

All Americans were adversely impacted by the loss of real States' Rights in the United States not just the people of the South. But unlike the rest of the United States, the people of the South were impoverished financially, culturally, racially, and made the scapegoat for all the ills of the United States. In 1930 renowned Southern author Frank L. Owsley lamented the fate of the defeated and impoverished South saying that future generation of Southerners would be consigned to sit "upon stools of everlasting repentance."[233] His predictions have become the reality of Southern life. It is not uncommon at all to see Southerners and their culture portrayed by liberal Hollywood media types as rude, uncultured, ignorant, and of course, racist. But it gets even worse for the South. Even though the South is the bastion of conservative voters, conservative talking heads on radio and TV never miss an opportunity to push the false narrative of the slave-holding, racist, bigots down South. These "conservative" talking heads will continually harp about how, during Reconstruction, the Republican Party was the friend of the African-American. These "brilliant" paragons of conservative knowledge forget to mention how the Republican Party used Northern spawned racism to divide the Southern people into warring camps not to aid the African Americans but to advance the interests of their crony-capitalists masters in the North. Conservative talking heads never inform their audience that the first

---

231 Robert E. Lee, as cited in, www.theimaginativeconservative.org/2014/08/acton-lee-conversation-liberty.html Accessed 5/16/2018.
232 Alexander H. Stephens, *A Constitutional View of the War Between the States* (1870, Sprinkle Publications, Harrisonburg, VA: 1994) II, 666.
233 Frank L. Owsley, as cited in, Kennedy and Kennedy, *The South Was Right!*, 19.

African American United States Senator, Hiram Revels of Mississippi, resigned from the Republican Party enraged over the way Republicans were using race hatred to aid the Republican Party and harm all Southerners. Republicans soon became weary of dealing with the Black element of its party and as soon as sufficient Republicans were elected in the newly forming states in the West, Southern African Americans were abandoned by the G.O.P.

Unfortunately for all Southerners, but especially Black Southerners, when the Republican Party abandoned the South, they left the South with the G.O.P. gift of Yankee induced racism. The bitterness caused by Republican Reconstruction and the near starvation of Southerners became rich ground for the harvesting of racist policies pushed by the Democratic Party. As such, the Democrats gained a "Solid South" which was just as faithful to the Democrats as Southern Blacks had been to the Republican Party. In each case the old divide and rule concept was used to keep Southerners from forming a united front to promote the best interests of all Southerners.

The consequences of the defeat and occupation of the Confederate States of America lives in the life of every Southerner today. Southern children can expect to grow up in a society where they will earn less money over a lifetime than their Northern counterpart — remember before Yankee invasion and conquest Southern children grew up in a prosperous and rich society. Southerners who are devoted to their religion will see their children taught a culture foreign to their faith and value system. All of this is just the tip of the iceberg that the ship of state, the CSS *Independence*, has struck. One can only hope the damage done can be repaired before all are consigned to the cold bleak waters of total tyranny.

PART II

Pictures Worth Thousands of Words

The truism a "picture is worth a thousand words" is especially correct when dealing with events and people removed from the present age by more than 150 years. On the following pages three sets of photographs are used to help dispel the myths about the South and the Confederate States of America. These photographs were selected as a representative sample of the men and events which will help to dispel the myths, half-truths, and outright falsehoods about the Confederate States of America and the War for Southern Independence.

The first selection of photographs is titled, "Great Men of the South." This group of photographs will demonstrate the high quality and influence these Confederate leaders possessed both in service to the South and to the United States. These men were military and political leaders in their own right and/or members of families who notably served, not only in the military defense of the United States, but also many were highly placed members of the government of the United States.

The second group of photos titled, "Northern Defenders of the Constitution," consists of a small sample of men from the North who resisted Lincoln's war upon the Constitution and the South. Much like Southern heroes, these courageous defenders of the Constitution have been maligned and slandered as traitors by the victor of the War for Southern Independence. These brave Northerners understood real patriotism is displayed by standing up for the principles these United States were founded upon and not "goose-stepping" down an all-powerful government's boulevard of tyranny. These defenders of the original United States government took their stand alongside America's Founding Fathers. In doing so, they were ostracized and defamed as enemies of the United States. Actually, they were noble defenders of the Republic of the Founding Fathers. As they often pointed out, Lincoln, who was elected with only 39 percent of the popular vote, was advocating a system of federalism utterly unknown to previous American presidents. Fifteen men from all sections of the United States held the office of president before Lincoln, yet none of these men ever declared the states were not sovereign or the Union created the states or the Federal Government had the right to wage war upon a state of the Union. Nevertheless, Lincoln pursued war and these brave Northerners, at the risk of death, imprisonment, or banishment from their country, resisted Lincoln's tyranny.

The third and most poignant set of photos ask the question, "What Price Union?" This question has been avoided by most standard "historians" or answered to obscure the total cost to the South and the nation. To be honest about the War, the question of how much did "saving the union" cost America must be asked and honestly answered. But even more important than the cost to nineteenth century Americans is the answer to the question, "What type of union has been saved?" The so-called "saved union" directly impacts the lives of all Americans today. When tabulating the cost of saving the union, one must consider more than just the loss of life and property. While the loss of life and property is significant, it does not qualify as a complete accounting of everything that was lost. To adequately account for what has been lost, one must look at things such as the human cost of the loss of home and of food supply which impacts not only the generation who suffered that acute loss but also the harsh consequences of that loss on generations far removed from the actual smell of battle. And to completely cover the cost of "saving the union" one must critically evaluate what type of union has been "saved" or more correctly stated what type of new union has been created by the Federal Government's invasion and conquering of once sovereign states. When Great Britain opted for war with its American Colonies after they seceded from the British Union, British political philosopher Edmond Burke issued a stern warning which holds true for Lincoln's war upon the Confederate States of America. Burke, in 1777, noted England promoted the principle of the "Rights of Englishmen" for many years. Americans were now demanding these freedoms and if the English fought against America, it would ultimately be attacking English freedom itself. Yes, as Burke noted, they might be able to subdue the Americans and restore the union of America and Great Britain but the pride of English freedom would be "depreciated, sunk, wasted, and consumed in the contest."[234] Burke warned Parliament that by waging war upon the seceded colonies, Great Britain would,

---

234 Edmond Burke, Speech on Conciliation with the Colonies, in *The Norton Anthology of English Literature*, Third Edition (New York: W.W. Norton and Co., 1974) I, 2352-366.

"depreciate the value of freedom itself."[235] Lincoln's invasion and conquest of the Confederate States of America depreciated, sunk, and wasted the value of freedom in America just as Burke had warned the British Empire in 1777. The same warning of "depreciating freedom itself," was given to the United States in 1861, and it is still being given today.

Edmund Burke (1729-97) British orator, philosopher, author, and political theorist.

Burke's warning about depreciating freedom by waging war upon a people seeking freedom held true in his day, in Lincoln's day, and holds true in modern America.

---

235 Ibid.

Great Men of the USA and CSA

Major General John C. Breckinridge (*Library of Congress*)

John C. Breckinridge (1821-1875) holds the distinction of being the youngest Vice President of the United States, having been elected at age 36, one year over the minimum age requirement for a vice president. Breckinridge served as vice president during the presidential term of James Buchanan (1857-61). Prior to serving as vice president, Breckinridge served in both the US House of Representatives and US Senate as a delegate from Kentucky. After the Democrat Party split into Northern and Southern wings in 1860, Breckinridge was nominated as the Southern Democrat Party nominee for president. With four parties contending for electoral votes, three of which were heavy in Democratic supporters, Lincoln won the election in the Electoral College with only 39 percent of the popular vote. Breckinridge ran second in both electoral votes and popular votes ahead of Bell (Constitutional Union Party) and Douglas (Northern Democratic Party).

Breckinridge's maternal great-grandfather was John Witherspoon of New Jersey. Witherspoon, a Presbyterian minister, served as president of the College of New Jersey which later became Princeton University. Witherspoon was an advocate of American independence and signed the Declaration of Independence for his state of New Jersey. Breckinridge served as a major in the Mexican War and rose to the rank of major general in the Confederate Army. In February 1865,

President Davis appointed Breckinridge to fill the position of Secretary of the Navy.

Jefferson F. Davis, President, Confederate States of America

Few men have stirred more passion, both positive and negative, than Jefferson Davis. Davis was born in Fairview, Kentucky, in 1808 and died in New Orleans, Louisiana, in 1889. He was the son of Samuel E. Davis, a Revolutionary War soldier. Samuel Davis was a follower of Thomas Jefferson's political philosophy, which has led many to speculate that is why he named his last child Jefferson in honor of Thomas Jefferson.

Jefferson Davis graduated from the United States Military Academy at West Point in 1828. He was commissioned a second lieutenant and assigned to a post in the Mid-West under the command of General Zachary Taylor. It was here that he met and fell in love with a young lady, Sarah Knox Taylor, his commander's daughter. After the two were married, Davis resigned his military commission and moved to a small plantation in Mississippi. Both Davis and his wife soon became critically ill with Yellow Fever or Malaria; Sarah died six months after their wedding. Davis did not recover from this loss for many years. He subsequently married a young lady from Natchez, Mississippi. During the Mexican War, Davis raised a regiment of volunteer infantry and was appointed its colonel. He distinguished himself on the field of battle. After receiving a wound to his foot during the Battle of Buena Vista, Davis returned to a hero's welcome in Mississippi.

Davis served in the US House of Representatives and in the US Senate as a delegate from Mississippi. From 1853-57, Davis served as Secretary of War in President Franklin Pierce's administration. Davis, as was true with so many other Southerners in 1860, was a reluctant secessionist. Nevertheless, he never questioned the right of secession, only its wisdom, when considering the vast disparity in population and recourses between the North and the South. Despite these considerations, when his state seceded from the Union, Davis followed his state. Many historians have criticized Davis' handling of the Confederate War effort but few have ever offered a name of one who could have done better than Davis or even as well as Davis. Unlike Lincoln, when Davis was sworn in as president of the Confederate States of America, he did not have a nation with a standing army, navy, armaments factories, and a mature functioning government. Starting from near nothing, Davis and the South stunned the world and bewildered the invader of the Confederacy by putting into motion a strong response to the invasion of the South. After the War, Davis stood by his defeated people and never apologized for fighting for Southern independence.

Lt. Gen. Richard Taylor, the "Patton" of the Confederacy

Taylor was the son of President Zackary Taylor (12th US president) and brother-in-law to President Jefferson Davis. Taylor was born in Kentucky, educated in private schools in both Kentucky and Massachusetts and graduated from Yale University, New Haven, Connecticut. A prolific reader of military history, Taylor's interest in battles and leaders served him well as commander of Confederate troops during the War for Southern Independence. Upon the death of his father, Zachary Taylor, Richard Taylor inherited his father's estate in St. Charles Parish, Louisiana, which included a large sugar plantation. Taylor was one of only three non-West Point Lt. Generals in the Confederate Army. A man with zero military experience before the War, Taylor, at the Battle of Mansfield and Pleasant Hill, Louisiana, delivered one of the most stunning defeats ever suffered by the United States military. Economically devastated by the War, Taylor relocated to Virginia after the War. With the publication of his memoir, Destruction and Reconstruction: Personal Experiences of the Late War, Taylor made a major contribution to a factual account of the War for Southern Independence. Few Americans hold these distinctions: son of a US President, Yale graduate, successful businessman, brother-in-law of Jefferson Davis, victorious military leader, and accomplished author.

John Tyler, 10th president of the United States, 1841-45

President Tyler is pictured here in 1826 while serving as Governor of Virginia. Tyler was a strong supporter of Thomas Jefferson's views of States' Rights and held firmly to the Jeffersonian concept of limited government for his entire life. During the stressful days following Lincoln's election, Tyler opposed secession. He hoped that war could be avoided and pursued every available avenue toward that objective. By February 1861, he became convinced that Lincoln preferred war to compromise. Upon hearing that Lincoln believed that war was not the worst of evils in dealing with secession, Tyler withdrew from the efforts of seeking a compromise with the Republicans. Tyler, the tenth president of the United States and an early opponent of secession, returned to Virginia and informed his wife, "I shall vote for secession."[236] Reversing his early stand, Tyler voted for secession in the Virginia Secession Convention. After passage of the secession ordinance, Tyler signed the document on July 14, 1861. In August, Tyler was elected to the Confederate Congress and served there until his death in 1862. At his funeral in Richmond, Virginia, his coffin was draped with the flag of the Confederate States of America. He is the only US President to have his coffin draped with a flag other than that of the United States. Many historians and Federal sycophants have condemned Tyler for supporting the right of secession. How could he have done otherwise if he was to remain faithful to his Jeffersonian States' Rights view of the Federal government? Tyler, just like Jefferson, Madison, Peirce, and virtually every other president before Lincoln believed in real States' Rights. He was faithful to his belief in States' Rights and for that and that only, he has been condemned. But for those who love real limited government, i.e., a government that fears the people and not one that puts fear in the people, Tyler is the real American Patriot.

Senator Hiram Revels of Mississippi

Hiram Revels, the first African American United States Senator. Revels disappointed many Radical Republicans who were advocating a harsh treatment of the defeated South during Reconstruc-

---

236 John Tyler, as cited in Gary May, *John Tyler* (New York: Times Books, Henry Holt and Company, 2008) 136.

tion. Revels favored a more conciliatory approach to the "reconstruction" of the South. Revels championed civil rights for former slaves but did not desire to use governmental power to force people into a social relationship that was not desired by all parties. It is somewhat ironic that America's foremost founding father who opposed "Jim Crow" type of laws was Saint George Tucker of Virginia, while the first African American Senator who championed equal rights before the law was from Mississippi, and the only Federal Supreme Court Judge to oppose the national establishment of Jim Crow laws (*Plessy v. Ferguson*) was from Kentucky. In all three cases it was Southerners who were blazing the way toward equal rights for all.

Revels understood that both races in the South needed to work together for the benefit of all citizens — punishing the South with poverty was harmful to all Southerners regardless of race. The use of racial animosity by the Republican Party to secure votes for their Party so enraged Revels that he resigned from the Republican Party in 1875. In his letter to President Grant, resigning from the Republican Party, Revels stated: "The bitterness and hate created by the late civil strife…would have long since been obliterated in this state, were it not for some unprincipled men who would keep alive the bitterness of the past, and inculcate a hatred between the races, in order that they may aggrandize themselves by office, and its emoluments, to control my people, the effect of which is to degrade them."[237] The process of inculcating hatred between the races is commonly known today as "playing the race card." During Reconstruction playing the race card provided the Republican Party a solid South voting mass. After Reconstruction and with the advent of so-called Jim Crow laws, playing the race card provided the Democratic Party a solid South. Although the ruling elite in each party prospered by using this method of "getting out the vote," the average citizen of the South, regardless of color, receives little long-lasting benefits and much social strife, just as Senator Revels noted in 1875.

---

237 Hiram Revels, Hiram Revels Letter to President Grant, November 6, 1875 as cited *N C Pedia*, http://ncpedia.org/biography/revelsletter (Accessed 4/20/2016).

Northern Defenders of the Constitution

Sen. Joseph Lane, Oregon

Joseph Lane was born in North Carolina in 1808 and moved to Indiana, where he began his life as a businessman and politician. Lane's father, John Lane, was a veteran of the American War for Independence. Lane was the quintessential self-made man moving to Indiana, educating himself while working, and saving money to acquire a small business. His business was a success and he subsequently entered Indiana politics. Lane was elected to several terms in the Indiana House of Representatives and the Indiana Senate. At the outbreak of the Mexican War, Lane helped raise a company of Indiana volunteer infantry and was subsequently elected captain and later colonel of the 2nd Indiana Volunteer Infantry Regiment. Lane was wounded twice during battle and displayed courage and skill as an officer; he was therefore promoted to the rank of brigadier general. At the conclusion of the Mexican War, Lane moved to the Oregon Territory where he served as the first territorial governor of the Oregon Territory. Politically, Lane was a strong supporter of the Jeffersonian view of strict-construction of the Constitution and therefore was an enthusiastic proponent of real States' Rights. Lane, a Democrat, served as one of the two first US Senators from the State of Oregon. He accepted the vice-presidential nomination of the Southern Democrat Party in 1860. With the election of Lincoln and the Republican Administration threat of invading the Confederate States of America, Lane warned Americans that the Republican Party's war against sovereign states would transform the American Republic into a vast empire. This new empire, he warned, would transform the states into mere provinces of the empire. Lane warned Americans that provinces of an empire exist for the benefit of the empire and not for the benefit of the people of the once sovereign states. His strong stand for the old republic of Jefferson and Madison was condemned by Republicans as treason against the United States; this charge effectively ended his political career.

Lysander Spooner, Abolitionist, Author, and Political Philosopher

Few people would ever think of a Massachusetts abolitionist as a friend of the South and defender of the right of secession, but Lysander Spooner was that kind of a man. Born in Massachusetts in 1808, Spooner spent his adult life fighting against the growth of big government. Spooner believed no taskmaster could be more intrusive to and destructive of individual liberty than the taskmaster of big government — simply put, Spooner was an anti-authoritarian libertarian. His two best-known works are: *The Unconstitutionality of Slavery*, where he proposes that, if read correctly, the Constitution did not defend slavery but condemned it. While his first work firmly places him in the camp of the Radical Abolitionists, his second work, *No Treason: The Constitution of No Authority*, places him in the camp of those defending the Confederacy's right to exist. Spooner defended the right of any state to secede from the Union and utterly rejects the idea Southerners committed treason when they seceded from the Union. After the War Spooner chided Northerners for proclaiming they "preserved or saved the Union." Spooner declared Northerners may proclaim they "Saved our Country" or "Preserved our Glorious Union" but those statements were "frauds."[238] Spooner criticized Northerners by insisting that, instead of preserving the nation of liberty, the followers of Lincoln simply "have subjugated, and maintained their power over, an unwilling people."[239] Spooner also stated the real reason for the War was for "purely pecuniary consideration … a control of the markets of the South."[240] Spooner noted that, although Southerners, after surrender, had given oaths of allegiance to the United States, those oaths were not valid because they were given under duress, that is, the threat of further violence or confiscation of their remaining property. Spooner courageously defended the rights of the slaves on both the Southern plantations and the slaves of an indivisible big government. In the introduction of his work, *No Treason: The Constitution of No Authority*, Spooner gives the "Union at any cost" Americans a much needed wake-up call, "On the part of the North, the war was carried on, not to liberate slaves … the number of slaves, instead of having been diminished by the war, has been greatly increased … there is no difference in principle — only in degree — between political and chattel slavery."[241] Spooner was a great American!

George Lunt, Massachusetts lawyer, editor, author, and historian

George Lunt's family history extends back to 1635 during the early days of the Colony of Massachusetts. Lunt graduated from Harvard in 1824 becoming notable for his mastership of Greek language

---

238 Lysander Spooner, *No Treason: The Constitution of No Authority* ((1870, Free Patriot Press, http://Freepatriot-Press.com 2009) 76-7.
239 Ibid.
240 Ibid.
241 Ibid.

and history. After college he established himself in the practice of law and soon became involved in politics. He was a strong advocate of the Jeffersonian small government view of the Constitution. He demanded that any action taken by the Federal government must follow the letter of the law *vis-à-vis* the Constitution. In his book, *Origin of the Late War* (1866), he demonstrated the Republican Party and Lincoln were in the process of overthrowing the existing form of government as handed down to Americans by the Founding Fathers of the United States. Lunt also laments the fact that sovereignty no longer belonged to the people of each state but now resided with the Federal government — this killed any hope of real States' Rights in the new America. As Lunt explained it, this was a monumental change in the nature of government in the United States. Lunt also boldly proclaimed the North had engaged in the act of aggression and conquest against the South. To add insult to injury of Northern feelings, Lunt boldly announced the war was not about slavery but about negating Southern influence in the Federal Congress and controlling Southern markets. As Lunt points out, slavery caused the war like property causes theft. In a more modern truism we could say, "Slavery caused the War like cars causes carjacking!"

Clement L. Vallandigham, Ohio Congressman

Clement L. Vallandigham attended Jefferson College in Pennsylvania, studied law and began the practice of law in his home state of Ohio. A Democrat with a traditional, limited government view of the Constitution, Vallandigham was elected to the legislature of Ohio and as United States Representative from Ohio in 1858, serving in that office until 1862.

While opposing secession, he nevertheless was a vocal critic of Lincoln's war policy. As a well-respected leader of the Democratic opposition to Lincoln, he incurred the ire of Republicans. Vallandigham reminded Americans, "A union founded in consent could not be cemented by force."[242] He asks a most critical question about "saving the Union" when he criticizes the Republican demand for war, "War for the Union; a union of consent and good-will. Our Southern brethren were to be whipped back into love and fellowship at the point of the bayonet. O, monstrous delusion! I can comprehend a war to compel a people to accept a master … in short a war of conquest and subjugation! Was the Union thus made?"[243] This speech and other such as this led to his arrest by military police, being tried in a military court, and banished from the United States — Vallandigham was a civilian, not a member of the United States military or in the active service of the militia at this time. Even a novice lawyer would recognize these acts as violating not only the letter and spirit of the Constitution but also every aspect of English jurisprudence all the way back to the Magna Carta! It must be remembered that all of these un-Constitutional acts were committed with the full knowledge and support of Lincoln and the Republican Party. Sycophants of Lincoln will proclaim all these illegal acts were done out of "necessity." It was necessary in order to "save the Union." Such a union, enforced with bloody bayonets, is like unto the union of a sheep's throat and the jaws of a wolf. "Necessity" is the typical "fig leaf" used by every tyrant to cover the nakedness of their aggression and illegal actions. Lincoln and the Republican Party found it "necessary" to play the part of tyrants in order to reconstruct the Federal system of America's Founding Fathers.

---

242 Vallandigham, C. L., *The Record of Hon. C. L. Vallandigham on Abolition, The Union, And The Civil War*, 7th ed. (1863, Johnson graphics, Decatur, MI) 178.
243 Ibid, 1.

What Price Union

As the United States Army blazed its way across an exhausted South where once peaceful happy homes populated the area, the Northern army left behind cities, towns, and villages which became known as "Chimneyvilles." Like a Biblical plague of locust, the invader of the Confederate States of America consumed or destroyed all food, pillaged and burned homes, smokehouses, barns, and destroyed both private and public property within their reach. When computing the human cost of the war to "save the Union," it must not be forgotten that homeless people suffer, hungry people suffer, sick and injured people who have no access to medicines or medical care suffer, and if there be no means of replacing the losses caused by war, the suffering will simply morph into genocide. When everything of value such as gold, silver, fine clothes, books, and furniture are stolen or destroyed, what kind of life will be bequeathed to future generations? The displaced population of the South had no way of obtaining food or shelter — everything had been destroyed. Food had to be grown and stored but Yankees had raided Southern smokehouses and barns where food was kept. Furthermore, even if they could live for six months until a new growing season began, all draft animals (oxen, mules, and horses) had been taken or killed by the invader. Seed to plant new crops was also taken or destroyed by the invader — the chance of survival was very slim for displaced Southerners.

Even those Southerners who were not directly impacted by war had to share what meager supplies they had with their fellow Southerners. By the middle of 1864, starvation and disease became a constant companion of most Southerners. At the end of the War, there was no Marshall Plan where the victorious conqueror would pour food and assistance into the devastated, defeated nation. Even as late as 1943 (78 years after the conquest of the South), Governor Sam H. Jones of Louisiana complained about the poverty Southerners were still suffering as a result of the conquest of the Confederate States of America by the United States.[244] Jones noted that, due to its natural resources, the South was once a rich and prosperous section of the nation, yet after the War, it seems as if, "that section of America which was ordained by nature to be the richest has become the

---

[244] Sam H. Jones, 199 *The Plundered South*, The Abbeville Institute, www.abbevilleinstitute.org/blog/theplundered-south/ accessed 5/23/2018.

poorest."[245] Over a million lives (military and civilian) lost, a people reduced from prosperity and health to poverty and disease, and a people forced to live in a government by coercion rather than consent — these are just a few details that must be considered when calculating the cost of "saving the Union."

Sadly, the cost is neither static nor fixed in "times past" but continues to the present generation and on to future generations of Southerners. Each new generation of Southerners must learn that their place in America, which they are expected to quietly and obediently occupy, is upon the 'stools of eternal repentance.' How then can the question be correctly answered, "What was the price of 'saving the Union' and, even more importantly, 'was it worth the price?'" For non-Southerners looking at the rapid and immense growth of wealth and power in the North after the War, the answer is of course, yes, it was worth it. But for those reduced to poverty, disease, and political slavery, the answer should not be a joyful affirmation of Yankee victory. Answering that question is somewhat problematic for Southerners if they are to remain seated upon the "stools of everlasting repentance."

Stereograph photo of destroyed locomotive
Richmond, Virginia, 1865.
In the margin of the original photo (above) are printed the words, "The War for the Union."

---

245 Ibid.

Richmond, Virginia, 1865

Columbia, South Carolina, just after a visit from Sherman in 1865

The United States Army destroying the South in order to "save the Union." This is one more example of Yankee "brotherhood by bayonet." Thirty-three years after this incident, the Native Hawaiians would refer to their Yankee enforced Constitution as the "Bayonet Constitution."

Part III

The Myth Lives On

The following four articles were written in response to various actions of big government and its acolytes in the United States over the past few years. This "over-reach" by the Federal government was not only made possible by Lincoln's war upon REAL States' Rights but it was made inevitable. Lincoln and the Republican Party were the standard bearers for an all-powerful big government which has, since the days of Lincoln, metastasized into the Deep State, the all-powerful big government of today.

As amazing as it sounds to modern-day conservatives and Republicans, even radical socialists, Marxists, and communists were drawn to Lincoln and the Republican Party no doubt because it was the party of strong central government. The close relationship between the origin of the Republican Party, Lincoln's election, the war upon the South and Marxism is examined in the first of four articles herein, 'Christians Marching with Marx.' The second article, 'Paddling One's Own Canoe,' looks at how too many Americans have lost the incentive in taking care of their own lives and families and are looking to big government as their lifelong savior. The third article, 'Ron Paul is Too Radical,' demonstrates just how little modern-day Americans understand the "radical" ideas that are the foundation of American liberty and government. The fourth and final article, '*The Wall Street Journal's* Confederate Animus,' demonstrates the ongoing campaign of anti-South cultural genocide.

Christians Marching With Marx
Walter D. Kennedy
2008

In our modern age of political correctness, it is not uncommon to find various Christians, including many noted ministers and evangelists, snuggling up to the detractors of the South. In Mississippi during the fight to keep the Confederate flag emblem on its State flag, Mississippians heard "leading" ministers of various denominations condemn the so-called "hated symbol." In Georgia the same scenario was played out, only this time the preacher was in the Governor's chair and did all within his power to destroy any effort to protect the real flag of Georgia. In churches across the South the Fourth of July is celebrated with the shameful sounds of "The Battle Hymn of the Republic," but God protect anyone who requests the playing of "Dixie" in church.

Political correctness has descended upon the South with a near fatal impact and all too often it is Christian leaders who are leading the assault. Warning the people of England about the lethal results of embracing Christian Socialism, Charles Spurgeon stated: "I would not have you exchange the gold of individual Christianity for the base metal of Christian Socialism." When one understands that virtually every radical socialist and communist in the United States at the time of the War for Southern Independence joined in the struggle against the South, the words of Spurgeon, a London Baptist minister, begin to have real meaning. The South had barely begun its struggle for independence when radical socialists, communists and even Karl Marx, began a war of words and of deeds against the cause of Southern independence. In an article written for *Die Presse*, a Vienna newspaper, Marx asserted that (1) the South was fighting to promote slavery, (2) the Confederate Constitution was a pro-slavery document, (3) Jefferson Davis was a Southern dictator, and (4) the United States Supreme Court was a willing tool of Southern slaveholders. The founders of modern-day communism, Karl Marx and Fredrick Engels, both served as Lincoln's unofficial European propaganda ministers during the War. Simply put, modern-day anti-South political correctness is an outgrowth of 19th century Marxist propaganda.

In an article written in late 2008, David Barton of Wall Builders fame and noted Evangelical Christian activist wrote an article excoriating and otherwise condemning the South for (1) defending slavery, (2) adopting a Constitution that defended slavery and (3) having leaders and a constitution that compelled states to accept slavery. While each of these charges can be easily debunked, what is so upsetting is to see an otherwise good Christian and defender of what he calls Constitutional government, embrace Marxist philosophy. And just for lagniappe, this Louisiana writer would like to know why is Barton attacking Southern heritage when he is the leader of an organization charged with defending Christian virtue and rights? According to more than one recent poll, it is and has been for a long time the South that accords religion and the Bible with the highest respect of all Americans. Why insult the people who are most likely to embrace the work of Wall Builders?

In 1894 Robert Ingersoll, a former Captain in the Illinois Cavalry, a radical Republican and a free thinker (the 19th century equivalent of today's secular humanists) gave an address in which he defended Lincoln's legacy as a free thinker. Ingersoll made a telling statement about why the so-called Civil War was fought: "The great stumbling block the great obstruction in Lincoln's way and in the way of thousands, was the old doctrine of State's Rights." Removing this "stumbling block" to the growth of big government was the very reason that none other than Adolph Hitler heaped praise upon Lincoln's action during the War for Southern Independence. Hitler also had to remove the last vestiges of what he called "Statal Rights" before he could establish his "perpetual and supreme" Reich. Marx's philosophical twin, Fredrick Engels, told Joseph Weydemeyer, a fellow communist, future leader in the Republican Party, and future Union General, that by forging one large and "indivisible" republic instead of many small republics, they would establish the ground work for the communist movement. With the death of real States' Rights everything that the advocates of big government desired became not only possible but also inevitable. Today nationalized banking is a reality; abortion on demand in any State is a reality; the removal of the Ten Commandments from a State building by Federal authorities is a reality. All of this happened because real States' Rights was destroyed by Lincoln's war — a war fought not to end slavery but to end REAL States' Rights. This is reality in modern America — a reality that was praised by Hitler and made possible by Lincoln, Marx, Engels and a host of other free thinkers. Marching with Lincoln and Marx is tantamount to exchanging the gold of constitutionally limited government for the base metal of Federal empire.

Paddling One's Own Canoe While Reflecting on Katrina
Walter D. Kennedy
2005

If ever there was a time in America when the fine art of "paddling one's own canoe" was needed it was during the trying times just after Hurricane Katrina. As the Biblical floodwaters rose in the City of New Orleans, the chant of "we need help" seemed to be the one common message heard from the rooftops, the mayor's office and the governor's office. During such perilous times one does not stop to chop logic, one must go about the business of saving lives. That time having come and gone, it is now time to "chop logic" about what has transpired.

During the early days of this republic, i.e., when States were sovereign and the Federal government was a limited government, most Americans held the view that they would not accept private charity and surely never accept governmental charity. Rather than depending upon others for one's well-being, each man would prefer to "paddle his own canoe." Anyone not willing to do so was viewed as less than a complete man and one to be shunned by respectful society. This dogged determination to "fend for one's own self" was instrumental in establishing a society that was capable of overcoming savages, wilderness, isolation, foreign invaders and poverty itself to create the most free and prosperous nation on earth. This willingness to do for one's own folk and not depend upon someone else to pull your irons out of the fire was sorely missing in and around the flooded plains of New Orleans, September 2005. But should we have expected any different response from a people who for generations have been taught that government will take care of your needs? During the flood, pontificating talking heads from every major T. V. network overlooked this reality: Those who look to government for their well-being are seldom capable of "paddling their own canoe." During the first few days of the disaster every commentator, whether liberal or conservative, tearfully bemoaned the fact of "the poor choice those people made" by staying in New Orleans. Opting to stay eight feet below sea level while a category four hurricane is bearing down upon a city whose levees can only withstand a category three hurricane was not the first "poor choice" those people have made. For many of the people trapped in New Orleans their life has consisted of a long series of "poor choices." At age 13 they choose to get pregnant; they choose not to study and to drop out of school; they choose a life of drug abuse; they choose to wear clothes and speak in a manner that does not positively impress potential employers; and, they choose to vote for the very people who have made making these poor choices bearable and therefore inevitable. One must ask, "Why have they not learned by their mistakes?" The answer of course is nanny government. As all traditional conservatives know, when nanny government, i.e., the socialist state, is determined to "paddle their canoe for them," a people will always be a dependent people not an independent people. As distressful as it was viewing the pitiful condition of the wards of the government, it was even more distressing and disgusting to hear so-called conservative leaders appealing for even more government involvement in the disaster which big government had fostered. According to Newt Gingrich large parts of Louisiana, Mississippi, and Alabama needs to be converted into Federal districts and the Federal government should "reconstruct" those States. Like fingernails scraping across a blackboard, those words set my ears ringing; but of course, if I were born and raised in Pennsylvania, I might have a different view of "Federal reconstruction." Even discounting the poor choice of words by Mr. Gingrich, the eagerness of so many neo-conservatives to embrace big government as the solution for problems differs little from the liberal/socialist's view of governmental assistance. If Katrina proves anything it should make it clear that government is not the entity that people should look to for their welfare.

Government at every level failed to function properly during this disaster. Yet many things went very well. In sub-divisions, towns and rural areas across three states, people cleared roads, cooked meals, provided shelter and most importantly, armed themselves and protected their lives and property. While the unruly citizens of the welfare state in New Orleans looted, other citizens all around that area were "paddling their own canoe." Before the bureaucrats of government could cut through its barrier of red tape, local folk had already cut through 36-inch trees and open up highways and roads that would have stopped a tank. Before FEMA could get its act together, the Salvation Army, Red Cross and numerous church groups were on site providing relief. What works in America? Free people work in America and do so much better than government. Big government is and always has been the problem, not the answer (something to many "conservatives" forgot in the wake of Katrina). Adding insult to injury, our conservative Republican president came to New Orleans looking and sounding more like Lyndon B. Johnson or Franklin D. Roosevelt and declared that the Federal government would rebuild New Orleans. So now we can expect something akin to FDR's social security boondoggle or LBJ's war on poverty fiasco combined with big government bureaucrats, rules and regulation as they reconstruct New Orleans. What more could a liberal Democrat have asked for from big government? Our conservative Republican has out done the liberals! With one last slap in the face for the people who were "paddling their own canoe," the President in an address at the National Cathedral declared that the lawlessness in New Orleans was a reaction to the legacy of "discrimination and injustice" those unfortunate looters had to endure. What kind of airhead wrote such a speech and better yet, what kind of airhead would give such a speech? The government of New Orleans has been under the control of the Black population for over twenty-five years. Jim Crow died with the passage of the 1964 Civil Rights Act, over 41 years before Katrina hit New Orleans. The current mayor of New Orleans, as well as many previous mayors, is Black; the current [2005] governor of Louisiana is a liberal Democrat who was elected by over 80% of the voters in New Orleans. Even in the face of such evidence, our conservative Republican President asserts that "discrimination and injustice" is the root cause of lawlessness in New Orleans. Who is left to blame for the lawlessness if the looters are not responsible? Here we see our conservative Republican President once again sounding more like LBJ than the conservatives who elected him; the only people left to blame are the middle-class folks who were busy "paddling their own canoe" during these tragic times. For traditional Southern conservatives Katrina once again proves that as for the National Republican Party is concerned, Southerners must still sit upon their "stool of eternal repentance."

One question that few people have asked is "Why did local government fail?" One can understand the failure of a big far away government but why did the local government prove to be such a failure? In representative government the elected office holders are a reflection of the people that vote them into office. Since the enactment of the South only Voting Rights Act in 1965, there has been a constant lowering of the qualification to vote. Today in Dixie, the only thing one must prove in order to vote is that he is alive (in close elections even that rule does not apply). When people depend upon government for a check each month, who live in a society with 80% single parent homes, who cannot read or understand any basic function of government, when these people are allowed to elect the mayor of a city eight feet below sea level, guess what happens when strong intelligent leadership is needed? Unfortunately for New Orleans and the Nation, the backup for the mayor of New Orleans was the governor of Louisiana, Kathleen Blanco. Governor Blanco, a liberal Democrat, rode into office on the back of the same group of voters that elected the mayor of New Orleans. Is it any wonder she could not find the will power to order the National Guard to "shoot to kill" looters in New Orleans? Only after the world nightly saw the lawlessness in New Orleans did the governor find the courage to act, by that time it was much too late. At some point in time this country must come to the realization that quality in the electors is just as important as quantity. If we are to safe guard those few freedoms that we now barely subsist upon, we must address the issue of voter qualification. If we as a nation fail to address the issue, we are doomed to enter into that most unhappy and un-free state of mobocracy. Virtually all of the founding fathers of this nation unequivocally voiced their fear of mass democracy or as John Randolph of Roanoke referred to it the tyranny of "King numbers." What will be the fate of those who at present prefer to "paddle their own canoe" when the non-paddlers become the majority and elect all officer holders in this country? At that time the looters will be in firm control and liberty will be doomed. Here are a few lessons learned from Katrina: 1. Don't depend on government to meet your needs, learn to paddle your own canoe. Imbued with a sense of self-reliance, free people are more likely to positively respond to a crisis than those who consistently suckle at the breast of nanny government. This is not to denigrate the positive influence that free government can have within the milieu of a liberty-based society but in a liberty-based society, everyone knows how to paddle their own canoe. 2. When faced with an emotional crisis, even the most "conservative" neo-conservative will sound more like a socialist, i.e., a liberal, than they will sound like a traditional conservative. Newt Gingrich offers a classic example of a neo-conservative selling out his "limited government" mantra for liberal big government ideas when faced with emotional images on TV. Promoting the expenditure of billions of dollars of Federal funds, placing large parts of three States into Federal reconstruction districts and doing away the *posse comitatus* act, Gingrich sounds more like Hilary Clinton than a real conservative. 3. Anytime a race related issue causes neo-conservatives any embarrassment, they find Southerners useful as a scapegoat. After many days of looting and violence in New Orleans President Bush dutifully noted that the lawlessness was a legacy of "racial injustice." If the looters are not responsible for the lawlessness, then who is responsible for the lawlessness? The inference in Bush's remarks is that if it is not the looters' fault for the violence down South then it must be the arch villain in America, Bubba and his cohorts. According to the manager of the New Orleans Walmart, the only thing not looted in his downtown store was the Country Music CDs. You see, Bubba was busy "paddling his own canoe" and didn't have time to do any looting; yet, it is the South, the hard working, conservative voting South that is, by inference, held up to the world as the villain for race problems in America. 4. Until we place quality for voters on the same level as quantity of voters, we will continue to elect officials with the lowest common denominator of the voters. When the tax consumers out vote the taxpayers both the property and the liberty of the minority is held hostage by the tax-consuming majority. It's shocking when one considers that more knowledge has to be demonstrated earning the privilege of driving a car, getting a hunting license, or cutting someone's hair than it takes to qualify to vote. Why should someone who is a convicted felon be allowed to vote? Why should someone living on government subsides be allowed to vote? Why should someone who files bankruptcy be allowed to vote? In all of these cases the individual has proven he is not responsible enough to manage his own affairs. Being unable to manage one's own affairs should not be a qualification for running the affairs of state. From Louisiana my suggestion for all Americans is to keep paddling your own canoe but learn the lessons of Katrina!

[The following article was written in 2008. At that time, I was a delegate for Ron Paul in my congressional district. I wrote this article and published it on the Kennedy Twins web site after being confronted by a co-worker who thought that Ron Paul was too radical and Obama would be a better presidential choice than Paul. The message of this article is needed today just as it was needed back then. By-the-way, Mikey has seen the light about Obama!]

Ron Paul Is Too Radical
Walter D. Kennedy
2008

Recently I was talking with a friend at work about the current crop of contenders for the 2008 presidential election. During the conversation I noted that as a Southern conservative I could not find anything in the front running Republicans that appealed to me. At that point my friend glibly remarked that he figured that I would be a Ron Paul man because Paul and I shared a rather radical view of America. Letting that thought pass, we proceeded to discuss the downfalls of the four leading Republicans, where upon the only choice that was left was Ron Paul but my friend stated that he would rather vote for Obama than Paul because, as he put it, "Ron Paul is too radical." Having to get back to work, the conversation was ended on that note but the thought of that well-educated middle-class family man's statement that Ron Paul was too radical for him, never left me for the rest of the day. Driving home that day the thought of Ron Paul being too radical for my friend to vote for just would not leave me. Then it hit me, he was right, Ron Paul is too radical for most modern Americans to vote for. But surprisingly this man found Obama to be a poor but an acceptable choice. Thanks to the not so stellar education system and liberal political correctness, most Americans do not understand the "radical" nature of our founding fathers. Yes, my friend was very correct, judging by what is normal today Ron Paul is very radical. But is he and those of us who hold such views really radical when compared to what our founding fathers believed?

Talk about radical! The establishment of this nation was announced by one of the most radical documents ever written by free men, the Declaration of Independence. Now remember that when this document was adopted there were no nations on earth that held to the ideas embodied in the Declaration of Independence. In an age where nations were ruled by kings most of who held near absolute power, our founding fathers announced to the world that governments existed not for the benefit of the rulers but existed for the benefit of free men. The first radical concept announced by the men of 1776 stated that our rights do not come from a king, emperor or any government but were given to man by God. Not only were our rights a gift from God but these rights were unalienable, that is, government cannot destroy our rights. Yes, they understood that governments can trample upon our rights but those rights remained a living fact of nature. Our founding fathers noted that the only JUST government was that government that existed by the CONSENT of the governed. Here we see an absolute attack upon the long-held view of kings ruling by divine right, that is, God grants kings the right to rule the people. In 1776 the founding fathers of this nation put the shoe on the other foot; it is now we the people who rule ourselves according to God's ordained purposes. Here for the first time in the history of man we see free men declaring that they had the right to rule themselves and not some king or emperor—how much more radical can you get? Well for your information Mikey (my Obama friend), a lot more radical!

You see our founding fathers believed that we the people had every right to alter or abolish any government that did not rule us according to the will of the people. Now this is not a revolutionary right, it is an intrinsic right of free man. If our government does not do as we think proper then we can alter, that is, change the nature of that government or in an even more radical action, we can abolish that government and establish a new government more to our liking—note here that it is the people and not the government that has the right to make those decisions. The key point of the Declaration of Independence is that government is now going to be the servant of we the people and not our master—it is the rights and liberty of we the people that is of paramount importance and not the life of a king, emperor, or some government. Government exists only to serve and protect the liberty and freedom of we the people. This love for liberty was so pronounced that one Virginian, Patrick Henry, electrified his and many other generations of Americans when he declared, "give me liberty or give me death!" Now that is some kind of radical — I am sure my good friend at work would not vote for anyone like that.

Henry's love for liberty was similarly displayed while debating the adoption of the new government under the Constitution, when he stated, "The first thing I have at heart is American liberty, the second is American Union." Once again Henry points us to the very reason government exists, that is, to promote and protect the liberty of we the people. In the more radical day of Patrick Henry liberty always trumps kings, emperors, unions, or government — now that is a radical concept, just try and get a modern politician to say that.

Yes, our founding fathers did indeed have some radical ideas. In the Kentucky and Virginia Resolves of 1798, Thomas Jefferson, the virtual author of the Declaration of Independence and James Madison, who was often referred to as the Father of the Constitution, made quite a few radical statements. For example, they noted that the Federal government was not a government that has anything close to absolute power and it is we the people of the sovereign states who had the right to judge for ourselves if the Federal government was acting beyond the power granted by the Constitution. In other words, we the people of the sovereign states could and must be the final judge as to whether the Federal government was acting as our servant or our master — not the Federal government itself. Today, the Federal government is the only one who can say what the Constitution allows or does not allows it to do—in essence it has become its own judge — a surer formula for the establishment of tyranny cannot be found. In the Kentucky and Virginia Resolves Jefferson and Madison declare that the final choice of how a people are to be governed is held by "we the people" of each sovereign state — that is where we get the idea of real State's Rights.

Under the radical system of real state's right the Federal government is not the master but it is the servant of the people of the States. If the Federal government taxes more than it should or refuses to defend the borders of these United States or any number of other transgression of the Constitution, we the people of the sovereign states have every right, in the words of the Declaration of Independence, to "alter or abolish" that government and establish a new government more to our liking. Again, find me a modern politician who is radical enough to embrace that idea. Lest you think that these radical ideas only pertain to the functions of government and means nothing to your day to day life as a provider for you family, let's look at what some radical real State's Rights men in early America had to say about big banks and big government.

Early in the history of these United States, the advocates of big government who were first known as Federalists, later Whigs, and ultimately Republicans, pushed for the establishment of a Federal banking system that could produce paper money. The States' Rights men such as Henry, Jefferson, Madison, and Jackson among many others fought against the effort to establish a Federal bank for two reasons: First, the Constitution does not empower the Federal government to establish such a system, and secondly, such a system would tend to pull money and power into the great cities, New York, Boston, Philadelphia and away from the more rural agrarian parts of the nation. Also, by issuing paper money that was not backed by something of great value such as gold or silver, the government and its bank could increase its revenue flow while devaluing the money held by the common man. Until the advent of the Republican Party and the election of Lincoln, for the most part the evils of a National banking system and Fiat money — money that is not backed by a precious commodity — had been stifled. With the defeat of the State's Rights party at the end of the so-called Civil War, America now lives with a national banking system and continual inflation caused by the issuing of more and more Fiat currency — the warnings of Thomas Jefferson and Andrew Jackson, both very strong State's Rights men — has become a reality for modern Americans. Remember the warnings about banks pulling money and wealth out of the small towns and cities and into the large centers of banking — do the words Wall Street ring a bell? Did all that wealth just get up and walk to New York City on it own accord? Now, how about the loss of wealth every citizen has to put up with because the Federal Reserve System determines that it needs to print up a few billion more dollars? Please remember, these fiat dollars are not backed by any precious commodity — it's just paper. What happens to the value of the money you have in your bank account, CDs, your retirement account or just sitting in your pocket? The value of your money is reduced by the actions of a Federal government that cannot be called into account by we the people of the sovereign states — you lose because the radical folks like Jefferson and Jackson ultimately lost their struggle against big banking and big government.

    One of the things that many of those so-called radical founding fathers desired was to be able to live their lives unmolested by government — another radical idea. John Randolph of Roanoke, Virginia often stated that he did not desire to have government do for him what he should be doing for himself. He would often say that free men are those people who understood that they should paddle their own canoe. Both Randolph and St. George Tucker of Virginia noted that when government — any government, did not allow a person to live as a free man, unmolested upon his own homestead, that government was reducing the individual to the state of civil slavery. In other words, if while not disturbing others, you cannot live on your own land without paying the government for that right you are not really free. Today no American lives free on his land. You never own your home or land, you only lease it from the government — refuse to pay your lease payment and the government will take it away from you — just like any slave master would do if a slave refused to work for the master. Yes, these men understood that some form of minimal taxes had to be paid but at some point, a free man should have refuge from the eternal tax bite of government or else he is not a free man but a tax slave of the government.

Now with these thoughts in mind, let's look at that radical Ron Paul. Ron Paul is often criticized for his radical libertarian views. Libertarians view liberty as having greater importance than government. During his tenure as a Congressman Ron Paul has been an active advocate of liberty over governmental power. Just like that radical, Patrick Henry, those of us who love liberty more than government we believe that in a free society liberty trumps government every time and yes in today's world that is a rather radical concept. Ron Paul has gotten into some trouble with many conservatives because he has dared to question the logic of Lincoln's war against the South. After all, if the Declaration of Independence means what it says, that is, people have the unalienable right to abolish their government and establish a new one more to their liking and if as Patrick Henry noted that in America liberty trumps union, then one has to admit that Lincoln was wrong and The South Was Right!

The radical Ron Paul believes in a Federal government that only exercises those powers that have been delegated to it in the Constitution, you know, just like Madison, Jefferson, Henry, and a world of other founding fathers of these United States. You see, Ron Paul does not believe in an all-powerful omnipotent government. Mr. Paul has some very good radical company when he stresses that the Constitution should be followed if we are to be a free people. Now, just like Mr. Paul is doing, let us ask some Constitutional questions. Where in the Constitution is the Federal government authorized to give American taxpayers money to foreign nations in the form of foreign aid? You can look but there is no authorization for such an authorization. Any good Constitutionalist, like Mr. Paul, would have to be against giving away our tax dollars to foreign nations. Where in the Constitution is the Federal government authorized to take money away from taxpayers and give it to people who only consume tax dollars in the form of social welfare. And we won't stop there, where in the Constitution is the federal government authorized to take tax dollars from working people and give it to various businesses in the form of corporate welfare? Once again, it's not in the Constitution. Where is the Federal government authorized to send our military to foreign nations to fight their wars and defend their borders—especially considering that our borders are under defended? How often have we heard stories of jobs being lost to foreign companies in Japan, Germany, South Korea, Taiwan and the list could go on. Yet each of these foreign nations has one thing in common, they are defended by American troops at the expense of the working tax paying citizens of this nation. Has anyone ever wondered how much more competitive those nation's factories are because they don't have to pay taxes to defend their own country? No, it is the American worker who is having to shoulder that burden and his factory's output is less competitive and his job more likely to be lost as a result of those taxes. All of this because no one can or will force the Federal government to live by the Constitution like America's more radical founding fathers intended. And one other thought is appropriate here. Where in the Constitution is the president given the authority to wage a protracted foreign war without a Congressional declaration of war? In the past 60 years more young Americans have died fighting undeclared wars than died fighting the declared War for American Independence, War of 1812, the Mexican War, the Spanish American War, and WWI combined. Our radical founding fathers knew what they were doing when they limited the war making capacity of this nation by a Congressional declaration of war. Here again we see that the radical Ron Paul is more in line with our founding fathers than he is with America's modern conservatives. Yes, that ole radical Ron Paul does not like the Federal Reserve System and it's printing of fiat paper money either. Here again Mr. Paul stands right next to those radical founding fathers such as Madison and Jefferson. As a matter of fact, President Andrew Jackson was just as radically opposed to fiat currency and a national banking system as Ron Paul. Remember, it was the States'

Rights party that was the main stumbling block to the formation of a national banking system and the issuing of fiat currency. After the failure of the Federalist Party and then the Whig Party, both of which championed the idea of big government and national banking, it was Mr. Lincoln and his Republican Party that pushed through the concept of fiat currency and national banking.

Today as you read these words, your money is being devalued by the actions of the Federal Reserve System, a system made possible by the defeat of the States' Rights party at Appomattox. Yes, big government, big taxes, and fiat currency are the legacy of the Republican Party, Mr. Lincoln, and the defeat of the South at Appomattox. Unfortunately, most Americans have no idea of what I am talking about, they think real States' Rights have nothing to do with their jobs and bank account and they are wrong. With the death of real States' Rights all of the previously mentioned ills that have been visited upon America have been made not only possible but it was made inevitable. So, Mikey, I suppose you are right after all. Ron Paul is too radical. He is too radical for modern Americans who have been fed upon the illusion that it is the job of government to take care of us, that this same government therefore has the authority to limit the exercise of our rights so as to safe guard society. In modern America government is a near god. Anyone who holds views to the contrary, such as Ron Paul or any of us neo-Confederates are easily labeled as extremists, radicals, or for us neo-Confederates — secessionists. The very thought that anyone would think that people have the unalienable right to secede from the protective care of nanny government is outrageously shocking to modern effeminate milk-toast Americans. Like Patrick Henry, who could never be reasonably described as an effeminate milk-toast person, those of us who love liberty more than we love the heavy-handed care given by big brother government, we are viewed as radicals. But when one thinks about it, the shame is not upon those of us who must bear that label, the shame is upon a society, which does not fully understand and appreciate the God given blessings of real American liberty. How many people in the 20th century swapped their liberty for the illusion of governmental security and comfort — this is the path traveled by the people of post-WWI Germany as they embraced Der Fuhrer Adolph Hitler. Likewise, in Italy Il Duce, Benito Mussolini persuaded the people of a once free republic to surrender a portion of their freedom and follow his fascist's legions. Lenin and Stalin also offered the people a worker's paradise if only they would allow the government to become their all-providing big brother. Cannot it be said that in each of these nations there were men and women who decried the growth of big government and the loss of liberty? Surely this is true and surely, they were labeled as radicals or unpatriotic to the government.

The weak-kneed milk-toast attitude of letting the government take care of us is surely an attitude that will sound the death-knell of real American liberty. It is the attitude that fosters all forms of big government; socialism, fascism, communism, and our own home-grown variety of conservative/liberal socialism. These sycophants of big government see government as preeminent in the life of a society, which is a radical departure from the form of government envisioned by America's founding fathers in 1776 and defended for us by Dixie's Confederate forefathers in 1861. If a future generation of Americans will ever live to see a land where they are not slaves to their governmental masters, then surely, we must unite and that effectually to fight for the day when real American liberty is once again celebrated and not scorned as being "too radical."

Wall Street Journal's Confederate Animus Displayed in a review of Dr. Sandy Mitcham's book: *Vicksburg*
Walter D. Kennedy
2018

On the eve of the War for Southern Independence an article was published in The New York Times which unequivocally announced why the North had to invade and conquer the South. The author of the article declared, "The commercial bearing of the question has acted upon the North…. We were divided and confused [about Southern secession] till our pockets were touched." The Union Democrat of New Hampshire added this observation, "The Southern Confederacy will not employ our ships or buy our goods…. No—we must not 'let the South go.'" In an article titled "What Shall Be Done for a Revenue," the Evening Post of New York warned that without tariff income from Southern ports, "the sources which supply our treasury will be dried up…. the railways would be supplied from southern ports."

These three citations are a small representative sample of the numerous editorials by Northern newspapers warning of the dire consequences to Northern commerce and industry if the South was allowed to establish its independence. Rather than being the vaunted champion of freedom and equality, it is obvious that the worship of the "Almighty Dollar" was the driving force in the North's War to Prevent Southern Independence. Notice how the Evening Post of New York warned that Southern ports would be the recipient of railway commerce.

From early in the history of the Republic, the merchants of the Northeast lived with one great fear, losing its choke-hold on the nation's commerce. If the expanding nation's wealth flowed down the Mississippi River to the port of New Orleans and if Memphis became the hub for the nation's major railroads, commerce would flow into New Orleans and the ports along the Southern East Coast and Gulf South. This is why early in the Republic's history many Northeast merchants attempted to sell the Mississippi River to Spain (circa, 1779). Southern Historian, Francis Butler Simkins, noted the Yankee's "money grubbing" nature declaring, "Northern capitalism was eagerly imperialistic...its success was creating a nation of dollar-worshipers...who regarded themselves as the lords of creation." Empires are built and maintained by dollar-worshipers not by liberty-worshipers. According to James Madison, America's Founding Fathers did not create an Empire but created a compound republic. Lincoln, the Republican Party, and their crony capitalist allies destroyed Madison and Jefferson's compound republic and replaced it with an ever-growing supreme Federal government — from which has sprung the Deep State. The South's long-standing love for States' Rights stood in the way of the North's desire for a commercial empire. Therefore, the South had to be destroyed. Today, anyone who dares to proclaim any view that does not comport with the view of the Empire is assaulted in the well-used and jaded method of ridicule and questioning of one's "historical credentials." And if the Empire can produce a self-loathing Southerner who, like Judas, is willing to betray his people for a few Yankee coins, it makes the Empire's work of defending invasion and oppression much easier.

Recently the *Wall Street Journal* (WSJ) published a review of Dr. Sandy Mitcham's book, *Vicksburg*. The first portion of the review gave credit to Dr. Mitcham for his work but from that point forward a virtual anti-South tirade flows from the reviewer's keyboard. The reviewer insists that Dr. Mitcham's arguments and quotes are not properly "sourced" as is expected for "scholarly history." A Southern historian or writer can barricade himself up to his eyeballs in "citations," "references," "primary source materials," and it will do little to placate the running dogs and lackeys of political correctness. Traditional Southerners understand any book which does not "toe-the-line" of the Empire's view of the War will never be accepted as "scholarly." The WSJ reviewer condemns Dr. Mitcham's work on five broad grounds. (1) He claims that Mitcham's maps are "sparse and sketchy." Perhaps Dr. Mitcham understood that facts about the human element such as death, starvation, and terrorism inflicted on Southern civilians by the invader were of more interest and more important than "unsketchy" maps. (2) The reviewer found fault with Mitcham's description of Grant as "desperate." After unsuccessfully attempting to take Vicksburg four times, Grant was indeed becoming desperate. It was Grant who had more than 7,000 of his men killed trying desperately to break Lee's fortifications at Cold Harbor. Grant understood that it takes desperate measures to defeat men who are defending their homes and families from a cruel invader. (3) The WSJ reviewer was somewhat incredulous that Dr. Mitcham would condemn Sherman for his "overbearing cruelty." Sherman, who suggested to the Federal Empire's War Department that a whole class of Southerners "men, women, and children should be killed or banished" to secure victory is given a "get out of jail free" card by the reviewer. (4) Mitcham's view of Lincoln is also condemned. Lincoln, the man who had the civilian grandson of Francis Scott Key arrested, tried, and jailed by military police and given a military trial, is not one who should be given a pass when looking for tyrants! (5) Mitcham's refusal to kowtow to the Empire's god of political correctness was more than the WSJ reviewer could tolerate, especially as it relates to slavery!

As Henrik Ibsen noted in 'An Enemy of the People,' "You should never wear your best trousers when you go out to fight for freedom and truth." I can assure you that Dr. Mitcham had his fighting clothes on when he wrote *Vicksburg*. As a well-trained and honest historian, Dr. Mitcham abhors political correctness and its sycophants. Nevertheless, it is understandable why the WSJ would publish a review which criticizes Dr. Mitcham's book; after all, no one has more to lose from exposing the lies, myths, and falsehoods which prop up the Yankee Empire than Wall Street. Yankees and their sycophants will never understand Dr. Mitcham's view on the War because they do not understand that a conquered people never forget!

Conclusion

At the writing of these pages two major interrelated events are taking place in these once United States of America. First, after the most contentious confirmation process for a Supreme Court justice in over 100 years, America has displayed its political-cultural division to the world and second, the ever-growing campaign of cultural genocide against all things Confederate continues unabated.

Most Americans, including too many Southerners, do not understand just how these events are related. The use of mob-rule and guilt by accusation as orchestrated by leftists of the neo-Marxist cabal is very familiar to defenders of Southern Heritage. This use of force and intimidation to overturn the will of the people is the same spirit and action that is being used to remove all things Confederate from public display in Dixie. For example, when Southerners defend memorials of their Confederate ancestors, they are quickly and vociferously met with the charge of "defending slavery" and therefore being racists. When the neo-Marxists could not stop the appointment of Judge Kavanaugh to the Supreme Court by legitimate means, they used the tried and true method that has worked well in the South. Neo-Marxists quickly pulled from their playbook the well-used and successful technique of Accuse-Convict-Remove! After all, it works well down South why not in Washington?

To implement their technique of Accuse-Convict-Remove, neo-Marxists will find someone or a group of people that will bring a hideous and revolting charge against their victim, in this case, Kavanaugh. After the accusation the neo-Marxists simply announce his guilt, denigrate anyone who offers proof of his innocence, and ultimately remove him. Fortunately for Kavanaugh, by a narrow margin the neo-Marxists attempt failed. Nevertheless, they have doubled down on their steady drive to take down traditional American values—due process with its presumption of "innocent until proven guilty" is just one of these values under attack.

Anytime the neo-Marxist rabble desires to remove a monument or artifact which reflects positively upon Southern history, the same well used and successful technique, i.e., Accuse-Convict-Remove, is used. First it is announced that the "offending" monument or artifact was established to promote "white supremacy" and is therefore a harmful and a hateful racist symbol. As with Kavanaugh, the "guilt" is announced along with the charge. When Southerners (regardless of color or ethnicity) bring forth proof that said monument/artifact was not erected or placed as a symbol of racism, they are forcefully scorned and belittled as being "defenders of slavery" and therefore unworthy of being heard. Just as in the case of Judge Kavanaugh, no proof of innocence is allowed and the charge of guilt cannot be questioned. All that is then left to do is to remove the "offending" subject. Because Kavanaugh had a large group of well-established conservatives and the President as his defenders, he was spared the fate which has become so common for the defenders of the defeated nation, the Confederate States of America.

This hideous Accuse-Convict-Remove technique which has been so successful in destroying Southern heritage and history and which was used against Judge Kavanaugh is also being employed against traditional American values. Those attacking traditional American values from the Ten Commandments to Confederate monuments may call themselves "progressives" or "liberals" but at bottom they are neo-Marxists. Their ultimate goal is the destruction and/or banishing of America's traditional value system and replacing it with a Marxist system. All Americans should understand that if the neo-Marxists can have a Confederate flag removed because it "offends" someone, what will protect the Christian flag when it "offends" someone? If a Confederate monument must be removed because someone finds it "offensive," what will happen to a Christmas Nativity Scene when it is labeled "offensive?"

Traditional values as embraced by those who hold dear a Biblical world view and strict-construction Constitutionalism are anathema to Marxists. The left's hatred of these traditional values is one reason they often belittle Bible-believing, Constitution-loving Americans as "bitter clingers." The problem faced by the neo-Marxists is how do they destroy something that is so dearly held and loved by the majority of Americans? The answer soon became obvious to the leadership of the progressive mob. The answer was slavery and/or white supremacy! First attack the Confederate States of America as being the defenders of slavery and America's sole advocates of white supremacy. Neo-Marxists then continue their attack by stigmatizing anyone who defends the traditional values of the South, especially defenders of the Confederacy as vile, evil racists. They then announce to the world that anyone who seeks to defend Southern Heritage is using that term as a "code-word" for defending slavery and promoting white supremacy. Neo Marxists then use their control of the "fake news" industry to deny Southerners an equal voice in defending their well-studied and factual defense of their history. While the left is busy promoting its fake history about the South, neo-conservatives are busy agreeing with the left and therefore promoting the acceptance of the Accuse-Convict-Remove method of attack. Is it any wonder when the neo-Marxists began their attack upon Justice Kavanaugh, unfounded and undocumented accounts were believed by so many people? Every time a conservative talking-head on radio or TV announces the South is responsible for Jim Crow laws (as proven herein it was New England who introduced these laws), or that the burden of guilt for slavery belongs to the South (this said even though slavery existed much longer in Massachusetts than in Mississippi and longer still in New York than in Alabama), or the South committed treason when it seceded from the Union (even though the Declaration of Independence states that a free people have the unalienable right to "alter or abolish" any government they no longer like and have the right to establish a government they do agree with), the neo-Marxists agenda is advanced.

Americans need to understand that the ultimate objective of the neo-Marxists is the destruction of the Constitution and its replacement with a Marxist-style document. Remember that in three different places the Constitution either defines or defends slavery. Once the neo-Marxist rabble has conditioned newer generations of Americans to remove anything they say is associated with slavery, what do you think will happen when the Constitution has been so identified? The process has already begun. The day after Judge Kavanaugh became Justice Kavanaugh, the new darling of the Social Democrats, Alexandria Ocasio-Cortez, tweeted that the time has come to get rid of the Electoral College because it is anti-democratic and "a shadow of slavery's power."[246] It should be obvious to all that the neo-Marxists have no desire to just ban the Confederate flag or take down Confederate monuments. As already pointed out they intend to use the odious stigma of slavery and /or racism to take down all traditional values from Christianity to the Constitution.

Since the publication of the first edition of *The South Was Right!* in 1991 to the date of the publication of *The Confederate Myth Buster*, the Kennedy Twins have warned Americans about the danger of an

---

246 Alexandria Ocasio-Cortez@Ocasio2018, tweet viewed October 6, 2018.

out of control Federal Government. Early in 1861, Senator Joseph Lane of Oregon warned Americans of the danger of allowing the Federal Government to wage war upon sovereign states of the Union. He cautioned that if successful, the old union of sovereign states would be crushed along with the South and replaced by an empire. He succinctly noted that the territory of an empire exists not for the benefit of the people but the people of the former states, now mere territories, would exist for the benefit of the empire. Just nine months after the conquest of the Confederate States of America, General Robert E. Lee noted that with the defeat of the South, States' Rights had been eliminated and all power is now concentrated into an all-powerful central (federal) government. He goes on to warn that such an all-powerful central government would become "aggressive abroad and despotic at home."[247]

Americans today are living in an empire that has foreign military bases spread across the globe. The total number of such military outposts is greater than all military bases of every other nation in the world combined! Where before Appomattox America influenced the world with merchants and missionaries, today the use of the military and money is the most common way of imposing the will of the new American empire upon foreign nations. In the past fifty years the average American has learned to live in fear of his government. Few Americans can now reasonably doubt who is in charge of Washington, DC. The so-called Deep State is an acknowledged fact. The Federal Government no longer fears the people after all, what can the people do to Deep State operatives? Even if a "non-Deep State" president is elected and is able to trim back the power of the Deep State, everyone understands that it will be back after one or more elections. Enraged by their loss of power, the next time they gain power the Deep State will not allow those evil "bitter clingers" to up-root their lucrative and comfortable lifestyle again.

As is pointed out in *The South Was Right!*, it is time for a radical reformation of these United States of America so as to provide the means for "we the people" of the sovereign states to control our agent, the Federal Government.[248] If the government cannot be brought under our control then the ultimate break-up of this big empire will

---

[247] Robert E. Lee, as cited in James R. Kennedy and Walter D. Kennedy, *Yankee Empire: Aggressive Abroad and Despotic at Home* (Shotwell Publishing Co., Columbia, SC: 2018), Intro
[248] Kennedy and Kennedy, *The South Was Right!*, 11.

happen. The break-up will happen not because the South desires it but because Americans from all walks of life, sections of the nation, and political viewpoints are beginning to understand that such an immense and culturally/politically diverse and divided nation cannot be governed without the heavy hand of tyranny. Hopefully Americans will never submit to such a form of government.

Bibliography

Books and Periodicals

Barbour, R. L. *South Carolina's Revolutionary War Battlefields*. Gretna, LA: Pelican Publishing Co., 2002.

Bradford, M. E. *Founding Fathers: Brief Lives of the Framers of the United States*, Second Edition. Lawrence: University of Kansas Press, 1982.

Buchanan, Minor F. *Holt Collier: His Life, His Roosevelt Hunts, and The Origin of the Teddy Bear*. Jackson, MS: Centennial Press, 2002.

Carey, George W. and James McCellan, eds. *The Federalist, Student Edition*. Dubuque, IA: Kendall-Hunt Publishing Company, 1990.

Carson, Clarence B. *Basic American Government*. Wadley, AL: American Textbook Committee, 1993.

Cawthon, William L., Jr., *The South as Its Own Nation, The Free Magnolia*, Vol. I, No. 2, April-June, 2007.

Commager, Henry S., ed. *Documents of American History*, Eight Edition. New York: Appleton, Century, Croft, 1968.

Dabney, Robert L. *Discussions of Robert Lewis Dabney. 1897*, Harrisonburg, VA: Sprinkle Publications, 1979.

Dana, Daniel. *A Discourse Addressed to the New Hampshire Auxiliary Colonization Society at the First Annual Meeting, Concord, New Hampshire, June 2, 1825*. Concord, NH: Shepard & Bannister, 1825.

Davis, Jefferson. *The Rise and Fall of the Confederate Government*. 1881, Nashville, TN: William M. Coats.

DeRosa, Marshall L. *The Confederate Constitution of 1861: An Inquiry into American Constitutionalism*. Columbia: University of Missouri Press, 1991.

Gillamn, William H., ed. *The Journals and Miscellaneous Notebooks of Ralph Waldo Emerson.* Cambridge, MA: Harvard University Press, 1960.

Greene, Lorenzo J. *The Negro in Colonial New England, 1620-1776.* Port Washington, NY: Kennikat Press, Inc., 1966.

Henry, William Wirt, ed. *Patrick Henry: Life, Correspondence, and Speeches.* 1891, Harrisonburg, VA: Sprinkle Publications, 1993.

Hillquit, Morris. *History of Socialism in the United States.* New York and London: Funk and Wagnalls Company, 1910.

Hitler, Adolph. *Mein Kampf.* New York: Hurst and Blackett, LTD., 1942.

Hogan, William R. and Edwin A. Davis, eds. *William Johnson's Natchez: The Ante-Bellum Diary of a Free Negro.* Baton Rouge: Louisiana State University Press, 1993.

Hummel, Jeffery R. *Emancipating Slaves, Enslaving Free Men.* Peru, IL: Open Court Trade and Academic Books, 1996.

Jensen, Merrill. *The New Nation: A History of the United States during the Confederation, 1781-1789.* Boston: Northwestern University Press, 1981.

Johannsen, R. W. *The Lincoln Douglas Debates of 1858.* New York: Oxford University Press, 1965.

Jones, J. Williams. *A Memorial Volume of Jefferson Davis.* 1889, Harrisonburg, VA: Sprinkle Publications, 1993.

Kennedy, James R. *Reclaiming Liberty.* Gretna, LA: Pelican Publishing Co., 2005.

"Dixie's Unwelcomed Presence in Rosie O'Donnell's America," www.kennedytwins.com.

Kennedy, James R. and Walter D. *The South Was Right!* Gretna, LA: Pelican Publishing Co., 1994.

Kennedy, James R. and Walter D. *Was Jefferson Davis Right?* Gretna, LA: Pelican Publishing Co., 1998.

Kennedy, James R. and Walter D. *Punished with Poverty: The Suffering South.* Columbia, SC: Shotwell Publishing, 2016.

Kennedy, James R. and Walter D. *Yankee Empire: Aggressive Abroad and Despotic at Home.* Columbia, SC: Shotwell Publishing Co. 2018.

Kennedy, Ron. "Choosing Slavery in Mississippi Over Freedom in Pennsylvania," *Southern Mercury*, Vol. 1, No. 3, Nov.-Dec. 2003.

Kennedy, Walter D. *Rekilling Lincoln.* Gretna, La.: Pelican Publishing Co., 2015.

Kennedy, Walter D. *Myths of American Slavery.* Gretna, La.: Pelican Publishing Co., 2003.

Kennedy, Walter D. "SECESSION: The American Way," *Southern Mercury*, Vol. 1, No. 3, Nov.-Dec. 2003.

Kennedy, Walter D. and Al Benson, Jr. *Lincoln's Marxists.* Pelican Publishing Co., Gretna, La. 2011.

Kirk, Russell. *John Randolph of Roanoke: A Study in American Politics.* Indianapolis, IN: Liberty Press, 1978.

Langer, Elinor. *A Hundred Little Hitlers: The Death of a Black Man, the Trial of a White Racist, and the Rise of the Neo-Nazi Movement in America.* Metropolitan Books, 2003.

Litwack, Leon P. *North of Slavery: The Negro in the Free States, 1790-1860.* Chicago: The University of Chicago Press, 1961.

Locke, John. *Two Treatises of Government.* 1698, New York: The Classics of Liberty Library, 1992.

Marx, Karl and Fredrick Engels. *The Civil War in the United States*. New York: International Publishers, Co., Inc., 1953.

Letters to Americans. New York: International Publishers Co., Inc., 1953.

McDonald, Forrest. *A Constitutional History of the United States*. Malabar, FL: Robert E. Krieger Publishing Co., 1986.

McElroy, Robert McNutt. *Jefferson Davis: The Unreal and The Real*. New York: Harper and Brothers, 1937.

McManus, Edgar J. *Black Bondage in the North*. Syracuse, NY: Syracuse University Press, 1977.

McWhiney, Grady, *Jefferson Davis the Unforgiven, Journal of Mississippi History*, XLII, May 1980.

Melish, Joanne P. *Disowning Slavery: Gradual Emancipation and Race in New England 1780-1860*. Ithaca, NY: Cornell University Press, 1998.

Mills, Gary. *The Forgotten People: Cane River's Creoles of Color*. Baton Rouge: Louisiana State University Press, 1977.

Moore, George H. *Notes on the History of Slavery in Massachusetts*. New York: D. Appleton and Company, 1866.

Nichols, David A. *Lincoln and the Indians*. Columbia: University of Missouri Press, 1978.

O'Reilly, Bill. *Racism in Public Education*, www.worldnetdaily.com, reviewed May 30, 2001.

Owsley, Frank L. *The Irrepressible Conflict, I'll Take My Stand*. Baton Rouge: Louisiana State University Press, 1983.

The Pew Research Center, *Trends in Political Values and Core Attitudes: 1987-2007*, www.people-press.org , reviewed March 28, 2007.

Pollard, E. A. *Southern History of the War*. 1866, New York: The Fairfax Press, 1978.

Prescott, Arthur T. *Drafting the Federal Constitution*. Baton Rouge: Louisiana State University Press, 1941.

Rawle, William. *A View of the Constitution*. Walter D. Kennedy and James R. Kennedy, eds. 1825, Simsboro, LA: Old South Books, 1993.

Rutherford, Samuel. *Lex Rex*. 1644, Harrisonburg, VA: Sprinkle Publications, 1982.

Scott, Otto. *The Secret Six*. New York: Times Books, 1979.

Semmes, Raphael. *Memoirs of Service Afloat*. 1868, Secaucus, NJ: The Blue and Grey Press, 1987.

Sharf, J. Thomas. *History of the Confederate States Navy*. 1887, New York: The Fairfax Press, 1996.

Simkins, Francis B. *A History of the South*. New York: Alfred A. Knopf, 1959.

Stephens, Alexander. *The Correspondence of Robert Tooms, Alexander H. Stephens, and Howell Cobb*. U. B. Phillips, ed. Washington, DC: American Historical Association, 1913.

Vallandigham, Clement L. *The Record of Hon. C. L. Vallandigham on Abolition, the Union, and the Civil War*. Columbus, OH: J. Walter & Co., 1863.

Wainwright, Jonathan M. *A Discourse on the Occasion of Forming the African Mission School, Christ Church, Hartford Connecticut*. Hartford, CT: H & F. J. Huntington, 1828.

Weaver, Richard M. *The Southern Tradition at Bay*. New Rochelle, NY: Arlington House, 1968.

Wilson, Clyde N., ed. *A View of the Constitution of the United States: With Selected Writings*. Indianapolis, IN: Liberty Fund, 1999.

The Essential Calhoun: Selections from Writings, Speeches, and Letters.
New Brunswick, NJ: Transaction Publishers, 1992.

Woods, Thomas E., Jr. *The Politically Incorrect Guide to American History.* Washington, DC: Regnery Publishing, Inc., 2004.

Court Cases

Jacobson v. Massachusetts, 197, US 11, (1905) pts. 23 & 30.
Plessy v. Ferguson, 163 US 537 (1896).

Newspapers

Memphis Daily Avalanche, July 6, 1876
Portland Tribune, October 17, 2003
Shreveport Times, October 22, 1957

Public Documents

Abraham Lincoln, July 4th Message to Congress, July 4, 1861
American Declaration of Independence
Confederate States Constitution
Treaty of Paris
United States Articles of Confederation
United States Constitution
The War of the Rebellion: a Compilation of the Official Records of the Union and Confederate Armies

www.ingramcontent.com/pod-product-compliance
Lightning Source LLC
Chambersburg PA
CBHW071316110526
44591CB00010B/906